P9-DCE-286

*PRENTICE–HALL SERIES*
*IN WORLD RELIGIONS*

ROBERT S. ELLWOOD, JR., EDITOR

JAPANESE RELIGION:
A CULTURAL PERSPECTIVE

_____ *ROBERT ELLWOOD/RICHARD PILGRIM*

BEYOND "THE PRIMITIVE":
THE RELIGIONS OF NONLITERATE PEOPLES

_____ *SAM D. GILL*

HINDUISM: A CULTURAL PERSPECTIVE

_____ *DAVID R. KINSLEY*

ISLAM: A CULTURAL PERSPECTIVE

_____ *RICHARD C. MARTIN*

AMERICAN RELIGION:
A CULTURAL PERSPECTIVE

_____ *MARY FARRELL BEDNAROWSKI*

# Robert Ellwood

*University of Southern California*

# Richard Pilgrim

*Syracuse University*

*JAPANESE
RELIGION
a cultural
perspective*

Prentice-Hall, Inc., Englewood Cliffs, New Jersey 07632

*Library of Congress Cataloging in Publication Data*

Ellwood, Robert S., 1933–
  Japanese religion.

  (Prentice-Hall series in world religions)
  Bibliography: p.
  Includes index.
  1. Japan—Religion.   I. Pilgrim, Richard B.
II. Title.   III. Series.
BL2202.E45   1985        291′.0952        84–15878
ISBN 0–13–509282–5 (pbk.)

Interior/cover design by Maureen Olsen
Editorial production/supervision by Marina Harrison
Manufacturing buyer: Harry P. Baisley

© 1985 by Prentice-Hall, Inc., Englewood Cliffs, N.J. 07632

*All rights reserved. No part of this book
may be reproduced in any form or
by any means without permission in writing
from the publisher.*

Printed in the United States of America

10  9  8  7  6  5  4  3  2

ISBN 0-13-509282-5

Prentice-Hall International, Inc., *London*
Prentice-Hall of Australia Pty. Limited, *Sydney*
Editora Prentice-Hall do Brasil, Ltda., *Rio de Janeiro*
Prentice-Hall of Canada, Inc., *Toronto*
Prentice-Hall of India Private Limited, *New Delhi*
Prentice-Hall of Japan, Inc., *Tokyo*
Prentice-Hall of Southeast Asia Pte. Ltd., *Singapore*
Whitehall Books Limited, *Wellington, New Zealand*

# Contents

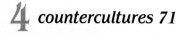 *countercultures 71*

# part 2

## SPECIFIC PATTERNS IN THE RELIGION OF JAPAN

 *religion and the arts 83*

6 *conceptual worlds 96*

# *Foreword*

The Prentice-Hall Series in World Religions is a new set of introductions to the major religious traditions of the world, which intends to be distinctive in two ways: (1) Each book follows the same outline, allowing a high level of consistency in content and approach. (2) Each book is oriented toward viewing religious traditions as "religious cultures" in which history, ideologies, practices, and sociologies all contribute toward constructing "deep structures" that govern peoples' world view and life-style. In order to achieve this level of communication about religion, these books are not chiefly devoted to dry recitations of chronological history or systematic exposition of ideology, though they present overviews of these topics. Instead the books give considerable space to "cameo" insights into particular personalities, movements, and historical moments that encourage an understanding of the world view, life-style, and deep dynamics of religious cultures in practice as they affect real people.

Religion is an important element within nearly all cultures and itself has all the hallmarks of a full cultural system. "Religious culture" as an integrated complex includes features ranging from ideas and organization to dress and diet. Each of these details offers some insight into the meaning of the whole as a total experience and construction of a total "reality." To look at the religious life of a particular country or tradition in this way, then, is to give proportionate attention to all aspects of its manifestation: to thought, worship, and social organization; to philosophy and folk beliefs; to liturgy and pilgrimage; to family life, dress, diet, and the role of religious specialists like monks and shamans. This series hopes to instill in the minds of readers the ability to view religion in this way.

I hope you enjoy the journeys offered by these books to the great heartlands of the human spirit.

ROBERT S. ELLWOOD, JR., editor
*University of Southern California*

# Preface

As the twenty-first century approaches, we stand on the brink of a global community caught between the glories of a new technology and the horrors of nuclear devastation. Perhaps at no time in the past has there been such a need for understanding the cultures and values of other peoples and for opening up conversation across cultural boundaries.

Within those cultures and values, the religious life has been—and remains—central. Religious values are traditionally the deepest and most strongly held values of a culture—the values that relate to central paradigms or understandings and assumptions about the nature and direction of life itself.

Although every culture calls out for understanding, Japan in particular makes its presence in the global community dramatically felt again (perhaps we could say for the second time) in the twentieth century: now, of course, not through the weapons of global war but through the wonder and quality of its technology and its culture. The Japanese genius is everywhere apparent, most obviously in its exported technology, which rivals the best made anywhere, but less obviously and more gradually through its influence around the world on everything from the arts of design and architecture to the arts of factory and labor management. Yet perhaps deeper and even more long-range than these is a potential influence arising from greater understanding and appreciation of its rich religious and cultural tradition.

What moves and motivates this nation and these people? What cultural, social, intellectual, spiritual genius is at work here? Wherein lies Japan's uniqueness as a culture and its power as an influence? These and a host of other questions stand before us as we try to look behind the images and power of modern Japan—images and power that seem to outweigh the size of this relatively small country situated on a few islands in the Pacific Ocean.

Our specific concern, of course, is the religious element in Japanese culture—an element that, although obviously present in the institutionalized religions of Japan, also permeates its traditional (and modern) life. This religious element, we think, tells us much about the inner workings of the Japanese way of life and is one of the central keys to understanding Japanese culture and values.

The way we address this concern in the present volume is through *interpretation* of that religious element and culture—an interpretation based in part on the categories of a common series outline and in part on the views of the two authors who have worked in harmony to present a single voice throughout the presentation. Speaking from a "cultural perspective" that grows out of the discipline of the study of religion, we seek to understand cultural phenomena for their religious meaning in their own right and to point out that religion and culture mutually interact within the larger fabric of a nation's life.

This book is an introductory textbook that is both like and unlike others of a similar genre. It is something of a summary statement indicating where we have come in a general understanding of Japanese religion. As such, it is dependent in some measure on the work of many people who remain hidden behind the words or in the footnotes. These people are fellow scholars of Japanese religion—both past and present, some Japanese and others not. They are a silent support system for such a volume, though they are not to be held responsible for our use of their work. It is in appreciation of these many scholars that we say "thank you" and encourage them as well as future scholars of Japan to keep up the good work.

We want to single out one scholar who deserves special mention as both our common teacher and our major inspiration for pursuing Japanese studies to begin with. Dr. Joseph M. Kitagawa, Professor of the History of Religion at the University of Chicago Divinity School, figures prominently in religion studies in America generally and Japanese studies specifically. He has done much—through writing, teaching, and professional presence—to change almost single-handedly the face of Japanese religious studies in America. To him we offer special thanks and congratulations for work well done.

We also wish to thank a variety of support systems without which this work would not have been possible. Our universities and departments provided facilities and resources, our colleagues and friends in Japan and elsewhere offered stimulation and help, and our wives and families created a network of bonding without which life and work would not move along as well as it does.

ROBERT ELLWOOD

RICHARD PILGRIM

1

## THE JAPANESE WAY

This book is an introduction to the religion and religious life of the Japanese. It is not an introduction to any particular religion but to a particular cultural tradition within which religious values and forms of expression have played an important role. Of course, specific religions such as Buddhism or Shinto are crucial to that tradition, and we will want to pay close attention to them as distinct elements within the larger picture; but our primary concern will remain the nature and variety of Japanese religion in general.

This book takes seriously the fact that any religion is lived out by specific human beings in a specific cultural, historical tradition. It also takes seriously the fact that the religion of a culture (like Japan) cannot merely be defined by the institutionalized religions that in great part make it up; "religion" is present wherever religious values or experience function. Religious values and experience, in turn, function in the depths of human consciousness and attitudes oriented toward what is sacred and ultimately real. Such values are not necessarily found only in the institutional religions, nor are they always defined and instilled by those religions, though they may certainly be influenced by them. Much modern, apparently nonreligious or secular literature, for example, may well express the human quest to come to terms with existence. Such values and issues can only be called religious or spiritual in some larger sense. Similarly, a Japanese landscape painting, though containing no explicit religious theme, may well express religious (spiritual) values and ideals, and thereby be called a form of religious art. Even a Japanese social custom, such as bowing to one another, is a ritual gesture sacred and meaningful to the Japanese.

The religion of a culture, in short, need not only be sought in the religions of that culture, but also in other key cultural forms (for example, literature, art, and social customs). In fact, wherever one finds these deepest values expressed, one can find "religion"; wherever paradigms—fundamental ways of perceiving and making sense out of existence—appear to be functioning, religion can be found.

A "cultural perspective" takes this understanding of the religious dimension in a culture like Japan seriously. Therefore it not only discusses the religions in and of themselves, but is also concerned with the influences those religions have on the larger culture and society. Moreover, it occasionally focuses on apparently nonreligious cultural forms to show religion taking place outside the religions.

Each chapter in this book, therefore, tries to be sensitive to this complexity of religion as actually lived out in human lives and human culture in Japan. The chapters of Part I, as a survey or panorama of Japanese religion, tend to focus on the religions of Japan in a historical context, although they suggest places outside those religions where one might find religion as well. Part II, an analysis of specific types of religious expression in Japan, emphasizes religious ideas as they permeate a variety of cultural or social patterns—for example, social structures, artistic form, a generalized worldview, and ritual.

Interestingly enough, the Japanese themselves have an understanding of religion which correlates nicely with our notion of religion in cultural perspective. Though the Japanese have a word for institutionalized religion (**shukyo**), that word is a rather recent development based, in part, on the influence of Western ideas about "religion." Much more deeply ingrained in Japan is the idea of religion or the religious life as any path or way (*do, michi*) that seeks spiritual depth and follows a spiritual discipline. The word *do* is the Japanese pronunciation of the Chinese word *Tao,* Way, The Great Path down which all that exists is moving, and any lesser path which ultimately harmonizes with it.

In Japanese, in fact, the major religions have been understood and called *do* or "ways" of religious significance: Shinto is **kami-no-michi** or *shinto,* the "way of the gods"; Buddhism is *butsudo,* the "way of the buddhas"; Taoism is *onmyodo,* the "way of *yin* and *yang*"; and Confucianism is *judo,* the "way of the gentleman". Beyond the major religions, however, other paths or practices have also been called "way"; for example, *karatedo* (the "way of the empty hand") and *chado* (the "way of tea"). In these cases, seemingly nonreligious practices and traditions are named ways and thereby carry religious meaning.

These and other ways in Japan carry religious meaning insofar as they seek to open human life to higher or deeper levels of spiritual awareness through particular practices and disciplines, and to help humans, individually and collectively, live as authentically as possible. They are religious insofar as they press human experience and meaning beyond the mundane level of day-to-day existence and seek to create a life lived in accord with some notion of a more sacred reality. Such ways are made up of particular forms, expressions, and practices that have a history and tradition and that help provide both meaning and direction to the lives of those involved.

Religion or religious life understood as "way" has an additional advantage—it emphasizes that religion is, indeed, religious *life,* that is, something lived out in human existence and not some abstract philosophy of life or mere belief system about reality. This life is, moreover, lived in community and culture, that is, in the specific context of a particular history, culture, and community. Although ultimately, of course, individuals are the locus of religious life, individual life cannot be separated from the communal, cultural, and historical contexts within which it is lived. A way of life that has religious significance is both individual and collective; it is shaped by personal experience as well as by the experience of the larger community.

One cautionary note may be needed at this point: The idea of distinct ways within Japanese religion should not be taken to indicate mutually exclusive beliefs and practices forming smaller or larger isolated religious traditions. As we have mentioned already and will stress throughout, the religions of Japan often merge in actual life. One can find Shinto elements in a Buddhist service or Confucian studies taking place in a Buddhist monastery. Shinto or Buddhist elements are also found in what otherwise seem nonreligious cultural forms or philosophies (such as **bushido,** the "way of the warrior").

Perhaps it is best to consider the various ways as strands within a larger rope called "Japanese religion" or the "Japanese way"—a rope that extends from prehistoric time up to this very day. The rope is not everywhere and always the same. The strands change and shift along its length, and the rope is flexible and changing. Nonetheless it is identifiable as the Japanese way. In fact, some have argued that this rope is itself the fundamental religion of Japan, and the strands that make it up are so many support systems to a larger religion called *nihondo,* the "way of Japan." Such an appeal to an overarching "civil religion" has some merit, but it can easily be overemphasized to the exclusion of the unique importance and specificity of the distinctive ways as particular religious modes of life.

Our task in this book is to try to indicate the ways that form the strands of Japanese religion, and to indicate how they constitute a unique way of life that has religious significance.

# 2

## moments and memories: an imaginary tour

The twentieth-century novelist Mishima Yukio*, with tongue in cheek, once described a room, called the "Japanese reality room," that was to serve an important training function for young Japanese writers. With a mere push of a button, the room could reproduce the total atmosphere and set of associations related to any theme important to Japanese perception. The button "rain over Japan," for example, would reproduce not only the atmosphere of a steamy, rainy day but also the related associations of sentimental melancholy, sorrowful occasions, and tears.

We might wish for such a room in this context. We could push a button labeled "religion in Japan" and sit back to enjoy a panorama of moments and memories suggestive of the range and atmosphere of the various "ways," or beliefs and practices of spiritual significance, that have made up Japanese religion. In a darkened Buddhist temple we might catch the smell of incense lingering in the air or feel the mysterious presence of serene and silent statues of Buddha. At a Shinto shrine we might hear the strange but provocative sounds of music played on ancient instruments or see the postured, gentle dance of young girls doing **kagura** (sacred dance). In a Zen meditation hall we might feel the charged stillness of monks in silent meditation or hear the gongs and bells that punctuate the chanting. At a religious festival in some small village we might experience the presence of **kami** ("gods") as the sacred *gohei* stick is waved over our heads in purification, or taste the festival rice cakes and *sake* (rice wine) that

---

*In this book, Japanese names are written in the Japanese manner, with surname first.

inevitably play their part in the festivities. At Mt. Fuji we might hear the quiet tread of pilgrim feet climbing the mountain or feel the rare and sacred atmosphere of the mountaintop. At the Zen temple Ryoanji in Kyoto we would be struck silent by the awesome emptiness of the famous stone garden.

These and countless more are the sights and sounds, the tastes and smells, of Japanese religion. Each of them carries its own meaning but implies a whole range of associated memories and meanings. Each of them implies not only a "way" that weaves experience and expression into some meaningful "world" but also a history of tradition and practice that, when taken together, constitute the totality of religion in Japan.

Unfortunately, *our* reality room cannot be quite so vivid. The next best thing might be an imaginary tour—much as we would take if we went to Japan as tourists looking for religion. An imaginary tour not only allows us to do things we might not otherwise be able to do, but it also brings us face to face with primary images and central paradigms of Japanese religion. It allows us to roam rather freely in time and space, stopping here and there to let moments and memories work on us and open our understanding.

In a happy coincidence, such a tour will put us on one important path of Japanese religious life, that of the wandering ascetic, the itinerant priest, or the traveling pilgrim whose wandering in itself carries religious meaning. Like the religious wanderer, we can seek out a sacred geography in which the power and the ghosts of a sacred past are experienced and one's life is restored and renewed. We can seek out both moments and memories of Japanese religion and whet our appetite for more.

## TOKYO

Our tour begins in Tokyo, the heart of a modern, industrialized nation living what many would claim is a fully secularized existence based on the "religions" of technological materialism and democratic humanism. From the bustling airport to the brightly lit Ginza area of downtown Tokyo, little suggests the presence of religious awareness. A closer look may, however, uncover what we are searching for. There are, in fact, literal and figurative islands of religiousness in what seems a sea of secularity, islands that then reach out with invisible peninsulas into the daily life of the Japanese.

One such island in Tokyo is Meiji Shrine, surrounded by elaborate gardens and wooded areas. Although a relatively new shrine (1921), and unique in enshrining the spirit of the Meiji period emperor (Mutsuhito, 1852–1912) and his consort, this manifestation of Shinto implies a whole range of important religious symbols and meaning. Behind this particular shrine lies a uniquely Japanese religious awareness called the "way of the kami" (kami-no-michi), or Shinto.

If we are fortunate enough to visit the shrine on some major festival day, such as New Year's or Children's Day, we find activity at its height, for Shinto

Meiji Shrine, Tokyo.

is bound up closely with festivals and ritual. Shinto has consistently been more an orthopraxis (right practice) than an orthodoxy (right beliefs) and more a right attitude or sensitivity than a right thought or conceptual understanding. Ritual or right practice helps order a world permeated by sacred, numinous power(s) (kami). It brings kami into presence, honors and celebrates that presence, seeks its blessings, and renews life.

The shrine and its surrounding area is a holy ground marked off by the large sacred gates (*torii*). Within the grounds, in a special building, the kami is enshrined. To visit the shrine as a believer is to leave the mundane world, to come into the presence of kami, and then to return to the world purified of the defilements of mind and body.

Particular kami within this polytheistic religion have specific functions, and specific festivals and rituals serve special needs. However, in general, the notion of right practice seeking purification and celebrating the vital forces of life permeates the Japanese religious sensibility and the whole of Japanese life. From the ancient mythic accounts of the actions of the original kami in creating the world to the ritual invocation of kami to bless a new oil tanker, from the most sacred ceremonies of the great Shinto shrines to a sense of proper social order and etiquette, the concern for right practice, purification, and life-celebration is evident. This religious awareness and form is deeply ingrained in the Japanese tradition. It is not merely confined to some particular historical tradition called Shinto; it permeates and influences the deepest values and smallest details of Japanese life, even a contemporary life of apparent secularity.

Two particular examples of this, as one looks more closely at Tokyo, are the care given to scenic gardens and the sense of order and cleanliness that pervades Japanese life, even in a large city. These patterns are in part an extension of the following Shinto elements.

For traditional Japan the kami are most evident and primarily manifested in the natural world, especially those more awesome aspects such as particular trees, majestic mountains, stone, or the sun. Perhaps even more important, mythic accounts of creation reflect an ancient feeling that the Japanese islands were created by the gods in the image of paradise—a paradise on earth, as it were, from which there was no subsequent "fall." This kind of awareness suggests a clearly religious appropriation of nature and a subsequent care for its importance to human life. Although other religious and nonreligious factors certainly play a part in the appreciation of gardens and nature, the Shinto connection is perhaps most fundamental historically and religiously. Nature, in its awesome power and beauty, is the manifestation of divine power. The power of kami is immanent in this paradisal world of nature. Humanity responds in adoration, supplication, and celebration, seeking to live harmoniously the way of the kami.

The place where kami reside must be clean and pure, for in a real sense order and cleanliness are next to godliness in Japan. In Shinto, the principles of light and ordered harmony far outweigh any principles of darkness and chaos. The pure, simple, sincere, clean, and tranquil take precedence over the crowded, chaotic, or dark mysteries of life. This religious awareness manifests itself in a Shinto aesthetic that permeates the whole of Japanese sensibility and culture—an aesthetic that seeks harmonious blending with the beauty and simplicity of nature and emphasizes the pure, the clean, the tranquil, and the natural character of things.

The Meiji Shrine is, however, a large and obvious Shinto presence in the bustling modern city. Smaller, more obscure shrines are scattered here and there, too, though one may have to look to find them. One such shrine is Kanda Myojin on Tokyo's north side, not far from the famous Ueno Park. Unlike Meiji Shrine, you could easily miss it as you drive by, since it is almost hidden by the high-rise buildings surrounding it; only the torii squeezed up against one of the buildings gives evidence that a shrine is there.

With interest aroused, you might decide to peek around the almost solid wall of concrete buildings to see what lies behind them. Going in through the torii you immediately find yourself in a small but decidedly different world—walled off now from the noisy street and surrounded by the silence of the trees and shrine buildings that draw you in toward the darkness of the main building housing the kami of this shrine.

Kanda Myojin and other shrines like it are islands of religious serenity amidst a sea of apparent secularity and indifference. People support such shrines with their money and their worship but, more than that, such shrines symbolize the slightly secret presence of Shinto in the hearts of most modern Japanese—a presence not always obvious to those who may be looking for other kinds of religious evidence.

Very different from either Meiji or Kanda Shrine, yet very much a part of Tokyo and what it represents, is the site of the 1964 Olympic Games. If one visited that site, it is not unlikely that the National Stadium would be hosting a huge gathering of people with a variety of festive displays, entertainments, and speeches. One might find there a mass gathering of the modern Buddhist sect, Soka Gakkai, or a similar event sponsored by any one of the other so-called New Religions of Japan. Although the New Religions are "old" in significant ways, one common characteristic is a reshaping of religious expression into distinctive "ways" to meet the changing religious needs of a changing world. The New Religions of Japan are an important aspect of contemporary Japanese religion. They are reminders that religion changes and can often take sectarian forms. Soka Gakkai, for example, finds its roots in the Japanese form of Buddhism founded by Nichiren in the thirteenth century. However, Soka Gakkai is definitely a twentieth-century Japanese phenomenon. Like many of the New Religions, it has great popular appeal; it is not culturally, socially, economically, or religiously elitist. It speaks appealingly and authoritatively to those seekers of meaning, purpose, and community in the midst of an apparently meaningless secular world or an apparently older, irrelevant religious world. Yet it does not deny the scientific materialism of the contemporary Western world. It is a society (*gakkai*) for the creation of value (*soka*), and the values to be created are beauty, goodness, peace, happiness, and benefit for all. Although it picks up an old theme of "becoming a buddha" (an awakened or enlightened one), it reinterprets that to mean the achievement of health and happiness in this life. It adapts a traditional enlightenment-Buddhism to a popular Buddhism of more immediate, practical benefits. Rather than the radical self-transformation of traditional enlightenment, it calls for perfecting and satisfying the self that we already are, and it holds out the promise of health, wealth, peace, and happiness for all.

Soka Gakkai and the other New Religions—whether Buddhist, Shinto, or of some other orientation—are to be reckoned with in understanding Japanese religion generally. They are the new popular religions of urban, industrialized Japan. They not only serve obvious religious functions for many people, but also provide a link to Japan's religious past. Both for practitioners and for students of Japanese religion, their oldness is as important as their newness and immediate relevance. For the practitioner they provide a link in the continuity of a religious/cultural identity. For the student they manifest many of the deep structures, modes of awareness, and forms or expressions that recur throughout Japanese religious history. To look carefully at a New Religion is to see something of the pattern of significant "ways" that permeate Japanese life, as well as to discover how new and distinctive movements take shape.

One other specific example of the presence of New Religions in Tokyo is the splendid new temple of Reiyukai—yet another Nichiren-based New Religion of great popular appeal. In this building we find symbolized the buoyant—if somewhat brash and expansive—spirit of many of the New Religions. Riding a wave of popular support, appealing to lower- and middle-class people of rural background, and offering a place and message of collective caring and happy success, this and similar groups erect magnificent centers for religious worship and gatherings—centers that bespeak with pride a new-found wealth and popularity.

This particular temple, dominating its immediate surroundings (especially a small Shinto shrine just across from its sweeping entrance) is a paradigmatic example of such structures and centers. Complete with inlaid granite and marble, light and sound shows to accompany worship, and ornate fixtures all around, it expresses a Buddhist way of simple faith, care for one another, group activities and worship, and a life of success and happiness amidst the modern materialism of the day. This is a Buddhism and a religion that have accommodated to the modern world in important ways, yet have managed to keep their religious identity.

Yet other places to find religion—though very different from all the above and much less obvious—are the museums, theaters, and bookstores of contemporary Tokyo. In these places we find contemporary (and traditional) expressions of artistic and literary interests. To find "religion" here one might have to stretch the term a bit, but it may be worth the effort nonetheless, for the finest and deepest of the contemporary arts and literature have an air of the religious or spiritual about them.

What this "air" means is that they point beyond the superficial, mundane character of life and somehow bring into presence the mysterious, transcendent, universal, or deeper aspects of existence. For example, as one commentator says of the writing of Ogai Mori (1862–1922): "For Ogai, art was something universally valid, and something endowed with the power to touch its audience on the deepest level of human existence. To attain these standards, a writer had to have full command of such professional skills as the use of the conventional language of symbols, allegory, and allusion, and be familiar with the achievements of past masters."[1]

One might look at any number of twentieth-century writers to find religious themes or intention in their work. A clear example is Mishima Yukio (1925–1970). Mishima embodies in both his personal life and his literary art themes suggesting a contemporary religious art.

In the first place, Mishima's career evokes a whole tradition concerning

1. Yoshiyuki Nakai, "Ogai's Craft," *Monumenta Nipponica*, 35, no. 2 (1980), 229–235

the spiritual hero or disciplined ascetic who strives to attain the spiritual depths of purity and devotion. Such a person is called, among other things, a *gyoja*—one who strives in pursuing some spiritual path or way. Aside from the particular character of Mishima's striving, imbued as it was with overtones of the warrior's code or way (bushido), he sought to supply precisely what he laments in the following passage: "Although it is true that we are living in a period of languid peace, we do not have an appropriate ideology or philosophy of life that enables us to live with a sense of spiritual satisfaction. People in this country do not know how to live in an age of peace: their lives seem to be floating along without direction."[2]

Mishima strove in his own life to realize this "spiritual satisfaction." His dramatic suicide by *hara kiri* (or *seppuku*) in 1970 was the ultimate gesture—the ultimate ritual and "right practice" by which he sought to prove his absolute dedication to the ideals he espoused. His life and his death were an open book (as it were) amidst his own literary work. Reflected throughout his art are the ideals he held dear, and many of them carry clearly religious meaning.

Key themes in his novel *Runaway Horses* bear this out. The underlying religious theme of that book is to unite heaven and earth—both for oneself and for the nation (Japan)—in acts of absolute purity and devotion. Heaven, in this case, is the transcendent principle of the "Yamato (Japanese) spirit" as embodied in the emperor and lived out in the traditional warrior code of absolute loyalty. As Yamato spirit it suggests the mythic beginnings of the imperial line and a sacred nation under divine guidance—a time of the pure and innocent origin of a holy people with a unique Japanese spirit.

Earth, in Mishima's work, not only means normal human existence but takes on interesting feminine characteristics as well. It is as though heaven is primarily male and transcendent, while earth is female and immanent—both representing two possible poles of religious experience (radical transcendence and radical immanence). Mishima expresses this in a fascinating passage in which the main male character, Isao, dreams he is a woman. In the dream he feels everything melting into a soft, languid, warm, silent, sensuous intimacy with things. The virile "outer world" of his existence gives way to a radically intimate inner world.

> A sharp-edged mechanism of steel had died. In its place, an odor like that of decaying seaweed, an entirely organic odor, had somehow or other permeated his body. Justice, zeal, patriotism, aspirations for which to hazard one's life—all had vanished. In their place came an indescribable intimacy with the things around him . . . an intimacy in which he seemed to flow into and merge with all the minutiae of gentle, beautiful things. . . . Things clung to him like paste, and, at the same time, lost all their transcendental significance.[3]

---

2. Yukio Mishima, "An Ideology for an Age of Languid Peace," *The Japan Interpreter,* 7, no. 1 (1971), 79.

3. Yukio Mishima, *Runaway Horses,* trans. M. Gallagher (New York: Pocket Books, 1975), p. 342.

Although Mishima flirts with this theme, it is finally the virile, male way that he opts for as a technique for uniting heaven and earth. This brings us directly to a second major theme in *Runaway Horses* and to Mishima's suicide.

For Isao in the novel, and no doubt for Mishima himself, one unites heaven and earth in decisive, dedicated, devoted action. In this case it is action devoted to the sacred principles of a divine nation: absolute purity, absolute devotion to the symbols of that nation (sun, emperor), absolute fearlessness, and absolute selflessness. It is action taken in the light of a higher standard or transcendent significance that is designed to let heaven's rays bathe all and to break through the darkness that obscures that heaven. For Isao and his friends (and probably for Mishima, too) the "darkness" represents self-serving politicians backed by a greedy materialistic society; it is a Japan in danger of forgetting its traditional spiritual values. It is also the human law that does not allow disobedience in the light of a higher law. As Isao says:

> [If it weren't for the law] we would have slipped marvelously through the thicket [of the law] and gone rushing headlong up into the bright sky of heaven. . . . The law is an accumulation of tireless attempts to block a man's desire to change life into an instant of poetry. . . . The mass of men, lacking valor, pass away their lives without ever feeling the least touch of such a desire.[4]

Unfortunately, however, as Mishima has another character say later:

> Heaven and earth are cruelly kept apart. . . . The sorrowful cries of the people cover the land but cannot reach the ears of heaven. . . . Who was to carry word to heaven? Who, mounting to heaven through death, was to take upon himself the vital function of messenger? . . . To join heaven and earth, some decisive deed of purity is necessary. To accomplish so resolute an action, you have to stake your life, giving no thought to personal gain or loss. You have to turn into a dragon and stir up a whirlwind, tear the dark, brooding clouds asunder and soar up into the azure-blue sky.[5]

The "decisive deed" for Isao and his friends is to murder a few well-chosen national leaders. The decisive deed for Mishima was perhaps to finish his final and major tetralogy of novels, "The Sea of Fertility" (of which *Runaway Horses* is the second), and then to break into the central headquarters of Japan's self-defense forces and harangue the troops on Japan's fate. In any case, this decisive deed is almost necessarily consummated in ritual suicide, for seppuku (or hara kiri) is a religious act, and it consummates a religious vocation that seeks to join heaven and earth in absolute purity. Isao says it this way:

> The greatest sin is that of a man who, finding himself in a world where the sacred light of His Majesty is obscured, nevertheless determines to go on living without doing anything about it. The only way to purge this grave sin is to make a fiery

---

4. Ibid., p. 337.
5. Ibid., pp. 391–392.

offering with one's own hands, even if that itself is a sin, to express one's loyalty in action, and to commit seppuku immediately. With death, all is purified.[6]

But the absolute purity of the sword and this death are only half the picture. For Isao and Mishima, as well as for much of Japanese culture, the life and symbolism of the sacred sword is matched by the life of beauty and poetic sensitivity. The "masculine virtues" are incomplete without the "feminine virtues." The *samurai* (warrior class) specifically, and the Japanese generally, sacralize both a masculine striving for transcendence and a feminine sensitivity to the beauty of things. It is not a matter of the chrysanthemum *or* the sword but the chrysanthemum *and* the sword. This theme runs throughout Japanese religion and culture as well as throughout Mishima's work. In *Runaway Horses* it is nicely expressed in the following excerpt:

> Purity, a concept that recalled flowers, the piquant mint taste of a mouthwash, a child clinging to its mother's gentle breast, was something that joined all these directly to the concept of blood, the concept of swords cutting down iniquitous men, the concept of blades slashing down through the shoulder to spray the air with blood. And to the concept of seppuku . The moment that a samurai "fell like the cherry blossoms," his blood-smeared corpse became at once like fragrant cherry blossoms. The concept of purity, then, could alter to the contrary with arbitrary swiftness. And so purity was the stuff of poetry.[7]

Although the religious themes in Mishima's work are in some degree representative of certain themes in Japanese religious culture, they should not be understood to be typical of all Japanese religion or typical of religious themes in other contemporary art and literature. It is simply that Mishima's work is one of the more obvious places to look in contemporary literature for religious expression. Similar analysis, with different themes, can be undertaken with other authors, dramatists, painters, calligraphers, poets, or composers. The central point is that art and literature of an apparently secular sort may well reveal rich religious expression. Religion, especially in a cultural perspective, is not confined to the institutionalized forms of sectarian religions.

## KAMAKURA

Moving south from Tokyo, our tour of Japanese religions makes a brief stop in Kamakura to visit the huge open-air statue of Amida Buddha built in the year 1252 C.E. This magnificent figure brings us face to face with one strand of traditional Buddhism and Japanese religion—the "pure land" type of Buddhism focusing on faith in **Amida Buddha.** The Buddha Amida symbolizes a popular form of Buddhism that swept through Japan in the thirteenth century and has subsequently been important in the religious life of many Japanese.

---

6. Ibid., p. 188.
7. Ibid., pp. 120–121.

Amida Buddha, Kamakura Period.

This particular statue shows Amida in concentrated meditation—the central "right practice" of traditional Buddhism. Just as Gautama, the historical Buddha (active in India circa 550 B.C.E.), attained his enlightenment through meditation, so also are meditation and meditative experience crucial to the Buddhist way. Through meditation and other forms of right practice, one may become an "awakened one" (a buddha) in this very life.

Enlightenment is the ideal of the elite tradition within Buddhism—a path suggesting the monastic life and full-time pursuit of **nirvana.** It is the ideal and right practice of what we might call enlightenment or nirvanic Buddhism; it is not necessarily the ideal or practice of millions of Japanese who have had other needs and sought other goals. For them an easier path was necessary, and the goal entailed more immediate benefits. Thus was born a more popular Buddhism, one that allows a different understanding of both goals and paths.

Kamakura contains other "moments" and evokes other memories. It speaks of an important time in Japanese history when the warrior class came to power politically and economically. Trained in strenuous self-discipline and dedicated loyalty, and ready to meet death head-on in the service of their feudal lord, the samurai were attracted to the disciplined practice of Zen Buddhism. Inasmuch as Kamakura symbolizes a previously dominant warrior class, it also symbolizes the samurai patronage of Zen Buddhism. Under this patronage Zen rose to heights of religious, cultural, and even political power.

As a distinctive sect of Japanese Buddhism, Zen represents a rich tradition going back into seventh- and eighth-century China and is a manifestation of enlightenment or nirvanic Buddhism. Based on the ideals of monastic practice and focusing on seated meditation (*zazen*), Zen seeks the awakening by which one becomes a buddha in this very life. By stilling the mind and overcoming the dualism of subject/object apprehension of the world, one breaks through the scrim of the named and descriptive world of normal consciousness. In a moment of radical realization (**satori** or *kensho*), all things become clear and "en-lightened" with the light of perfected wisdom—not the wisdom of words but the wisdom that grows out of the experience of emptiness (**ku**). To attain and to live this wisdom in everyday life is enlightenment and being a buddha.

Our imaginary tour must move on. Not far from Kamakura, as we head toward Kyoto, we pass in the shadow of famous Mt. Fuji, a place rich in religious meaning and exemplary of central features of Japanese religion. Mountains have always been important in Japan, and although Fuji is not the oldest or the most sacred, it evokes a variety of significant religious themes. For example, sacred mountains are often believed to be the residence of Shinto kami. As such they embody or "house" potent forces to which one might make offerings and from which one might seek blessings. For faithful Buddhists, on the other hand, mountaintops may represent buddha-paradises or the eventual destination of souls of the dead. In a variety of ways, therefore, the mountain has traditionally been a place permeated with sacred power.

Furthermore the mountain has often been the locus of various religious practices. Shrines and temples are built on them, pilgrimage is made to them, and ancient shamanic and ascetic practices are performed there. A pilgrimage to Mt. Fuji, for example, is more than a pleasant hike. It is a purifying austerity, a journey to a spiritual center, a means by which the spirit is renewed and the mind cleared and cleansed. To make pilgrimage in Japan is to go to the sacred sources and drink of the well of spiritual energy. Through ascetic austerity one leaves behind the mundane world of attachments.

One particularly important type of folk Buddhism has taken root around mountains. This is Shugendo, a sect made up of mountain priests or practitioners (*yamabushi*) who traditionally are said to gain magical powers through ritual austerities in the mountains. The story is told of one mountain ascetic who saw himself as an incarnation of the great "celestial" bodhisattva Miroku and devoted his life to Fuji as itself the embodiment of a bodhisattva. This man was Jikigyo Miroku, an eighteenth-century Tokyo merchant who was a lifelong devotee of Fuji. The story is told that he had visions of the dawning of the age of Miroku. To help bring this new age into existence he built a shrine on Fuji and practiced austerities such as fasting. For thirty-one days he is said to have fasted and become the living embodiment of Miroku. Proving his devotion by fasting to death, he helped stimulate a Fuji cult of great popularity in the eighteenth century.

This and countless other examples suggest the power of mountains and the practices associated with them. Like Mishima's purity in *Runaway Horses,* mountains "join heaven and earth" in an almost physical manner, therefore becoming powerful symbols uniting the worlds of the sacred and the profane.

Leaving Fuji and Kamakura, we move on to the cities of Kyoto and Nara, those ancient capitals of Japan symbolic of so much of Japan's religious and cultural past.

## KYOTO/NARA

Kyoto and nearby Nara are rich fare for the religious tourist. Some of the most famous Japanese temples and shrines are found there, many dating back to the earliest beginnings of Japanese Buddhism and organized Shinto. This area was the original homeland of the clans that created a unified culture and nation. It is the womb of Japanese culture. Nara was the first capital and center of imperial rule in the eighth century, and Kyoto (then called Heian) was the second capital, from the ninth through the twelfth centuries.

A visit to Kyoto and Nara is, in fact, a visit into the very center of much of Japanese religion. It is difficult to know where to begin or where to end as one wanders from historic sites to tourist sights. Two specific places, however, might capture something of this religious world. One of these is a nineteenth-century copy of the ancient imperial palace of Heian, for it is here that the ghosts of an aristocratic world are found. This elegant world centered in the labyrinthine buildings and grounds of the imperial palace, sealed off from the mundane world of other classes and other pursuits. It was a world well represented in one of the great novels of Japanese and world literature, Lady Murasaki's *Tale of Genji*. Murasaki, a court lady who lived in the late tenth and early eleventh centuries in Heian, spins a lengthy tale of the legendary Prince Genji and evokes a world permeated by the refined taste and spiritual attitudes of the time. Although the *Tale of Genji* is not necessarily history, it reflects history and becomes the stuff of myth as sacred story and paradigmatic model.

Genji's religious world is a wholistic one. He and the other characters of the novel move easily in and out of a variety of religious forms. They visit holy men in outlying Buddhist hermitages to seek cures or to see some relative who has taken monastic vows, they call in the services of a Buddhist exorcist to heal a person possessed by a spirit, they consult Taoist astrologers and diviners to determine if the time is ripe for a given trip or undertaking, and they engage in endless ceremonies under watchful Shinto eyes. Hanging over all this, though not dominating it, is a Buddhist sense of karmic retribution and the impermanence of life.

Perhaps even more fundamental, however, is the all-pervasive rule of taste—of etiquette and ritualized behavior and refined aesthetic sensitivity. In this world of elegant but careful communication, poetry is prominent. In poetry one can communicate all the levels of refinement and sensitivity and reveal one's own status and breeding. This world of taste is at least suggested in the following scene in which Genji is ending a visit to his former nursemaid who has taken sick. During the visit he catches a glimpse of a lovely young lady. Sending a poem to her comparing her to a flower (*yugao*), he then receives an answer as he leaves.

> So he spoke tenderly. The princely scent of the sleeve which he raised to brush away his tears filled the low and narrow room, and even the young people, who had till now been irritated by their mother's obvious pride at having been the nurse of so splendid a prince, found themselves in tears.
>
> Having arranged for continual masses to be said on the sick woman's behalf, he took his leave, ordering Koremitsu to light his way with a candle. As they left the house he looked at the fan upon which the white flowers had been laid. He now saw that there was writing on it, a poem carelessly but elegantly scribbled: "The flower that puzzled you was but the *Yugao*, strange beyond knowing in its dress of shining dew." It was written with a deliberate negligence which seemed to aim at concealing the writer's status and identity. But for all that the hand showed a breeding and distinction which agreeably surprised him.[8]

Thus Genji is off on another escapade involving a new love. In the meantime, however, the passage reveals the centrality of aesthetic and emotional sensitivity, the concern for breeding and status, the importance of indirect and suggestive communication, and the centrality of poetry. This rule of taste—this poetic, aesthetic, and "feminine" sensitivity—was fundamental to aristocratic culture. Genji becomes a paradigmatic example and "cultural hero" in a tradition in which aesthetic sensitivity takes on religious meaning by providing an orientation in life and transcendent value. It is at least one of the keys that unlocks the meaning of much that is fundamental to a Japanese way of being in the world and a Japanese identity. As with Isao in *Runaway Horses,* one way of "joining heaven and earth" in Japan is by turning life into "an instant of poetry."

The subject of poetry and aesthetic sensitivity, however, leads us to another moment and memory of a very different sort. This is a visit to a performance of *takigi* (firelight) *noh* drama at Kofukuji Temple in Nara. With this, we come face to face with another Japanese religious form—sacred music and dance.

The ritual of firelight noh plays, both at Kofukuji and the nearby Shinto shrine called Kasuga, dates back at least to the thirteenth century. Performed on important festival occasions, noh and other musical, dramatic forms are a part of the process of inviting, entertaining, and sending off the various kami or buddhas being honored. When performed at night, however, this dramatic art evokes the memory of a whole tradition of ritual dance and music especially related to the ancient Shinto kagura and often enacted at night before the shrines of kami.

---

8. Murasaki Shikibu, *The Tale of Genji,* trans. A. Waley (New York: Anchor Books, 1955), pp. 70-71.

Touring modern Kyoto, one finds important shrines and temples right in the midst of the city, not to mention ancient imperial palaces and villas. Starting in Kyoto's southeast corner at Fushimi Inari Shrine, one could go up the east side of the city where it lodges against the low mountains surrounding it, cross over to the west side along the northern boundaries, and come down the west side to Katsura Villa in the southwest corner of the city. In the process, one could visit such old and famous Zen temples as Tofukuji, Daitokuji, Ryoanji, and Myoshinji; or other Buddhist temples such as Zenrinji, Nishi and Higashi Honganji, and Niinaji.

Shinto shrines, too, dot the way. Starting with Fushimi Inari Shrine, dedicated to the kami of rice and agriculture, one could find such old and famous shrines as Yoshida, Heian, Kamigamo, and Kitano Shrines. A tranquil beauty in these places draws one to the central shrine that houses the kami. If one is lucky, one would see or hear a priest chanting prayers or hear the mysterious strains of Shinto music. Better yet, one might encounter a festival with its colorful participants and processions and its entertaining events. One might even be invited to participate by offering a small branch to the kami or by drinking the festival sake that flows at **matsuri** (festival) time.

Of course, the moments and memories of an imaginary tour, like the moments and memories of a real one, are practically endless. Our purpose here is merely to offer a taste and to stimulate the appetite for more. We hope the following chapters will satisfy at least some part of that appetite.

*japanese religion in historical perspective*

## THE STORY OF JAPANESE RELIGION

The long history of religion in Japan has been dominated by three major historical themes. As an introduction to this section, let us look at them in order. First, there is the theme of tension and accommodation between indigenous, native Japanese religion and spiritual influences coming in from outside Japan. The most obvious indigenous religious tradition is that which has come to be identified as Shinto, and the major outside influence has been Buddhism. But the actual situation is more complex than that. The tension and accommodation pattern undoubtedly goes back to prehistoric times when migrations from north and south brought about various religious patterns and practices that had to be reconciled. In early historic times, Confucian, Taoist, and Buddhist elements moved into Japan seeking reconciliation with the native kami. In more recent times, a Japanese religious synthesis made up of all these factors blended together—Confucianism, Taoism, Buddhism, and Shinto—has in effect stood over against new outside visitors such as Christianity and Western secularism.

Throughout this history Japan has swung from a welcome of outsiders as attractive contributors to a rejection of them as threats to Japanese integrity. In the end, though, Japan has managed with remarkable skill to preserve both sides of the dilemma. It has accepted innovations from without but succeeded in making them thoroughly Japanese, and it has done so without allowing indigenous traditions to be wholly submerged and lost.

This is partly due to the fact that Japan, unlike many countries, has never had an alien faith imposed by outside conquerors; the many foreign influences that have reached its shores have come peacefully as gifts, and the country has had time to accept, adjust, or reject them in its own way. Also, Japan's particular pattern of accepting religious pluralism has allowed the many paths of faith to maintain their identity while subtly smoothing off their rough edges until they are compatible with the function of religion in Japanese society.

Second, Japanese religion has been dominated by tension between strong, charismatic individuals on the one hand and the role of religion in providing social coherence on the other. Scholars have sometimes expressed this in terms of an archaic contrast between **ujigami,** or kami protecting the clan (*uji*) or community, whose role enforces the cohesion and continuity of established patterns of society; and the **hitogami** or visiting "outsider" god (often manifested through shamans) who brings innovation, strange messages, and nonordinary phenomena. Throughout Japanese religious history, especially on the Buddhist side and later among the New Religions, charismatic persons, sometimes called **hijiri** or holy men, have brought new messages. Kobo Daishi, Shinran, Nichiren, Nakayama Miki, and so forth, have all challenged conventional faith and started new movements based initially on individual conversion rather than on communal adherence.[1] In time, however, like all enduring religions, their causes have become institutionalized, firmly established in family and community groups. The interaction between established community religion and innovative charismatic figures has been a long-term dynamic in Japanese religion.

Third, in Japan as elsewhere there has been far-reaching and often creative tension between religion as contact with ultimate reality and means of salvation, and religion as a social and cultural system. Religion plays several roles at once: offering contact with the ultimate, bestowing salvation, legitimating the social and political order, and providing themes and inspiration to artists and architects, writers and poets. The tensions and opportunities presented by these several roles are common to religion throughout the world, but in Japan they have been especially subtle because Japanese religion has, insofar as possible, embraced them all as one. For example, despite the role of charismatic figures mentioned above, Japanese religion has generally encouraged individuals to make contact with the ultimate and find salvation in a way appropriate to their family and community roots, and it has placed severe sanctions against spiritual deviants. Despite possible tensions between religious faith and aesthetics, Japanese religion has tried to relate the two very closely. A thousand combinations of the sacred and the aesthetic in Japan, from temple gardens to the noh drama, testify to this spirit.

---

1. See Ichiro Hori, "On the concept of Hijiri (Holy Man)," *Numen,* 5, no. 2 (April 1958), 128–160; no. 3 (September 1958), 199–232.

## Archaic Japanese Religion

Although remains from the Stone Age going back many thousands of years have been found in Japan, the earliest culture that appears to have much relation to historic Japanese civilization is the Jomon, dating from around 8000 B.C.E. to about 200 C.E. It is classified as neolithic, possessing sedentary village life and rudimentary agriculture. The Jomon people gradually moved from a hunting, fishing, and gathering economy, largely along the seashore, to planting such tubers as yams.

Like many neolithic cultures, Jomon religion emphasized fertility. Female clay figures, perhaps goddesses or earth mothers, have been found at Jomon sites, as have male phallic representations at household shrines. Serpents, also associated with fertility, frequently decorate pottery, suggesting a snake cult. Other aspects of Jomon religion are indicated by clay masks that may have been employed by shamans.

Finally, Jomon culture produced the remarkable clay figures known as *dogu*—bizarre but exquisitely crafted, half-animal, half-human figures with peculiar slit eyes that have reminded some of ski masks. It would be strange if these figures did not have some magical or supernatural meaning, but since the Jomon peoples left no written records we can only speculate. We may note, however, that already the brilliant fusion of the religion and the artistic, which has characterized Japan so well, had arisen. Broadly speaking, Jomon culture and religion were probably comparable to that of Polynesia and Melanesia at the time of initial European contact.

A more advanced stage appeared in Japan during the next major prehistoric period, the Yayoi, dating from about 200 B.C.E to 250 C.E. Wet rice agriculture was introduced from Southeast Asia and gradually spread northward from Kyushu during this period. Metal was also introduced, probably from Korea. The earliest metal objects were of ritual rather than practical use: swords, spears, mirrors, and bells that probably served as sacred objects in shrines have been found buried with important persons.

Yayoi religion was centered on agricultural rites and shamanism. The *niiname,* the harvest festival that has been so important to Shinto and the rites of the imperial house down through the centuries, has its roots in this era. Female shamanesses, especially, had important roles both among the common people and as oracles on matters of state.

We get a vivid portrait of conditions in Japan at that time from the accounts of travelers from China. They tell us that people ate raw vegetables from bamboo or wooden trays, clapped their hands for worship rather than kneeling, were fond of liquor, long-lived, and generally honest. These chronicles tell us that the country was formerly ruled by a man, but more recently (apparently in the third century C.E., after a period of turmoil) by a woman named Pimiko. She was a shamaness who lived in seclusion with a thousand female attendants and a single male who mediated between her and the outside world. The narratives suggest that this sorceress queen remained unmarried and "bewitched the people."[2]

This was about the time that the Kofun era, 250–552 C.E., began. Kofun means "great tomb" or "tumulus" and refers to the most striking relics of this age, immense earthen monuments built for rulers and great men. These edifices were often a keyhole shape and surrounded by a moat. The goods found in these tombs give us a colorful picture of the life of the upper classes of the time. On the flanks of the artificial hills were clay figures, called *haniwa,* charmingly and skillfully executed and representing retainers intended to follow the deceased to the other world. Dancers, warriors, animals, and even figures thought to be shamanesses all share the same hollow oval eyes and tiny expressionless mouths that give these statues an odd, timeless, immortal quality, as though each were an archetype of the activity in which he or she was engaged. Within the tomb the body was surrounded by sacred mirrors, swords, and jewels (three items that are still the sacred regalia of the Japanese emperor) and by remarkable paintings and accoutrements, such as "soul boats" apparently designed to ferry the spirit to the other world.

All these objects show considerable continental influence. The comma-shaped jewels (*magatama*), important as holders of sacred power, are comparable to Korean models; large bronze ritual bells called *dotaku* are reminiscent of similar items in China's splendid Bronze Age. In fact, metalworkers of early Japan appear largely to have been Korean immigrants, and, as in many archaic societies, the blacksmith's art had sacred connotations: metal swords could fend off evil spirits and metal mirrors hold benign ones.

After a time of turmoil Japan was unified under the Yamato house, progenitors of the present imperial line, around 350 C.E. One theory is that a new wave of immigrants who were horseriders arrived around that time via Korea (although they may have originated farther north) and seized military power over the more sedentary older population; the leader of their chief clan was, in the later terminology, *tenno* or emperor, though actually he was no more than a first among equals or a paramount chief in a society of largely independent clans.[3] Each clan was under the patronage of the clan kami. This deity's priest was the chieftain. Frequently a female relative such as a sister or wife of the ruler would serve as shamaness giving oracles from the clan kami and other gods and spirits. But gradually the roles of chieftain and priest separated, with priests serving at specific shrines. Shamanesses called *miko* or *ichiko* delivered divine messages both at shrines and among the common people.

2. See Ryusaku Tsunoda and L. Carrington Goodrich, *Japan in the Chinese Dynastic Histories,* Perkins Asiatic Monograph no. 2 (South Pasadena, Calif.: P. D. & Ione Perkins, 1951). A selection of this material can be found in R. Tsunoda, W. T. de Bary, and D. Keene, *Sources of Japanese Tradition,* 2 vols. (New York: Columbia University Press, 1964), I, 5–14.

3. For a lively contribution to the debate on Japanese prehistory and the role of the horse people, see Gari Ledyard, "Galloping Along with the Horseriders: Looking for the Founders of Japan," *The Journal of Japanese Studies,* 1, no. 2 (Spring 1975), 217–254.

The world of clans and kami was modified irreversibly by the sixth and seventh centuries through the introduction of Buddhist and Confucian thought, as well as by the subsequent consolidation of state and society on a Chinese pattern with Buddhism as a state-patronized religion. But the world of archaic Japan did not wholly disappear, nor has it to this day. Its worldview is perpetuated in the rites of Shinto—both those of the court and of the ordinary shrine. Beneath the facade of continental bureaucracy the old loyalties and power structures of clan and family continued (and continue) to broker the real power in Japanese political and social life.

Before moving to the new world of Japanese religion after Buddhism, we would do well to pause for a moment to review what the old but still living world of clans and kami was like. This is the worldview reflected in the classic mythology of the *Kojiki* and *Nihonshoki*.[4] There a three-story universe comprised the "high plain of heaven" (*takama-no-hara*), where the sovereign deities lived; the "manifest world" (*utsushi-yo*), earth as we know it; and the underworld (*yomo-tsukuni*), abode of the dead and of unclean spirits. Kami were everywhere and able to move easily between these three levels; in particular, heavenly kami descended from above to give divine kingship to the people and fertility to the fields.

This pattern is evidenced in the sequence of agricultural rites. In the spring, fecundating kami were believed to descend into their shrines on high places, such as mountaintops, or by the seashore. They would be met by processions of worshipers who would greet them, lead them joyously into the fields, and dance to celebrate their divine labors as they planted and transplanted rice. In the fall would come the niiname or harvest festival, the greatest event of the ritual year, when the kami of the fields would be honored for the bounteous ingathering and seen off until the coming year. The niiname, commemorating as it did the turning of the seasons, also had New Year's overtones; masked visitors, like mummers or Halloween trick-or-treaters, would go from house to house.

The harvest festival also had, and still has, close links with sacred kingship. The emperor, like other rulers throughout the archaic world, had important magical responsibilities for fertility as well as for political stability. The same kami who descended from the high plain of heaven to bring forth the child of the harvest also mated with earthly kami to produce a kingly lineage. All this is consummated ritually at the harvest festival celebrated by the emperor as high priest each fall. The most significant performance of that rite, called the *daijo-sai* or "great food festival," is celebrated by a new emperor the year after his accession. In an elaborate and ancient ritual, rice and wine from special fields are twice presented by the new sovereign to the deities in the middle of the night as a sort of holy communion. This rite, still performed as the climax of an im-

---

4. The standard translations of the *Kojiki* and *Nihonshoki* are Donald L. Philippi, *Kojiki* (Tokyo: University of Tokyo Press, 1968), and W. G. Aston, *Nihongi* (London: George Allen & Unwin, reprint, 1956).

perial accession, is today perhaps the most archaic state ritual still intact in the modern world.[5]

Another vital aspect of ancient Shinto was its emphasis on purity versus pollution. Shinto shrines, like the kami they housed, were immaculate—places set apart and approachable only by the pure. Anything ritually impure—contaminated by disease, death, or blood—was prohibited; persons entering the clean, austere precincts of a shrine (in this period usually just an open-air altar in a sacred place, or at best a temporary shrine in the harvest fields) would first cleanse themselves with water. The spiritual importance of cleanliness, and of pure sanctuaries that the pollution of the world cannot touch, has had a deep, longstanding impact on Japanese values and culture.

## The Coming of Buddhism

The traditional date for the introduction of Buddhism to Japan corresponds to 538 or 552 C.E. We are told by the *Nihonshoki* that in that year a Korean king sent the Japanese emperor a Buddhist scripture and image with a letter extolling their merits. The permeation of the Buddha's **dharma** ("teaching," "truth"), and equally of Confucian thought (which may have arrived even earlier) was certainly a more gradual process than such an exact date would suggest, but the date does indicate approximately the time Buddhism began to be politically significant. The chief early source of mainland (Chinese) culture was Korea; therefore, with Buddhism came not only the envoys of Korean rulers but also immigrant Korean craftsmen. Thus, in addition to Buddhism's philosophy and faith, a technology and art much in advance of Japan's had come to Japanese shores in the sixth century.

The historical periods within which the new continental culture, including Buddhism, was slowly and often painfully assimilated are called the Asuka (552–645) and the Hakuho (645–710). The Asuka period began with disputes over the new Buddhist faith: some factions wanted Japan to adopt it, but others were opposed. The Buddhist cause was taken up by the powerful Soga family but was opposed by the Mononobe and Nakatomi houses, who had traditional Shinto priestly roles. The argument deteriorated into a civil war out of which the Soga prevailed. Soga no Umako completed his seizure of power in 592 by arranging the assassination of the emperor. He placed his own niece on the throne as the Empress Suiko. She was a devout Buddhist and appointed as her regent the imperial prince, Shotoku (573–621).

Prince Shotoku was among the most brilliant and influential rulers in Japan's history. His era was a turning point in the emergence of three important elements: a mature Japanese culture, Buddhism as a national religion, and a consolidated state. The prince sought to use Buddhism as a unifying ideology

---

5. See Robert S. Ellwood, *The Feast of Kingship: Accession Ceremonies in Ancient Japan* (Tokyo: Sophia University Press, 1973).

Prince Shotoku (573–621).

transcending the individual clan, since as an imported religion it was the special possession of no contentious chieftain but only of the imperial house and the national government. In this era and after, the Soga assiduously patronized Buddhist arts and architecture as well as learned monks to enhance their own prestige.

Shotoku founded the first major national temple, the famous Horyuji Temple outside of Nara, in 607. Although most of the present edifices were built later than Shotoku's time, Horyuji remains a treasure house of early Buddhist art. In 604, by traditional dating (some scholars would put it much later), the so-called "Seventeen Article Constitution" attributed to Shotoku was issued.[6] Though not a constitution in the modern sense, it was a set of lofty ethical principles for government servants—largely Confucian in inspiration, though Buddhism is mentioned. The importance of this document lies in the extent to which it shows that Confucian and Buddhist ideas had become normative in Japanese intellectual life, and that a state and civil service based on them was

---

6. The Seventeen Article Constitution can be found in Aston, *Nihongi*, pt. 2, pp. 129-133.

Miroku Bodhisatta, Nara Period.

at least an ideal to strive for. This constitution, whether by Shotoku or a later hand invoking his memory, was a first step toward the rationalized, bureaucratic administration undergirded by religion that Shotoku wanted.

Shotoku tried hard to give balanced attention to Buddhism, Shinto, and Confucianism. His own Buddhism was a practical, layman's faith indifferent to doctrinal quibbles and monkish squabbles. His interests are shown by the three sutras (Buddhist scriptures) on which he is said to have written commentaries: the *Lotus Sutra,* with its theme of universal salvation; the *Vimalakirti Sutra,* emphasizing the path of the lay devotee; and the *Srimala Sutra,* chanted for the protection of the nation by Buddhism. Shotoku appreciated not only the nation-building and cultural potentials of Buddhism but also its philanthropy: the temples he had built contained schools, hospitals, and orphanages under the care of monks and nuns, as well as rich halls of worship.

An enduring legacy of this period is the magnificent Buddhist sculpture in those seventh-century temples. It is still inspiring today—one can only imagine how it must have seemed to the Japanese when it represented the arrival of a culture and faith much more sophisticated than anything that had been known before. Consider, for example, the Miroku (Maitreya, the coming Buddha of the future) in Horyuji Temple and its near-relative in Koryuji Temple in Kyoto. These seventh-century figures are based on Korean models and were probably constructed by Korean master artists resident in Japan. Nevertheless they point to the spirit that was to emerge in the greatest Japanese religious art.

The Miroku figure is clad only in a light and simple robe. He is in seated meditation on a stool, but the feeling is not one of heavy, ponderous concentration. Rather, one senses a state beyond even that—a condition of infinite awareness so sublimely perfected that it has the appearance of casual ease. Yet his is a calm state worn with the easy grace that only the enlightened attain in this cosmos of anxiety and woe. The coming Buddha sits with one leg laid lightly across the other and rests his head gently on the fingers of one hand; his eyes are alive yet downcast in quiet inwardness. With clean, sure lines and exquisite simplicity the sculptor suggests the poise and equilibrium that, especially in Mahayana Buddhism, are the hallmark of transcendent spiritual achievement.

As we move down the centuries of Japanese religion we will find the same statement—that the eternal is best found in the simple grace of the natural—reiterated time and again, whether in the rustic Shinto shrine or in the Zen art that finds the Buddha-essence in a gnarled tree or in a Zen master's half-stern, half-laughing face.

Buddhism continued to be favored under the Soga rulers during the first half of the seventh century, although the quality of that rule after Shotoku's death diminished. Later Soga rulers engendered increasing popular opposition for their high-handed ways and favoritism toward the foreigners they brought in to serve their cultural revolution. In 645 resentment came to a head. Nakatomi Kamatari, later given the surname Fujiwara, overthrew the Soga regime. The Fujiwara clan were to become all-powerful a little later in the Heian period: the coup of 645, then, heavily influenced the course of Japanese history for many centuries. The first major result of the new administration was the Taika Reform of 646, which attempted centralization of the nation in an absolute monarchy working through a rationally organized bureaucracy. Land was transferred to the crown, which was then to redistribute it equitably. The reform was only partially implemented, and then only with modest success, but the precedent it set was also to have lasting consequences.

The Emperors Tenchi (r. 661–671) and Temmu (r. 671–686) and the Empress Jito (r. 686–697) were, despite somewhat troubled times, strong sovereigns who promoted Buddhism and government authority. Temmu and his widow Jito also assured that the court Shinto rites, dear to their Nakatomi supporters, were updated and given parallel status to Buddhism; the Nakatomi family's senior branch became chief court-Shinto chaplains and chief priests at the Grand Shrine of Ise around this time—positions they held until 1872.

It was during this period that such court-Shinto observances as the practice of sending an imperial princess to the Grand Shrine of Ise as priestess emerge from the mists of myth and assume their historic forms. Indeed, the Ise Daijingu or "Grand Shrine," located near the east coast of Japan and dedicated to two goddesses (Amaterasu, deity of the sun and ancestress of the imperial line, and Toyouke, goddess of food), appears to have come into national importance as the main imperial shrine around this time, too. The Emperor Temmu also ordered the production of the *Kojiki,* the invaluable collection of ancient myths and scraps of history that presents the court's understanding of Japan's origin and destiny, though the book was not completed until 712. (It was supplemented in 720 by the *Nihonshoki,* a much fuller chronicle of Japan from the first descent of the gods to the reign of Jito.)

The seventh-century reforms were institutionalized in the Taiho Code, promulgated in 702 by the Emperor Mommu. Supplemented by commentaries to form a legal system called *ritsuryo* (laws and regulations), it not only explained the new bureaucratic structure modeled on the Chinese but also regulated priests, monks, and nuns (showing their ultimate subordination to the state) and provided for various state Shinto rites, such as the seasonal cycle culminating in the niiname or harvest festival, the accession daijo-sai or food festival celebrated by a new emperor, and the sending of the princess to Ise Shrine. The emperor and the Nakatomi priests had central roles in these rites as celebrated in the palace shrines, indicating the state character of Shinto. Of particular interest is the fact that this Japanese constitution has one high bureau not found in the Chinese models, the *jingi-kan* or shrine office. It was dominated by the Nakatomi clan and it administered Shinto affairs, especially the court rites, independently of any other bureau.

## The Nara Period (710–794)

In 710, the first permanent capital of Japan was established at Nara, a new city designed after the capital of the splendid T'ang dynasty then ruling in China. Until then the capital had been a more or less temporary settlement that was moved after the death of each emperor because of the Shinto taboo against death pollution. With the ending of that practice a city could be built that reflected the full power of Japan's emerging Buddhist culture. Nara became an entire city of opulent palaces and lavish temples, spaced by lovely parks.

The visitor to Nara today can see something of that wonder. Walking through the famous Deer Park of Nara—with its scattered pagodas, temples, and tame deer—and up the pathways of stone lanterns leading to the vermilion-porched Kasuga Shrine, home of the patron kami of the great Fujiwara clan, is like stepping into a fairy-tale past. Not far away, in the Todaiji Temple, the Great Buddha (Vairocana Buddha) of Nara looms over fifty feet high, surrounded by many smaller buddhas like the central light of ultimate reality reflected in innumerable universes.

The realities of Nara during its golden age were not as idyllic as its living remains suggest, but before we come to that story let us examine the nature of Buddhism in Nara. Our focus will be on Buddhism because the Nara period represents a time when, perhaps more than at any other, Buddhism was the leading edge of cultural and social advance. Several different traditions of Buddhist teaching were welcomed in Japan, whether brought by imported Chinese, Korean, or Indian priests or by Japanese sent to study in China at government expense. These include the six sects of Nara Buddhism, though actually they were little more than intellectual schools sometimes based in particular temples. Two were Theravada teachings, now extinct as schools in Japan. Two others, of Mahayana background, are also now extinct as separate institutions: the Sanron (Madhyamika) and Ritsu (Vinaya) schools. The former was more philosophic, whereas the latter emphasized monastic discipline and correct lineages of ordination. During the Nara period certain Ritsu priests were prominent and gave lay ordination to members of the imperial family.

The most significant of the Nara schools, however, were the Hosso and the Kegon schools. Though small today when compared with the great Buddhist denominations that arose later, they remain the custodians of temples of great historic and artistic interest in and around Nara. Hosso, to which Horyuji and Kofukuji Temples in Nara belong, is the Japanese version of Yogacara or Vijnanavada, the "mind only" school of Mahayana Buddhism that teaches that all apparent reality is projected out of consciousness in accordance with patterns of perception embedded in it. The Kegon or Avatamsaka school, based on the *Garland Sutra,* is housed at Todaiji as well as in other temples. It emphasizes the infinity of universes, the interrelatedness of all things, and the worship of Vairocana (the figure portrayed by the Great Buddha)—a cosmic budda representing unlimited absolute reality itself.

Beyond the schools, however, Buddhism was developing in a different way out in the countryside. Popular Buddhist teachers and wonder-workers, often called *ubasoku* from the Sanskrit word for disciple, wandered about combining Buddhism—often superficially understood as a magical means to marvelous power—with native shamanism. They were not properly ordained, especially by strict Ritsu standards, but they and their admirers often considered them something far better than an ordinary ordained monk, namely, a *bodhisattva.* Their mystic path was called *bosatsu-do,* the "way of the bodhisattva." Like a bodhisattva who lives only for wisdom and compassion, they went from village to village consoling the sick, counseling the oppressed, performing divination and miraculous healings, and leading the populace in such practical works as building bridges and irrigation systems. Often these charismatic figures also spoke out on behalf of the common people, alluding to the grasping and hypocrisy of the upper classes and the orthodox monks who ministered to them.[7]

Such pointed sermons found ready audiences, for the social problems of the Nara era ran deep. Far from sharing in the splendors of Nara civilization, the lower classes only became poorer and more oppressed as the eighth century wore on. Rationalized government brought with it regimentation and heavier taxation. Temples themselves became wealthy landowners and were no less assiduous than lay nobles in collecting rents. In those days only sons and daughters of the aristocracy could aspire to ecclesiastical office or the convent. In short, the gulf between rich and poor, between those who enjoyed the splendid Buddhist culture and those whose labor supported it, became greater. It is not surprising, then, that the peasantry turned to an alternative form of Buddhism that was more congenial to the familiar shamanistic religion of the country.

By mid-century it was apparent that these two levels of Buddhism and of society would have to be reconciled. Edicts attempting to control the irregular clergy successively failed. The pious Emperor Shomu, desiring to build the Great Buddha as a national cathedral, found that donations of money and labor from outside the capital were in short supply. In a dramatic gesture Shomu appointed a man called Gyogi Bosatsu (670–749), an established leader and spokesman for the countryside shamanistic Buddhists, chief priest of the nation. This was despite the fact that Gyogi was not regularly ordained and had earlier (in 717) been arrested for preaching to peasants the heretical doctrine that one could be saved through good works. In exchange for his sudden elevation, Gyogi won his followers over to the Emperor's cause, and according to tradition he also visited the Grand Shrine of Ise and obtained the blessing of the great kami Amaterasu on the building of the Great Buddha. The temple was completed in 749, the year of Gyogi's death, and the Emperor Shomu himself took monastic vows, abdicating in favor of his daughter Koken.

Here was the beginning of a scandal that brought discredit on Nara Buddhism. Koken abdicated in 758 in favor of a young prince, the Emperor Junnin. She then, according to accounts, became romantically involved with the court chaplain, an ambitious priest called Dokyo, who had been trained in both shamanistic and orthodox circles. Dokyo convinced the former Empress to depose Junnin, whom she later had strangled, and regain the throne herself as the Empress Shotoku. Dokyo then plotted to seize imperial power for himself, but his conspiracy was thwarted by a timely oracle from the kami Hachiman at his main shrine in Usa on the island of Kyushu.

By now it was evident that the government ought to be separated from the steamy religious atmosphere of Nara. In 784 the new Emperor Kammu moved

---

7. See Joseph M. Kitagawa, *Religion in Japanese History* (New York: Columbia University Press, 1966), pp. 38–45.

the capital out of Nara. After a ten-year hiatus in Nagaoka it was settled in Heian, modern Kyoto, in 794. The vivid Nara period was at an end.

Two final points about this period should be made. First, not all irregular, shamanistic Buddhists were wholly reconciled to the political and religious "establishment." Those who remained outside were the first of a lineage of quasi-independent persons of spiritual power who depended more on charisma and shamanlike initiations than on legitimate ecclesiastical office. One example from this period is En-no-Shokaku, legendary founder of the order of yamabushi ("mountain adepts"), colorful practitioners of shugendo. Considering, as did indigenous shamans before them, the mountains of Japan to be "other worlds" where gods and buddhas dwelt and where supernatural powers could be obtained, they went into the mountains to practice such rigorous austerities as standing under cold waterfalls for hours to meditate and being hung by the heels over high cliffs in order to acquire power, to combat evil spirits, and to heal and divine. They usually belonged to lively bands or orders that would spend part of the year in the mountains to meditate, to initiate new members, and to practice mystic rites, and then descend to the villages to ply their magical trades. Buddhism of a tantric (esoteric) sort, like that of Tibet, fitted easily into this tradition since it also put great stock in words of power (*mantra*) and harsh initiatory disciplines to train the adept, whereas its sweeping Mahayana philosophy provided an intellectual undergirding for the practices. The yamabushi were nominally affiliated with one of the major Heian denominations, Shingon or Tendai (themselves deeply dyed with tantrism, Shingon most explicity). But, for most practical purposes, the yamabushi priests were free agents. In many parts of Japan they were mainstays of popular religion, whether as magical healers or pilgrim guides, and down to modern times they can still be found.[8] In the nineteenth and twentieth centuries, this charismatic tradition received a vigorous revitalization in the New Religions, many of whose founders were influenced by shugendo and experienced initiations comparable to the yamabushi practitioners.

A second point to note is that Shinto, although perhaps lacking the glamour of Nara Buddhism, was not eclipsed but survived and, indeed, played a vital role in legitimating Buddhism as well as actions of the government. The traditions claiming that Gyogi sought and received approval from Amaterasu at the Ise Grand Shrine for the construction of the Great Buddha, and that a word from Hachiman at Usa countered the schemes of Dokyo, are significant. Further, during the Nara period the foundation appears to have been lain for synthesizing the two religions, so Shinto kami were made to be guardians, pupils, or manifestations of the great buddhas and bodhisattvas of the alien faith. Thus Amaterasu the sun goddess, for example, was identified with Vairocana as the

---

8. See H. Byron Earhart, *A Religious Study of the Mount Haguro Sect of Shugendo* (Tokyo: Sophia University Press, 1970).

"Great Sun Buddha" (Dainichi), who is the supreme expression of the universal essence.

## The Heian Period (794-1185)

The Heian period was the golden age of classical Japanese culture and imperial court society. Its great ideal, among the upper classes, was *miyabi,* courtly elegance and taste, that elusive quality of utter grace and refinement so well illustrated in Lady Murasaki's *Tale of Genji* (*Genji Monogatari*). This book, considered the greatest masterpiece of Japanese literature, portrays life at court—a life that centered on refined aesthetic sensitivity, poetic expertise, and proper ritual decorum.

The Heian state was nominally ruled by the emperor, but real power was held by the Fujiwara family. The most powerful Fujiwara rulers became virtual dictators. They perpetuated their power by marriage: Emperors customarily made Fujiwara women their consorts and abdicated after producing an infant heir for whom the chief Fujiwara minister could serve as regent. The greatest of the Fujiwara statesmen, Michinaga (966-1027), was, whether in or out of office, the real power in the country throughout no less than eight such brief imperial reigns. Michinaga lived a regal life, complete with a private temple designed to reproduce the wonder of a Buddhist paradise; it had jeweled nets on the trees and peacocks around the pond. "My aspiration," he allegedly said, "is fully satisfied like a full moon in the sky."

Others were less well pleased with Fujiwara domination, and when the Heian era finally ended, with it ended effective rule by that house. The Heian state was weakened and finally felled by complex struggles on the one hand between the Fujiwara and retired emperors who increasingly strove to exercise power as the era wore on, and on the other between the capital and the restive warlords in the provinces. In fact it was the growing gulf between the court and the warrior class (who came to realize they held the true economic and military might) that precipitated the end of the Heian period.

The old court at Heian, for all its flaws, has ever since held a nostalgic charm for the Japanese. In more warlike or crassly materialistic ages, its leisurely pace of life, humanistic values, and elegance have hovered brightly at the back of the national mind. Always more of a dream than a reality, the old capital's meaning was never better expressed than in a few lines by the great haiku poet Basho in the seventeenth century:

> *I am in the Old Capital*
> *Yet still I yearn for the Old Capital—*
> *Ah, the Bird of Time.* *

*The last line speaks of the *hototogisu,* the Japanese cuckoo, here written with characters meaning "bird of time." Like the Western nightingale, the hototogisu is a bird of rich, poetic associations, whose call evokes feelings of pathos, yearning, and unattainable beauty.

Characteristically, Heian religion appears in the literature and general culture more as bits and pieces, and as instruments of mood and feeling, than as systematic philosophy or practice. The miyabi or "courtly elegance" spirit was more emotive than logical. Theoretical inconsistencies involved in relating, as the Heian world did, to several religion or value systems at once—Buddhist, Shinto, Confucian, Taoist—bothered it not at all; they accepted anything that added to the present a nuance of depth or allayed a superstitious fear. Thus we find in Heian literature and history a melancholy Buddhist awareness of the transitoriness of beauty and love, plots turning on such Shinto observances as the sending of an imperial princess to Ise where she would serve as priestess, the keeping of a Taoist calendar and directional taboos, and the rhetoric of Confucian ethics in state documents. There were exceptions, of course. We are told of one Ise princess, a devout Buddhist, who bemoaned the peril her service of Amaterasu might bring to her ultimate salvation since no Buddhist worhip was allowed in the Saigu, the ritually pure lodge near the Grand Shrine of Ise where the vestal priestess lived. Among priests there were theologians quite capable of rigorous thought and trenchant argument, but the Heian nobility for the most part (and, we must suppose, the illiterate peasantry who have left few traces) seemed satisfied with their syncretistic spirituality of diverse strands.

Institutionally, Heian religion was dominated by two great Buddhist denominations, Shingon and Tendai. Each was founded by a powerful charismatic individual and was headquartered on a particular mountain. Thus these two schools represented styles of Buddhism that went far toward accommodating the new religion to the old shamanistic spirituality.

Shingon was founded by Kukai (773–836), called posthumously Kobo Daishi, a brilliant monk whose life spanned the transition of the center of power from Nara to Heian. Originally trained for government service, Kukai's interests turned toward religion in the course of his education. As early as 797 he produced his first major work, the *Sango shiiki.* Endeavoring to harmonize Taoism, Confucianism, and Buddhism, this book is a foretaste of Kukai's lifelong concern to reconcile various religions, as well as the diverse schools of Buddhism, on deep levels of profundity.

Around the same time, however, Kukai discovered the *Mahavairocana Sutra,* a work of tantric or esoteric Buddhism that emphasizes that Vairocana is the central deity and personification of the essence of the universe, the *dharmakaya* ("truth body"). For Kukai this teaching represented the crown of Buddhism and the perspective from which all other teachings were to be appreciated and interpreted. Vairocana was also shared with the Kegon school, but Kukai's school, called Shingon or "True Word," goes further in its instruction about spiritual practice and achievement. Kukai believed that an adept could, through mystic means, become one with the essence of the universe and so achieve Buddhahood "in this body, in this lifetime" (*sokushin jobutsu*).

The means for doing this centered on the esoteric "three secrets" he taught: *mudras* (hand gestures), *dharani* (chants aligned to the tantric spiritual beings), and yogic meditations, including evocations of those powerful allies. Furthermore, Shingon makes great use of complex **mandalas,** rituals, and works of art. The two basic mandalas, or symbolic arrangements of cosmic buddhas, are the womb and diamond mandalas representing universal essence at work, that is, wisdom lived out in compassionate action.

Art, like ritual, is of great importance to Shingon because it is a vehicle for the realization of buddhahood. It is not surprising, then, that Shingon made extremely important contributions to the continuing development of Japanese religious art and, even more significant, to the spiritual attitudes that down to the present have shaped artists' approaches to their craft. For, in this perspective, art becomes meditation since artists must themselves be in touch with their buddhahood. Furthermore, Japanese art has always been, through a kind of secularization of the Shingon principle, highly medium-oriented—as much concerned to portray the "essence" of the mood or ink itself as of the subject it is made to depict.

Shingon's emphasis on sacred art had another consequence of tremendous import: the popularization of Buddhism among the common people. Shingon art portrayed extremely deep and esoteric matters, but these same pictures and statues became the "books" of the illiterate. Commoners might not have understood the doctrines behind the strange and powerful figures who increasingly graced local temples and wayside shrines, but they could feel elevated by the sense of wonder and mystery they conveyed. Moreover, esoteric buddhas and bodhisattvas stepped out of the mandalas, so to speak, to become elements within folk religion: Jizo, friend of children, travelers, and the dead; Kannon, bodhisattva of compassion; and Amida, savior of those who call upon his name.

It is characteristic of Shingon that it operated at once on many levels, from unsophisticated peasant faith to that of erudite monks, while providing the nobility with eloquent preachers and spectacular rituals. This was entirely in accord with the syncretizing thought of Kobo Daishi who strove to unite all religions and all aspects of human experience into one vast but coherent system. Kukai's writings include the *Jujushinron,* a remarkable survey of all known religions and schools of Buddhism arranged according to levels in the quest for total enlightenment. Thus Kegon, because it was based on the interrelatedness of all things and on Vairocana as the universal essence, is next to the top; Shingon, offering not only this intellectual teaching but also, through its tantric techniques, the means to realize them, is seen as the supreme school. But the listing indicated that Kukai saw other sects and devotional practices that fell short of the highest not as heresies or rivals but as lower stages on the way—imperfect but valuable in their appropriate time and place. In another major work, *Sokushin jobutsugi,* Kukai outlines how this is done: making manifest Vairocana as one's true nature through practice of the "three secrets."[9]

---

9. See Yoshito S. Hakeda, trans., *Kukai: Major Works* (New York: Columbia University Press, 1972).

The second sect dominating Heian Buddhism was Tendai. Tendai was the Japanese form of the school of Buddhism known in China as T'ien T'ai, after a mountain of that name in southeast China where it flourished, particularly under the great monk and scholar Chih-I (538–597 C.E.). It was brought to Japan by a monk named Saicho (767–822, posthumous name Dengyo Daishi) in 806, and was located at the monastery he had already established on Mt. Hiei just northeast of the city of Heian (Kyoto)—a location that gave him and his order great influence in the capital.

Tendai offers a particularly expansive Mahayana vision. Its fundamental concern is to reveal the deep unity of all Buddhist practices and teachings and all of existence. To this end it ranks the Buddhist sutras on various levels according to their revelation of ultimate truth, with the *Lotus Sutra* placed at the top as the supreme statement of the Buddha's wisdom. This powerful scripture emphasizes the universality and eternity of buddhahood or nirvana and suggests that it is not limited in space or time, that all may find it, and that the historical Buddha and all other buddhas are but conditioned manifestations of this ultimate reality that showers the entire earth like rain. The various spiritual teachings and practices are equally partial and equally valid, being seen by the wise as but a single "way." Under the spacious umbrella of this perspective many forms and schools of Buddhism flourished: Zen, Pure Land (or Amidism), an esotericism similar to that of Shingon, Vinaya (Ritsu) with its emphasis on monastic discipline, devotion to Kannon the great bodhisattva, and much else. As we shall see, many of these movements nourished by Tendai later took independent courses to become mighty sects in their own right.

As one might expect, Tendai's accommodating stance made possible a relation to Shinto as well. Ichijitsu ("One truth") Shinto, the school founded under Tendai auspices and centered at the Sanno Shrine at the foot of Mt. Hiei, emphasized that buddhas and kami can be identified with one another, each representing common lines of spiritual force. Although the full development of this theory, like the corresponding Shingon-influenced Ryobu-shugo ("Unification of both sides") Shinto, did not come until much later than the time of Saicho, its roots go back to earlier practices and attitudes, and it was greatly influenced by the *Lotus Sutra*'s concept of absolute and relative expressions of buddhahood. This theory related the buddhist pantheon to the indigenous Shinto deities as **honji suijaku** ("original nature—trace manifestation").

Tendai was scarcely behind Shingon in supporting the Heian period's love of spiritual diversity, esotericism, and pilgrimage. Like Shingon, it supported a love of lavish ritual and quasi-magical piety. It also established its easy relation to Shinto and supported the mountain priests who practiced shugendo. We will later look at some of these features of Tendai in more detail.

Although the Buddhism of Shingon and Tendai dominated the Heian period, and much of Shinto was even brought under its influence, the Heian period tells another story, too. Under the aegis of governmental support, and sustained by ongoing popular religious traditions relating to kami and local shrines, more orthodox forms of Shinto continued, as they have up to the present. Although this Shinto may have lacked the spectacular visibility of the dynamic new Buddhist sects, it showed a remarkable power of endurance.

Little is known about popular Shinto in the Heian period. Court Shinto, however, was theoretically the ritual foundation of the state. It centered around four major institutions: (a) the *toshigoi* or spring prayers for a good harvest; (b) the rites of the Grand Shrine of Ise, especially the *shikinen sengu* or ritual rebuilding of the shrine every twenty years; (c) the *saigu* or sending of an imperial princess to Ise to serve as high priestess at the Grand Shrine; and, most significant of all, (d) the already mentioned daijo sai or harvest festival celebrated by a new emperor as the keystone of his accession rites.

Heian Shinto rites were slow and stylized, lacking the drama of Buddhism. However, they were extremely important, for they kept alive archaic religious patterns. Moreover, through these rituals, with their characteristic emphasis on simple offerings and sacred purity, the nation showed itself as it wanted to be seen by the kami.

## The Kamakura Period (1185–1333)

The Gempei War (1180–1185) brought Fujiwara rule to an end. It was not simply a battle among factions of the old Heian aristocracy. In contrast, a series of conflicts involved segments of the newly arisen samurai or *bushi* (warrior) class, and ultimately led to political dominance by this class. In the process, the old Heian aristocracy's power was eclipsed. The way was now opened for a strong feudal system in which provincial landed barons (*daimyo*) ruled over their own samurai retainers and vassals.

The victory of the Minamoto (Genji) clan over the Taira (Heike) clan in the Gempei War signaled not only the defeat of the Taira and the Fujiwara but also the coming to power of a whole new class. Perhaps symbolic of this, the Minamoto leader Yoritomo (1147–1199) moved the capital from Heian to Kamakura. Though in terms of contemporary geography and travel this may not seem significant, by twelfth-century standards it was a major geographic shift that represented a new direction in politics, social order, religion, and culture. It symbolized a revolution and new day, releasing energy for the blossoming of a variety of new cultural forms.

In the meantime a new governing structure was established at Kamakura (eventually under the Hojo clan) called the *bakufu* and ruled by the chief military ruler of the country (*shogun*). Although the ruling house changed after the Kamakura period, this structure, and the de facto rule of feudal militarists continued well into the nineteenth century. Throughout this time the imperial house continued to exist and even nominally to rule, but by and large the country was in the hands of a new and different group.

Religiously the situation was also quite new in spite of the continued existence of the Heian Buddhist denominations and Shinto. But the power of Heian

Buddhism and its aristocratic patrons was now eclipsed, giving opportunity for new movements to flourish. At the same time the social, political, and religious turmoil was seen as proof that life itself might be coming to an end—or at least that impermanence (*mujo*), karmic retribution (*inga*), and the degeneration of time itself (*mappo*) were seriously jeopardizing the human search for order, purity, and salvation.

New religious movements in the Kamakura period flourished because of these conditions. Zen Buddhism was established by Eisai (1141–1215) of the Rinzai school and Dogen (1200–1253) of the Soto school. Both had been Tendai monks who became dissatisfied and sought a "truer" form of Buddhism in China. The Zen they brought back, with its strict discipline and emphasis on absolute loyalty to a master, was immediately attractive to the warrior class, which quickly became its major patron.

Nichiren Buddhism, a second major new Buddhist movement, was founded by another former Tendai monk, Nichiren (1222–1282). This teaching, emphasizing salvation via faith in the *Lotus Sutra,* gained strong support among the masses.

The third major new movement of the early Kamakura period was **Pure Land** Buddhism. Although the scriptures, teachings, and practices of Pure Land Buddhism had long been present in Japan—especially as one possibility within the eclecticism of Tendai Buddhism—only now did they become embodied in sectarian groups solely devoted to them. As taught by Honen (1133–1212) and the Jodo (Pure Land) sect inspired by him, and his disciple Shinran (1173–1262) and his Jodoshin (True Pure Land) sect, Pure Land teachings increasingly pervaded Japanese religion, from high courtiers of Heian to peasant villagers. Helping in this task were later men and groups such as Ippen (1239–1289) and the Ji (Time) sect. The message of Amida Buddha's saving grace was taken around the country by itinerant preachers. Such missionaries had great appeal. They provided a message of paradisal existence beyond this sin-laden and degenerate world, and they offered an "easy path" of dependence on the "other power" of Amida Buddha.

Both Honen and Shinran had been Tendai monks who became dissatisfied with its aristocratic, elitist, and esoteric tendencies. They increasingly moved to establish new Buddhist centers and to take the "gospel" of Amida's grace and mercy directly to the people. The most important Pure Land theme was that the cosmic Buddha Amida had already, in effect, saved all beings by his infinite compassion and mercy. The second theme follows directly from this: human beings need only call on Amida in faith to bring about the salvation he has already won for them. This calling is **"namu Amida butsu,"** or "praise to Amida Buddha," called the **nembutsu,** and is the central practice of most Pure Land groups.

Although there are theological exceptions—especially in the teachings of Shinran and in more contemporary Pure Land circles—the popular view of salvation focused on rebirth in Amida's Pure Land after death. Amida came to receive the soul at the moment of death. Subsequently, in the paradisal Pure

Land, one had easy access to nirvana, total release from the wheel of birth and death. In the popular mind, however, rebirth in the Pure Land was a sufficient goal in itself.

The sectarian developments in Pure Land Buddhism were built on the factors mentioned above, but they were related to other issues as well. Not only were the times ripe for moving out from under the umbrella of Tendai and establishing separate movements, but these and other sectarian developments in the Kamakura period also depended on strong, charismatic leaders who gathered about them loyal followers who then sought to perpetuate that leader's teachings. Furthermore, the message of these leaders often claimed to be the only true way, and this fostered separatist movements adhering exclusively to that particular group. Finally, many of these movements preached a kind of "priesthood of all believers" within which the distinctions between monk and layman were largely erased. In such a context a sectarian orthodoxy and orthopraxy could be established outside the normal transmission lines of institutional (monastic) Buddhism—one could, as it were, "set up shop" on one's own.

While various Pure Land movements increasingly dominated the Kamakura period, other movements already mentioned continued to grow. Prominent among these was Nichiren's Hokke (Lotus) sect. One of the more colorful figures in Japanese religious history, Nichiren was something of a militant zealot who claimed for himself and the *Lotus Sutra* (*Myohorenge-kyo*) sole authority and power by which individuals as well as the nation might be saved. Like the Pure Land groups, he put great stock in the idea of a degenerate age and, in fact, saw all other Buddhist groups of the day as examples of it. Nichiren was not, however, merely a variation on the Pure Land theme. Not only was the object of faith and the character of the practice different, but also the content of salvation was more clearly a mode of realization in this life rather than one of rebirth in the next. However, salvation for Nichiren was inevitably related to a collective, national salvation—an eschatological vision in which Japan, under the cosmic Buddha, would usher in a new Buddhist age and be the home of a new historical Buddha. It is easy to see how some of the millennialist religious movements of contemporary Japan, for example Soka Gakkai, find their inspiration in Nichiren.

Unlike both the Pure Land and the Nichiren sects, Zen represented a normative, monastic Buddhism that had little mass appeal and relatively little to do with a Buddhism of faith, devotion, and calling on other powers. Zen was more representative of the traditional "hard path," "self-power" forms of Mahayana Buddhism. In fact its very name means "meditation" and, more specifically, a particular form of seated meditation (zazen) that is best practiced in monasteries. Its ideals were more in keeping with the traditional Buddhism of Nara and Heian days insofar as enlightenment and the bodhisattva realization were its religious goals. Yet Zen was not simply another form of Heian Buddhism; it was just not the same kind of Kamakura alternative as represented by the Pure Land or Nichiren groups.

Zen thrived under the blessings and patronage of the new rulers, at Kamakura and later at Kyoto. By the end of the Kamakura period Zen was firmly entrenched with an extensive, strong temple system and close ties to both the old Heian aristocracy and the new military ruling class. Though Zen never garnered the numbers that the more popular movements did, it nonetheless wielded increasing influence in Kamakura society—religiously, culturally, educationally, and even politically. These developments continued only as Japan moved into its next period when Zen became, in effect, the state relgion.

Although the three Buddhist sects just discussed dominated the religious scene of the thirteenth century, other paths were also developing. Primarily, these were ways related to warrior codes and to the arts.

The way of the warrior, initially called *yumiya no michi* ("way of the bow and arrow") or *kyuba no michi* ("way of the bow and horse"), and in later history called bushido ("way of the warrior"), indicated primarily the ideals and values of the feudal samurai: loyalty, bravery, discipline, duty, and a fearless willingness to meet death in the service of these ideals and one's superiors. This life-defining code presumed an honoring of buddhas as well as kami, and its prestige and popularity grew throughout the Kamakura and subsequent periods.

In the arts, the idea of a "way" was particularly important in late Heian and early Kamakura poetry. In the hands of such famous court poets as Fujiwara Teika (1162–1241) or such priest/poets as Saigyo (1118–1170), there was a clear and explicit notion of a "way of poetry" (*kado*) that carried religious meaning. In fact, poetry in Japan had long had a sacred, even magical, character to it, but by the Kamakura period it was a sophisticated, clearly defined, Buddhist-influenced way in which aesthetic ideals such as **yugen** (sublime mystery) and *sabi* (solitariness) carried religious meaning.

Such sentiments, and the Heian courtly sophistication in the arts generally, continued on through the Kamakura period. The ideal of the Buddhist hermit or recluse related artistic (especially poetic) endeavor to spiritual experience and practice. One can see this at the end of the Kamakura period in the writings of Yoshida Kenko (1283–1350). In his *Essays in Idleness* (*Tsurezuregusa*) he clearly represents these forms of religio-aesthetic sensitivity and the model of the recluse literati. On the one hand he displays a continuing nostalgia for Heian sophistication when he says: "They speak of the degenerate age, yet how splendid is the ancient atmosphere, uncontaminated by the world, that still prevails within the palace walls." On the other hand he represents the bittersweet tension of the detached recluse in a world of attachment to beauty when he says: "A certain hermit once said, 'There is one thing that even I, who have no worldly entanglements, would be sorry to give up, the beauty of the sky.' I can understand why he should have felt that way."[10]

Still another important development in the Kamakura period was taking place in Shinto. As we have already seen, in the Heian period rationalizations

---

10. Donald Keene, trans., *Essays in Idleness: The Tsurezuregusa of Kenko* (New York: Columbia University Press, 1967), pp. 22–23.

had appeared to reconcile Shinto and Buddhism. These theories focused on the idea of honji suijaku (''original essence, manifest traces'') in which the buddhas and bodhisattvas represented spiritual ''essences'' of which Shinto kami were ''manifest traces.'' During the later Kamakura period, however, moves were afoot to purify Shinto of its Buddhist overlay and to see in Shinto, rather than Buddhism, the superior spiritual essences. Perhaps stimulated by the idea that the national kami had helped drive out the Mongols in 1274 and 1281 through a divine wind (*kami kaze*), this movement sought to reassert the superiority of Shinto and the uniqueness of ancient indigenous patterns.

Such Shinto views are clearly evident in the writings of Kitabatake Chikafusa (1293–1354) who was concerned to reassert the divine descent of the imperial line as well as the divine uniqueness of Japan and the superiority of Shinto. It is also evident in the Yui-itsu Shinto movement that spanned the medieval period. Such sentiments in Shinto indicated a growing national self-consciousness that became increasingly strong in later years and stood behind not only attempts to restore the emperor to power but also sentiment for establishing a theocracy based on an ''imperial way'' (*kodo*).

## The Muromachi Period (1336–1573)

Looking at the broad sweep of Japanese religious history, the Muromachi period represents less of a change from the Kamakura period than the Kamakura period was from the Heian period. The dominant Buddhist groups and movements of the Kamakura period, especially Zen and Pure Land Buddhism, continued to gain in strength and support. In fact Zen grew to such lengths among the upper and ruling classes that it became a de facto state religion. Pure Land movements grew as well.

But after the repulsion of the Mongols, the Kamakura shogunate was in a weakened state in the early fourteenth century. Strong rival clans and determined moves to restore the emperor to power brought it to an end in 1333. For the next three years the Emperor Godaigo ruled a shaky coalition with a weak hand, and by 1336 a new bushi clan—the Ashikaga—had established a new shogunate and moved it to the Muromachi section of Kyoto. Once again the bushi were in control and a military-based government ruled in a feudal society, though the site of this government had returned to Kyoto.

The Muromachi period was definitely a troubled time. Although the first half of the period was governed by relatively strong and able leadership, the second half degenerated into civil war, beginning with the Onin Wars of 1467–1477 and continuing with a period of Japanese history known as the *Sengoku jidai* (''Age of warring provinces,'' 1467–1568). Kyoto and the Ashikaga rulers remained symbolic centers in these later years, but the country was essentially partitioned among the great landed barons of the time, who continually vied for power.

This history, however, is only a part of the larger tale of the Muromachi period. Religiously and culturally there is a different, though related, story. From this perspective we not only look at patterns of religious expression that persist in spite of the turmoil, but we also focus on Kyoto, and the Ashikaga family as cultural/religious patrons, to the arts and literature, and to the growing influence of Zen.

The Ashikaga, like many others of the bushi class, were neither country bumpkins nor unwashed soldiers. They were representative of a class which now sought to emulate the older courtly aristocrats. In addition they brought to Kyoto the general bushi interest in Zen Buddhism. Under the relatively strong leadership of Ashikaga Yoshimitsu (1358–1408) Kyoto became a thriving center for religion, art, and culture.

Zen Buddhism was instrumental in the development of what stands out as the distinctive religious feature of the Muromachi period. Under the leadership of such Zen priests as Muso Soseki (1275–1351) Zen established a strong temple system in the Kyoto area that became the hub of religious, artistic, educational, and even political activities. Zen imported and produced art and literature, taught the children of the upper classes in temple schools, fostered interest in the Chinese classics, and provided its own monks as the scribes and advisers to commercial/ political interests in the government. In all this, however, it is the unique relation of Zen to the arts that stands out.

Zen's relation to the arts in the Muromachi era was based on several features. The primary feature lies in the nature of Zen experience itself. For much of Zen, and for much of the Taoist tradition that influenced Zen's early development in China, religious experience was closely associated with aesthetic experience and was naturally expressed in artistic/literary forms. Therefore, although Buddhist art as iconography and symbol has played a part in Zen as in other sects, Zen went beyond iconography and symbolic expression. In Zen even secular subjects could express religious experience. The whole range of the arts, especially calligraphy, monochrome ink painting, poetry, and the tea ceremony, was open to Zen as potentially religious.

Zen had become a vehicle for Sung dynasty Chinese culture and learning. On its temple walls and in its temple halls these arts were displayed and practiced. Monks and priests were often poets and painters as well, and professional painters and poets who were not monks found a ready place and patron for their work.

Zen's understanding of the discipline and practice of artistic creativity made art a natural ally of meditation itself. For Zen the arts were "ways" of spiritual significance, especially as practiced within a Zen context. Calligraphy (*shodo,* the "way of the brush"), painting (*gado,* the "way of painting"), and many others forms were adjunct disciplines to meditation. Within such a context many of Japan's greatest artists flourished. Although not all were equally and intimately involved in Zen practice, all were influenced in some degree by the general Zen taste or style of the day. Among the most prominent of these were Zeami Motokiyo (1363–1443) and Komparu Zenchiku (1394–1481) in the noh theatre, Sogi

(1421–1502) in *renga* or linked verse, Noami (1397–1471) and Shuko (d. 1502) in the tea ceremony, Ikkyu Sojun (1394–1481) in Zen poetry, Shubun (d. 1450) and Sesshu (1420–1506) in landscape painting, and Soami (d. 1525) in garden design.

Finally, Zen was in a very favorable position vis-a-vis the ruling powers. The Ashikaga shoguns and family were firm patrons of both the arts and Zen. This, of course, gave Zen a unique opportunity to pursue and spread its artistic interests. Muromachi Zen and its aesthetic influences permeated the culture of the times and brought both Zen and its art to a pinnacle of popularity.

The danger in this, of course, was that artistic interests would overtake religious ones. In fact, as early as the first half of the fourteenth century the great priest Muso Soseki admonished his monks to keep their Zen practice pure and not "befuddle their minds in non-Buddhist works or devote their efforts to literary endeavors" lest they be considered mere "shaven-headed laymen." Although many Zen practitioners were able to balance the religious and the artistic quite well (including Muso himself), in the later Muromachi period Zen became increasingly unexceptional religiously and produced few notable leaders.

In the meantime, of course, other religious activities and developments were taking place. In 1549, Catholic missionaries under St. Francis Xavier arrived in Japan. Although they met with initial success, by the mid-seventeenth century the Christian presence had all but been stamped out by anti-foreign and anti-Western sentiment.

Within sectarian Buddhism, the "easy-path" devotional sects continued to rise in power and popularity. Nichiren Buddhism, for example, continued its activities until a suppression at the hands of religious and political opponents in 1537 took much of the wind out of its sails. Pure Land Buddhism, especially the True Pure Land sect, became increasingly popular, well organized, and widespread. Under Rennyo (1415–1499) especially, the centers in Kyoto flourished, and the Pure Land message was taken into the northern and eastern provinces to form new sectarian groups such as Ikko ("single-mind" sect).

Shinto and folk religion, long the mainstay of Japanese faith, continued to operate in age-old ways at shrines and in homes and villages throughout Japan. Sentiments for a "purified" Shinto, which had already surfaced during the Kamakura period, continued to grow. One Shinto spokesman Yoshida Kanetomo (1435–1511). The following statement indicates the direction his thinking was going to assert the national tradition and the unique and sacred imperial way (kodo):

> During the reign of Empress Suiko, Prince Shotoku [573–621] stated in a memorial that Japan was the roots and trunk of civilization, China its branches and leaves, and India its flowers and fruit. Similarly, Buddhism is the flower and fruit of all laws, Confucianism their branches and leaves, and Shinto their roots and trunk. Thus all foreign doctrines are offshoots of Shinto.[11]

---

11. Tsunoda et al., *Sources,* I, *op. cit.,* p. 265.

Although Shotoku seems not to have actually said such a thing, Yoshida not only wanted to say it but also wanted to find such sentiments in the heroic golden age of Japan's early years. Furthermore, it must be understood that "Shinto" in this view is not merely a shrine system with rituals and festivals but indicates the all-important sense of a sacred national polity (*kokutai*) and tradition, a divine descent for the imperial line, and the sacred uniqueness of Japan within the world.

As one pursues the story of Japanese religion in this period or in any other, it is important to remember that in the actual religious life, as lived out in daily life, these distinctions between Buddhism, Shinto, purified Shinto, and so forth tend to break down. Most Japanese were in some degree involved in all of them, and these distinctions are better thought of as strands woven inextricably together. The noh plays help show this for the Muromachi period. Within their plots and their aesthetic ideals one can find most of the elements of fourteenth- and fifteenth-century religious life—all the way from shamanistic exorcism to Pure Land theology, and from Zen priests to demons and ghosts.

## The Tokugawa Period (1600–1868)

In contrast to the Muromachi period the characteristic marks of the Tokugawa period were unity, order, and stability. Though changes certainly took place, compared with the previous era it represented some two hundred and fifty years of calm under a relatively strong central government. Religiously speaking, there was a general shift away from Buddhism and Buddhist culture to Confucianism, Shinto, and a growing secular culture.

Although the history of the transition from civil war in the sixteenth century to centralized order in the seventeenth century is complex, in essence it has to do with the emergence of particularly strong and determined regional barons in the later sixteenth century who increasingly exercised control over the other feudal lords and over the last vestiges of power in Kyoto. These barons, although generally of the samurai class, represented a new breed of tough, provincial, even "lower class" men who gathered power by their own strength and wit—practical men bent on unifying the country and stabilizing it.

Chief among these barons were Oda Nobunaga (1534–1582), Toyotomi Hideyoshi (1536–1598), and Tokugawa Ieyasu (1542–1616). Each built on the advances of the previous one until by 1600 a new shogunate could be established—the Tokugawa shogunate and government at Edo (Tokyo). With determination and sometimes ruthlessness these men and their supporters took control of the whole land, including not only the holdings of other barons but also such power centers as the Tendai Buddhist headquarters near Kyoto.

Two symbols of the times are castles and the city of Edo. The castle was a new architectural structure at this time and represented not only a practical form of defense in times of civil war but also the sense of individual, autonomous strength that characterized the new breed of rulers. Simultaneously, however, the Japanese castles evidenced older patterns of aesthetic, decorative taste and thus symbolize the continuance of previous cultural features as well.

The move to Edo, too, symbolized these new times and new rulers. Eschewing both Kyoto and Kamakura, these rulers moved to yet another city—young, provincial, and bustling—that was in many ways far removed from the older centers of cultural, religious, and political/economic power. The move to Edo signaled a major turning point toward the modern era in Japan's history and away from an earlier, more traditional culture. Although the Tokugawa period did not see the modernization of Japan or Japan's entry into the ranks of a modern nation state, it certainly prepared Japan for that development. Especially, it witnessed the dramatic rise of the merchant class to a position of economic, if not political, power.

The Tokugawa shogunate maintained a relatively stable government until 1868. In order to do so, it entered deeply into the daily lives of the people through hierarchical structures, and controlled them by means of law and maxim. It tended to resist the new or the innovative and be very protective of its control, especially against foreign influence. Japan resisted foreign trade until well into the nineteenth century.

Religious history took a decided turn. Buddhism had tended to dominate in previous centuries. Now, Confucianism began to come to the fore under state patronage. This orientation is particularly important to trace since it became both the dominant religio-philosophic teaching of the period and an ideological tool in the hands of the Tokugawa rulers. Confucian and Neo-Confucian ideas permeated the thinking, planning, and action of the Tokugawa rulers as it did the intellectual/educated elite of the times. It was pervasive within an important class of people and filtered down to the masses through the laws and maxims of the government.

Of course Confucianism had long been present in Japan, though somewhat ''hidden'' because of its lack of any clear institutionalized structure. From early times, however, it had infused the Japanese value system with the virtues of loyalty and filial piety. Later it was studied in the temple schools of Zen Buddhism. With the new times and new rulers in Edo, however, Neo-Confucianism came into its own in Japan. It promoted a vision of ''paradise'' as an ordered, just society, and it instilled values of loyalty, sincerity, order, and stability. For the Tokugawa elite this was a life-defining ''way'' that satisfied not only the quest for intellectual/religious meaning but also the quest for hierarchical order, political/social loyalty, and the rule of moral law. The spirit of this new orientation is graphically represented in a comment by one of its early heralds, Hayashi Razan (1583–1657), a Neo-Confucian scholar and an important adviser to the Tokugawa government:

> The Way of Taoism and Buddhism is the Way of quiescence and nonstriving, and of entering the original undifferentiated state of nature. But man is born into the world of today; how can he put himself in his original state where ''no thought''

is said to reign. Such arguments based on withered trees, dead ashes, and old faggots are of the same sort—all weird, perverted talk. The Way of Confucianism is different from this, and consists in nothing but moral obligations between sovereign and subject, father and child, husband and wife, elder and younger brother, and friend and friend. These and the five virtues [loyalty, filial piety, sincerity, decorum, justice] are rooted in the mind and in the principle of mind in the nature of man.[12]

This not only exemplifies the central message of Neo-Confucianism (especially as based on the Chinese Neo-Confucian philosopher Chu Hsi, 1130–1200) but it also suggests the growing anti-Buddhist sentiment of the period as well. Although Neo-Confucianism owes much to Taoism and Buddhism in China, it tended to eschew those influences in seventeenth-century Japan. As a life-defining "way" of human action, it focused very strongly on moral obligation and behavior.

Such a focus was perfect for the Tokugawa government. It looked to Neo-Confucianism to rationalize and inspire its policies. In a sense, the government and the educational system it fostered became a Neo-Confucian "church," that is, the primary institutional locale and embodiment of this religio-philosophical system.

Exemplary of this were the laws promulgated by the government that set out the duties, ethical maxims, and obligations of the varying classes in the society—all designed to establish and maintain heirarchical order and stability and to instill Neo-Confucian values. As early as 1615, in fact, laws such as the following were issued:

1. Drinking parties and wanton revelry should be avoided.
2. Offenders against the law should not be harbored or hidden.
3. All innovative ideas or factional conspiracies should be reported to the government.
4. Restrictions on the type and quality of dress to be worn should not be transgressed.
5. The *samurai* of various domains shall lead a frugal and simple life.[13]

Based on such laws—written or unwritten—the duties and obligations of various groups were set. Earlier notions of a particular way of the warrior (bushido), for example, were now codified and preached. People such as Yamaga Soko (1627–1685) were saying:

The business of the *samurai* consists in reflecting on his own station in life, in discharging loyal service to his master, in deepening this fidelity with friends, and in devoting himself to duty. Though these are also the fundamental moral

---

12. Ibid., I, 348.
13. Ibid., I, 327–329.

obligations of everyone in the land, they have no leisure to fully pursue this Way. Therefore, the *samurai* confines himself to this Way and becomes a model for the people.[14]

In fact, the ideal samurai was, in this "religion," the paradigmatic model for both orthodoxy and orthopraxis.

Other classes, however, had their own particular obligations and "ways." The merchant class was instructed in *chonindo* ("way of the merchant"), which consisted in diligent labor, frugality, honesty, loyalty, and obedience to superiors. Peasants, too, were expected to adhere to these obligations. "Salvation" in this religion consisted in fulfilling the moral duties and maintaining the social order.

While Neo-Confucianism developed new schools and new emphases during the seventeenth and eighteenth centuries, another aspect of Japanese religion was slowly and steadily evolving. This had to do with a resurgence of Shinto nationalism. We have already noted such views in earlier centuries, especially as tied to ideas of an "imperial way" and the sacrality/superiority of the national tradition and structure (kokutai). These sentiments had long been a part of Japanese thinking, but especially during the second half of the Tokugawa period they blossomed into increasing dominance. The central features of this movement included affirming and honoring the divine emperor and the imperial line; the indigenous, ancient traditions of mythology and literature; and the sacrality and superiority of Japan's unique structure. On the other hand this same movement fostered hostility toward all foreign (even Chinese) ideas.

One of the first people to herald this development in the Tokugawa period was Yamazaki Ansai (1618–1682), a Neo-Confucian thinker who sought to merge those teachings with Shinto ideas. For Yamazaki this meant a reassertion of uniquely Japanese ideas of inner devotion merged with Confucian notions of outer decorum. For Nakae Toju (1608–1684), the founder of the Wang Yangming school of Neo-Confucianism in Japan, it meant a theistic understanding of the ultimate Neo-Confucian principles (*ri*) underlying all life.

One particularly important direction this movement took was to reassert interest in the study of Japan's own classical, literary tradition. Whereas Neo-Confucianism had already stimulated interests in classical, quasi-scientific, and language studies, this new direction focused much of that interest on Japan's own past. Kada Azumamaro (1669–1736), for example, was a Shinto priest who petitioned the government to start a school for "national learning" (*kokugaku*) and thereby to stimulate study of ancient Japanese poetry and literature.

Others took up this same cause. Under such people as Kamo Mabuchi (1697–1736), Motoori Norinaga (1730–1801), and Hirata Atsutani (1776–1843) the movement came to full flower. Its main concern was the study of the ancient Japanese classics (mythology, literature, and poetry) but its agenda was to dis-

---

14. Ibid., I, 390.

cover and instill the unique Japanese spirit and to "purify" Japanese institutions and ideas of all foreign influences. In its later forms this movement, and much of Japan with it, became increasingly anti-foreign, including anti-Buddhist and anti-Confucian as well.

The sentiments of these "national learning scholars" (*kokugaku-sha*) are well summed up in the following comment by Hirata:

> People all over the world refer to Japan as the Land of the Gods, and call us descendants of the gods. Indeed, it is exactly as they say: our country, as a special mark of favor from the gods, was begotten by them; therefore the difference between Japan and other countries defies comparison. Ours is the Land of the Gods, and each Japanese is a descendant of the gods.[15]

These and similar views led to a religion of the state—a "civil religion," a theocracy, a life-defining way called the imperial way. Although the Tokugawa period did not see the full institutionalization of this way, it set the stage for later developments up to World War II.

Other religious factors, of course, functioned during the Tokugawa period—albeit upstaged by the developments in Neo-Confucianism and Shinto nationalism. For example, it is clear that the fortunes of Shinto increased during the period, but the fortunes of Buddhism declined. Institutional Buddhism came steadily under the direct control of the Tokugawa rulers, though popular Buddhist ideas and practices continued to play a key part in the religious life of the masses. Buddhism also suffered, however, from internal stagnation and failed to produce either creative leadership or compelling answers to the challenges of Neo-Confucianism and Shinto revivalism. The traditional and medieval artistic ways were eclipsed in the Tokugawa period. Although there were exceptions to this, particularly in the tea cult following Rikyu (1522–1591) and the haiku poetry of Basho (1644–1694), not only were such arts now understood as either Confucian ritual or mere entertainment, but also other cultural/artistic forces were becoming prominent, particularly the bourgeois culture of the merchant class, which took a decidedly secular turn.

Finally, the later Tokugawa period evidenced a growth in popular, peasant religious movements focused on charismatic leaders. These movements—including Shinjaku (mental culture) founded by Ishida Baigan (1685–1744), Hotoku (returning virtue) founded by a peasant named Ninomiya Santoku (1787–1856), and Tenrikyo (heavenly wisdom teaching) founded by Nakayama Miki (1798–1887)—borrowed from the various religious patterns of Japan and adapted them to their particular situation. It remained for a later period in Japanese history to witness the culmination of such movements in the New Religions of the later nineteenth and the twentieth centuries.

---

15. Ibid., II, 39.

## The Meiji Period (1868–1912) and Beyond

Although the Meiji period is short, it makes up for its brevity in political/social significance. Whereas the Tokugawa period set the scene for Japan's coming-of-age as a modern nation-state, the Meiji period saw it happen. A variety of factors brought the downfall of the Tokugawa shogunate, but among these were internal governmental weakness, liberal pressures to reform the political structures more in line with Western ideals of democracy, kokugaku pressures to restore ancient Japanese imperial institutions, and foreign pressures to open Japan to international trade and political involvement. Unable to handle these pressures, the Tokugawa shogunate fell at the hands of younger members of the samurai class who were calling for a "return to antiquity" (*fukko*). In a relatively bloodless coup these people restored the emperor to power in 1868.

The emperor's position, however, remained symbolic. The actual rulers after the coup ironically became the progressive wing of the reform movements, less interested in restoring ancient ways than in modernizing Japanese economic, political, military, and social structures. Throughout the 1870s this faction carried the day, and by 1889 Japan had established a constitutional and parliamentary system while maintaining the imperial symbolic center.

In the process of these changes feudalism—including the shogunal system itself—collapsed. Class privilege also began to crumble as Japan moved toward more popular democratic principles. International trade and the growth of the great merchant houses in Japan also hastened these changes. Industrial families like Mitsubishi gained power and prestige and took an active part in the political realm.

The Western-influenced reformers, however, remained Japanese samurai at heart and relatively authoritarian in their rule. Japan moved toward true constitutional democracy, but much of that movement was in name only. Even after 1889 Japan was governed by a very few nonelected officials who invoked imperial will as their basis for authority. Especially in the 1880s, in fact, the reform movement took a decidedly conservative, nondemocratic turn. The Imperial Edict on Education of 1890 exemplifies these traditionalist sentiments. It opens with the following:

> Our Imperial Ancestors have founded Our Empire on a basis broad and everlasting, and have deeply and firmly implanted virtue. Our subjects are ever united in loyalty and filial piety, and have illustrated the beauty thereof from generation to generation. This is the glory of the fundamental character of Our Empire, and herein also lies the source of Our education.[16]

As is clear in the rest of this document, and from subsequent history, this signals a reassertion of the Shinto/Confucian-inspired ideals so prevalent in the

---

16. Ibid., II, 139.

Tokugawa period. With the divine emperor at the center and loyal subjects ranged around, the sacred national structure (kokutai), the imperial way, and the return to antiquity (fukko) could all be realized in this theocratic vision of the new nation-state.

Such views grew increasingly strong throughout the Meiji period and beyond. In fact, they received official sanction by being declared a "nonreligious" form of Shinto in the constitution of 1889, and were made central to a governmental system that ostensibly abided by the separation of religion from government. Whether "Shinto" is the best name for this civil religion may be disputed. This "nonreligious" religion of the state, however, was based on the idea of the unity of government and ritual (*saisei itchi*), the imperial way, and the sacrality of the national structure. Moreover, it brought with it Confucian ideals of filial piety and loyalty and such samurai values as self-discipline and a "sacred martial spirit."

The early twentieth century saw the further development of these ideals, often used to inspire and rationalize military excursions into neighboring countries. Movements such as the Amur Society, formed in 1901, sought the extension of the imperial way beyond Japan's own borders. In 1930, for example, this group announced that "We stand for Divine Imperial Rulership (*tenno shugi*). Basing ourselves on the fundamental teachings of the foundation of the empire, we seek the extension of the imperial influence to all peoples and places, and the fulfillment of the glory of our national polity (kokutai)."[17] By World War II this view was voiced in the desire to bring the "whole world under one roof" (*hakko ichi-u*). In fact, Japan's involvement in the war was inspired in part by such ideas. For example, the Imperial Declaration of War of 1941 states:

> The basis of the Imperial Way lies in truth, in sincerity, and in justice. Its range is wide and there is nothing it does not embrace. It expels evil, subjugates injustice, absolutely maintains the tenets of justice, and itself occupies a position which can never be violated. The august virtue of the divine imperial lineage has not a single instant when it did not arise from these three virtues. In other words, they form the national character of Japan, and, at the same time, the national trait of the people. It is in the service of these virtues, and not mere arms themselves, that Japan must resort to war.[18]

While this "imperial way" was the dominant and characteristic feature of Meiji and subsequent religious history through World War II, other religious patterns continued to emerge. Christian ideals were particularly influential among intellectuals of the early Meiji era, and Buddhism remained active— albeit officially out of favor. Traditional Shinto, as distinct from the imperial way discussed above, remained important in the daily lives of the Japanese as did other smaller sectarian groups that had begun in the nineteenth century and

---

17. Ibid., II, 258.
18. Ibid., II, 292.

were slowly developing in the twentieth. In fact, it is to such groups that we now turn as we look to religious developments in modern (i.e. post-World War II) Japan.

## MODERN JAPAN

The period since World War II has been marked by political stability, economic growth of unprecedented proportions, social change, and abundant religious activity. Although traditional sectarian Buddhism and Shinto, and a small but influential Christianity, have been active, the major story about modern Japanese religious history lies with the many New Religions that have grown up and flourished, especially since the war, thanks to the disestablishment of the imperial way, and true religious freedom.

New religious groups large and small have garnered impressive support across Japanese society. Although several groups, for example Tenrikyo, date back into the nineteenth century, many either came into existence or were revived since 1945. Though they generally may be typed as Buddhist, Shinto, or eclectic in their teachings and practices, they are probably better distinguished by their separation from the traditional religions, their tendency to win mass or popular appeal, their formation of communities around charismatic leaders, their this-worldly eschatologies, and their interests in practical, immediate benefits. Similarly, it might be more useful to indicate some of the factors that led to their eruption on the scene than to try to assign them to some typology or to list their many names.*

The New Religions have flourished, in part, because of a vacuum of religious meaning. This vacuum was caused by many factors, but primarily by a postwar stagnation of the major religions of Japan, the general secular turn of much of Japanese life, the loss of national identity after World War II, the loss of a sense of continuity and connection with the past, and the breakdown of traditional family structures due to urbanization. These factors have tended to undercut the deep-meaning structures by which the Japanese have known who they are both culturally and religiously. The New Religions have filled this vacuum for many people and provided important connections and continuities between old and new in Japanese life.

One example is Soka Gakkai, a large and powerful group whose presence in Japan (and elsewhere) has at times been controversial. Finding its inspiration in Nichiren Buddhism and the *Lotus Sutra,* this group has taken the old and sought to adapt it to the modern situation. It is a popular religious movement that appeals to the broader middle or lower classes of Japan. It emphasizes practical, concrete, and immediate benefits; the importance of charismatic leaders; communal experience and structures; and a relatively easy accommodation with an urban, industrialized, materialistic society.

Other groups shift the focus and emphasis a bit. Some lean toward tra-

---

*See Appendix, pp. 149–51, for brief descriptions.

ditional Shinto and folk religious patterns. In these cases one often finds shamanistic women, spirit-possession, magico-religious practices, sacred mountains,
and concern for purification and healing.

These groups are perceived as dynamic, modern, and directly related to
individual personal life. They are often evangelical in their concern to reach out
for new members, and they provide for those members an important sense of
collective identity and belonging. However "new" they may be, they remain
uniquely Japanese and make connections with traditional religious patterns. They
provide valuable links with the past as they meet religious needs in the present.

The New Religions, however, are only one of the more obvious places to
look for religious meaning and expression in modern Japan. Not only might one
look at traditional Buddhism, Shinto, Confucianism, and Christianity as they
are present and active in today's Japan, but perhaps more in keeping with a
"cultural perspective" on Japanese religion, one might look in less obvious places
as well.

A recurring theme in Japanese religion has been the literature and the arts.
In modern Japan this is particularly true of certain forms of literature, film, and
architecture. Authors such as Kawabata Yasunari (1899–1972), Mishima Yukio
(1925–1970), and Tanazaki Junichiro (1886–1965) have evoked in their work
not only the "ghosts" of ancient Japanese religious values but also the whis-
perings of deeper realities and values by which the human condition in general
is probed and expressed. Contemporary architects such as Kurokawa Kisho and
Isozaki Arata have sought to express ancient religio-aesthetic values such as emptiness (ku) and spatial/temporal intervals (*ma*) of spiritual significance.

The religious character of these artistic forms may be less obvious than
some institutionalized sectarian practice, but they nonetheless carry religious
meaning and entail involvement in a life-defining "way" of religious/spiritual
significance. In every culture, and certainly in Japan, the religious dimension
of being human cannot be confined to the more obvious religions; rather, it
permeates a culture's life and is often found in unlikely places. As the modern
world and Japan continue to develop and change, one will need to be open to
changes in religious expression and prepare to see such expression in surprising
places.

## SCENES FROM THE PAST

### The Coming of Buddhism

It was long ago and ways were simple. The people of Japan were fishermen,
hunters, and farmers gathered into numerous uji or clans. The clan chieftain
was the priest of his people; he presided at a shrine to the tribe's ujigami or
patronal kami located in a pure place, perhaps on a high hill or across a clear
rushing stream from the village where his people dwelt. The shrine would not

be a building but a simple outdoor altar in a clean site, like the open-air altar of the Munakata Shrine in Kyushu today. Not far from it, however, might be a house, perhaps itself temporary and erected only for the harvest festival, where stayed a female relative of the chieftain who served as a shamaness delivering oracles on matters of state.

This was the era of the great Kofun tombs with their charming haniwa figures portraying a way of life on which the sun has long since set and with their mute relics of early continental contact: mirrors and swords of metal intended more for magical than for practical use, and the even more sacred magatama jewels and bells.

We picture a way of life close to nature and the agricultural cycle, punctuated by worship offered in places of more natural than artificial beauty. These sites were blessed by kami who descended from heaven or came in from the sea regularly. Incoming kami swelled the bounty of the fields to their climax and also filled rulers with sacred power. Above all the kami was the sun goddess (Amaterasu), the clan deity of the Yamato house, which was, in turn, chief over all the scattered clans.

Into this archaic world arrived something very different in the sixth century C.E. The *Nihonshoki,* the chronicles of Japan published in 720 C.E., mark it by a specific event at the Yamato court and a specific year, 532 or 552 C.E. The actual process was undoubtedly much more gradual and involved persons of much less exalted rank, but let us trace the introduction of Buddhism from Korea (which had received it from China, and China from India by way of central Asia) as it is told in the *Nihonshoki,* for the narrative is of no small interest in illuminating Japanese attitudes.

According to the *Nihonshoki,* in that year the King of Paekche in Korea, hard-pressed by his neighbors and anxious to consolidate an alliance with the island empire, sent the Japanese sovereign certain gifts he declared of greater worth than immeasurable treasure. These gifts included an image of the Buddha in gold and copper, several ornamental flags and umbrellas used to honor such figures, a library of sutras, and a letter stating that:

> This doctrine is amongst all doctrines the most excellent. But it is hard to explain and hard to comprehend. . . . [It] can create religious merit and retribution without measure and without bounds, and so lead on to a full appreciation of the highest wisdom. . . . [With it] every prayer is fulfilled and naught is wanting. Moreover, from distant India it has extended hither to the three Han, where there are none who do not receive it with reverence as it is preached to them.[19]

Thus into the midst of the active, dynamic culture of old Japan came an image of one seated in the great peace of profound meditation, together with scriptures suggesting thoughts and ideas from far-off lands and carrying lines like these from the *Diamond Sutra:*

---

19. Aston, *Nihongi,* II, 66.

*All composite things*
*Are like a dream, a phantasm,*
*a bubble, and a shadow;*
*Are like a dew-drop and a flash of lightning . . .*

We cannot be surprised that the archaic Japanese did not fully comprehend Buddhism all at once. But it is clear they all recognized that in the imported faith was something new and deeply impressive, not only new in an ordinary sense but also of an entirely different order from anything they had encountered before, representing a thus-far unexplored range of human thought and experience.

Not only was the strictly spiritual nature of the Korean gifts of an unprecedented depth but so also was the cultural sophistication they implied. We can probably assume this first Buddhist statue was wrought with a fineness that opened new windows to the potential loveliness of forms shaped by the human hand. The sutras, if not the first exposure of the Japanese to the art of writing, undoubtedly gave them fresh impetus to master that skill and all it could unfold.

Yakushi Buddha, Nara Period.
John Weatherhill, Inc.

With Buddhism, then, came not only religion but also culture, and not only Buddhist culture but also the whole wealth of Korean and Chinese culture. Over the next three centuries these riches were brought into Japan in the luggage of traders, artisans, and ambassadors as well as in the ranks of priests in search of new sutras and doctrines. Together with the paraphernalia of faith, though, came Confucian and Taoist learning as well as the crafts and ideas of statecraft.

The situation in Japan was quite comparable to that of less developed peoples around the world who, in the nineteenth and twentieth centuries, were nearly overwhelmed by the influences of European-American civilization carried in massive doses by missionaries, traders, settlers, and colonial governments—with the important exception that Japan was not, then, in danger of being subjected to the rule of a foreign empire. The Japanese were in the uniquely happy state of being able to receive the foreign high culture truly as a gift from which they could take what they wished and assimilate it at their leisure.

Nonetheless, a jolting infusion of such magnitude could not but create problems and controversies. The *Nihonshoki* account of the introduction of Buddhism explains it well. The Emperor Kimmei, receiving the Korean religious/cultural bounty, commented: ''Never from former days until now have we had the opportunity of listening to so wonderful a doctrine. We are unable, however, to decide for ourselves.'' He turned, therefore, to his ministers for counsel and received mixed advice.

The chief minister of the Soga house argued for acceptance of Buddhism, saying that all the other nations of the continent (India, China, Korea) did honor to the Buddha and Japan should not be the sole exception. But the other two counselors were of the Nakatomi and Mononobe families. Both had important hereditary positions in the Shinto priesthood. The Nakatomi, in fact, were later to beget the powerful Fujiwara house, and until recent times their senior branch held responsibility for the major Shinto rituals of the imperial court. Understandably, they were wary of competition in the realm of religion and contended before the throne that the ancient kami would become enraged if foreign deities were worshiped in their stead.

The Emperor, with a wisdom worthy of Solomon, settled the matter by asking the Soga chief to take the image as an experiment and worship it in his own house. Radiant with joy he knelt to receive the precious object.

Shortly thereafter a pestilence occurred in the country. The Nakatomi and Mononobe statesmen lost no time in suggesting that this tragedy represented the anger of the native gods at the presence of the copper and gold rival. The Emperor conceded the plausibility of this argument and had the offending image thrown into a canal. But immediately a mysterious fire consumed the great hall of the imperial palace, though it was a clear day with neither lightning nor wind, suggesting that the buddha-power of the image was also capable of vengeance. Thus Japan vacillated between remaining true to its own soul and being fascinated with foreign splendors. As in later times as well, ''foreign splendors'' won out and Buddhism steadily increased its fortunes.

## The Tendai Umbrella

It is now three centuries after the introduction of Buddhism. The capital is the new and splendid city of Heian (now Kyoto). On the broad streets of this carefully planned metropolis merchants hurry with delicacies for the ruling aristocrats—the people "above the clouds" who dwell in great mansions—while priests go about their rounds, and a gala oxcart passes by carrying a fine lady to a flower-viewing party or other appointment. Above the city, on lofty Mt. Hiei to the northeast, a great spiritual empire is taking shape.

The northeast is significant. That was the direction, according to Chinese belief, from which evil influences were likely to come; the vast monastery founded there would serve as a bulwark to protect the nation's premier city from the angle of most grievous danger even as smaller temples were set to block the other approaches. Though Japanese Buddhism had grown in sophistication since its earlier importation, the old combined perception of Buddhism as a spiritual path and as a source of sheer spiritual-magical power lingered, as did the powerful alliance of church and state consolidated by Prince Shotoku.

Nowhere was this alliance more evident than on Mt. Hiei. The high ecclesiastics of the Tendai empire were from aristocratic families, and its subtle theologians devised ways by which all the religious views of the nation, (Shinto and Buddhist, popular and esoteric) could be harmonized. Mt. Hiei and Tendai were long the cultural and educational centers of early Buddhist Japan, but as time went on Tendai grew in wealth and power until the Heian palace itself seemed weak beside it. Time and again the soldier-monks of Mt. Hiei would demonstrate with holy objects in the capital until the government was intimidated into meeting their demands, or would form alliances and engage in skirmishes like any other feudal lords. Finally, in 1571, the Mt. Hiei monastery with its hundreds of temples was razed and its denizens slaughtered by troops of the warlord Oda Nobunaga who suspected them of conspiring with his enemies. The sacred summit is today but a shadow of what it once was, though still a place of compelling and numinous beauty.

The origins of this empire lie in a more distant past, however. It was in the year 788 that a young monk, just ordained in Nara, left the former capital to establish a place of meditation in a more solitary place. He found Mt. Hiei suitable for his holy purposes. He was Saicho (767–822, known posthumously as Dengyo Daishi), and as he ascended the peak he sang over and over a prayer he had devised:

> *O Buddhas*
> *Of unexcelled complete enlightenment*
> *Bestow your invisible aid*
> *Upon this hut I open*
> *On the mountain top.*[20]

---

20. Tsunoda et al., *Sources* I, 116.

A special blessing seems to have been granted: Saicho and his temple on Mt. Hiei were in a very favorable position when six years later the capital was moved to the marshy fields at the foot of his mountain, and the mountain priest himself received much imperial patronage. In 804 the Emperor sent Saicho to China to study, and he received training in the teachings of T'ien-t'ai (Tendai in Japanese). Tendai was among the most profound of all the deep-thinking Mahayana philosophies; it constructed a vast umbrella under which a variety of types of Buddhist practice and views might be securely followed.

Tendai taught that all sutras and all forms of Buddhism were paths to truth, but these truths operated on various levels to accommodate the state of the individual's spiritual preparations. First came the "lesser vehicle" (Hinayana) tractates, then the more profound Mahayana sutras, and finally the *Lotus Sutra*—to Tendai the crown of them all. This was the *Lotus Sutra* that taught the emptiness and relativity of all principles, however subtle, yet also told of the Buddha's grace coming down like rain on all beings. For the *Lotus,* children simply presenting an offering of flowers crushed in their tiny hands were closer to realization than the proud *arhats* or liberated saints of Hinayana Buddhism.

These views undergirded Tendai's basic philosophical position: the triple truth that (a) all things are empty (*sunyata,* ku), (b) all things nonetheless have a "real" if temporary existence, and (c) all things are therefore simultaneously empty absolutely yet existing as temporary reality. Finally, then, the transitory phenomenal world of appearances is reality as it really is, to be seen as the buddha-nature and showered with a buddha's grace.

This seemingly abstruse doctrine offers extremely significant insights into not only the Tendai umbrella but the Japanese mind in general. Coupled with comparable insights from Shingon, Zen, and Neo-Confucianism, it helps explain the Japanese tendency in art and letters to dwell on the transitory nature of phenomena yet hold the idea that the phenomenal world is ultimate reality itself. This reality can be caught in words or brushstrokes—the bird or branch of a Zen artist, the grimacing face of a kabuki actor in an *ukiyo* (floating world) portrait of the worldly Edo period, and the frog of which the haiku poet Basho wrote in lines said to sum up the whole meaning of Buddhism for those who understand:

> *Old pond—*
> *Frog jumps in—*
> *Sound of water!*

Each of these is not just a token of some greater, more abstract idea or reality that lies behind them. Though everything comes and goes, each *is* reality, and the only greater reality is that which can be neither named nor drawn.

On Mt. Hiei, this vision expresses itself in the multiplicity of spiritual paths. As there are many trails to the summit of the sacred mountain, so are there many paths to enlightenment, depending on the temperament and state of development of the individual. Even today, scattered like fairyland palaces under the forest eaves, one can find temples dedicated to one Buddhist mystery and way to salvation after another. Here is a shrine to Amida, the buddha of faith who has promised that all who merely call upon his name will be brought into the Western Paradise or Pure Land. Over here is a temple of Kannon, the many-armed bodhisattva of compassion whose countless acts of mercy not only work concrete good but also let a glow of transcendent wonder fall through answered prayer into the lives of those mired in the world of darkness and despair. Over there is an incense-laden temple of Fudo, the Immovable One—the fire-surrounded, fierce-visaged Myoo or Mysterious King whose wrath is not demonic but rather directed against enemies of the Buddha's truth; he holds the sword of discrimination and a lasso with which to ensnare error.

Finally, we come to a temple of Dainichi, the Great Sun Buddha favored by Shingon. This is a temple for mystics and philosophers, for Dainichi personifies the ultimate essence of the universe itself, the dance of the atoms and galaxies. His meditations sustain the rise and fall of all worlds. Between this massive image and the worshiper is a deep pit containing a table for the flower and incense offerings of Buddhism; it represents the gloomy world in which buddhas, bodhisattvas, and priests must labor for the salvation of all sentient beings.

Shinto is not excluded from the Tendai umbrella. At the foot of Mt. Hiei, near Lake Biwa and on the far side from Kyoto, rest the lovely white and vermilion buildings of the Sanno (Mountain King) Shrine. The Sanno Shrine is dedicated to the primordial divinity who ruled that mountain long before Buddhism arrived on Japanese shores and whose protection is still sought on behalf of the monastery. Moreover, in the broad view of Tendai, all divinities ultimately are temporal manifestations of the same unity, so the Mountain King kami was said to be both a Japanese form of that which in India was the historical Buddha, Sakyamuni, as well as one form of the great Shinto goddess at Ise, Amaterasu.

## Princess and Priestess in Pilgrimage and Sacred Place

An extremely important recurring theme in Japanese religion is pilgrimage—physical movement to a religiously important place. A pilgrimage is transformative, giving the pilgrim fresh grace and spiritual status. Indeed, the pilgrim is frequently transformed into a mediator who represents the sacred to the community and the community to the sacred.

An interesting early Japanese institution known as the saigu (abstinence palace) reflects this pattern.[21] From ancient times until the fourteenth century the accession of a new emperor was accompanied by the selection of an imperial princess to serve as priestess at the saigu near the Grand Shrine of Ise dedicated

---

21. This discussion is based on Robert S. Ellwood, "The Saigu: Princess and Priestess," *History of Religions*, 7, no. 1 (August 1967), 35-60.

to Amaterasu. The latter was and remains the premier shrine in the land—a kind of Shinto national cathedral. In the Heian era, when the institution of the saigu was most important, the shrine was considered so sacred that only members of the imperial house and its priests and envoys could worship there. Later, as we shall see, the situation was quite different, though the Grand Shrine's sacred and national significance was not diminished.

The progress of the princess to Ise had all the forms of a pilgrimage and so was a slow and graduated affair. She was selected by divination and, after that selection, a delegation of governmental shrine officials proceeded to her house, purified it, and placed green branches to indicate its new role as a sacred dwelling.

Entering a preliminary abstinence hall the princess had to purify herself in a colorful ceremony in which she went in procession to the banks of the river in an ox-cart, accompanied by twenty-two runners, twenty-four companions in carriages, and numerous bearers. There, a high-ranking Nakatomi priest of the governmental shrine office held a *nusa* or sacred wand with streamers, and the sacred princess knelt by the edge of the stream to cleanse her hands and lips.

While the princess was dwelling in this first hall another preparatory house, the *nonomiya* or palace in the fields, was being built in accordance with the ancient belief that buildings used for sacred purposes should be constructed anew for each new use. After a year or less the princess moved to the nonomiya in a purifying and processional rite similar to the entry into the first preliminary hall. Then, after a year at the nonomiya, long and elaborate preparations began for the princess's great pilgrimage to lonely Ise and its solemn shrines.

The procession to Ise took place during the ninth month. It was the occasion of national observance appropriate to a sacred and special season. Solemn rites of purification were held. The whole month was known as an "abstinence month" when impurity in all things must be avoided. Taboos were fixed, burial and reburial were forbidden, and such non-Shinto, Chinese imports as the Taoist worship of the north star were proscribed.

When the princess finally reached the Grand Shrine, she lived with an entourage in a simple residential compound a few miles from the shrine. There the same annual cycle of Shinto rites as those of the Heian court was kept. Three times a year, however, the princess left the saigu to go up to the Grand Shrine to preside over great rituals connected with the Ise deities. Her ceremonial duties were relatively light—chiefly just receiving and holding a great purificatory wand. She was not so much a priestly performer in these solemnities of prayer and offering as a sacred, silent presence in the midst of the rite.

What was the meaning of this strange mode of life? Behind it lies the Japanese image of the miko or shamaness—a pure woman who lives secluded in a holy place, far from humanity and close to the gods. In early times highly placed women like this were confidantes of rulers and gave oracles on matters of state. Furthermore, the saigu was intended to represent the court and the capital of Heian before the great ancestral and national deities at Ise. But it was not to be the court as it was, compromised by the corrosions of alien religions and various pollutions. It was the court as it would like to be seen by those clean and ancient spiritual powers, the kami who had guided Japan in the divine age long before Buddhism and elegant civilization had been heard of—pure as a young priestess.

## Later Pilgrims to the Grand Shrine

Many centuries later, after times had changed, the Grand Shrine attracted a new kind of pilgrim. Ise still represented a pilgrim's goal. It was, in Victor Turner's phrase, "the center out there;" a place having no geographical relation to the concentrations of political, economic, or even ecclesiastical power; a place isolated and holy, whose access required planning and a journey marked by watchfulness but increasing purity; a place where the transformative powers of the holy seem especially close to earth.[22] As an ancient Japanese scripture puts it: "Ise, of the divine wind, where repair the waves from the eternal world, the successive waves."[23]

Ise has always seemed a place like this. In the Nara and Heian eras, its lovely but lonely groves knew only the footfall of priests and princely envoys, so awesome was its sanctity. But later, especially in the Tokugawa period, the same sanctity brought thousands upon thousands of people of all walks of life to the Grand Shrine. *Ise-mairi,* going up to Ise, then became a national passion. Everyone, it was felt, ought to go at least once in one's life; *Ise-ko* (Ise clubs) were set up in innumerable towns and villages to pool the meager resources of their humble adherents to allow one person, chosen by lot, to go each year to pray for all and bring back an Ise charm or talisman.

Why Ise? No doubt its ageless mystery, the opportunity to register a covert protest against the Tokugawa shoguns by honoring the shrine of the legitimate imperial house they had rendered impotent, and clever promotion by priests all combined to set countless pairs of feet on the Ise road. For the Tokugawa masses pilgrimage was one of the few modes of escape from long hours of hard work in a regimented society, and they took full advantage of it.

Ise pilgrimage was scarcely a totally solemn affair. The great Tokaido road south from Edo that branched off to Ise, and the other highways to the sacred shrines, were lined with lively inns that catered to the pilgrim's every comfort and desire and entertained them with song and dance. In Ise city itself the thing to do after a day visiting the holy sites was to watch a lively dance performed by charming girls in one of the huge inns or teahouses. Even the three-mile road between the inner and outer shrines was lined with beautiful kimono-clad entertainers who would sing and dance for a handful of coins.[24]

---

22. Victor Turner, "The Center Out There: Pilgrim's Goal," *History of Religions* 12, no. 3 (February 1973), 191–230.

23. Aston, *Nihongi,* I, 176.

24. For a readable and accessible account of the Ise pilgrimages, see chap. 9 of Oliver Statler, *Japanese Inn* (New York: Random House, 1961). See also Winston Davis, "Pilgrimage and World Renewal: A Study of Religion and Social Values in Tokugawa Japan," *History of Religions,* Part I, 23, 2 (November 1983), pp. 97–116; Part II, 23, 3 (February 1984), pp. 197–221.

Not every Ise pilgrim, of course, had even a handful of coins. Some were skipping out of town with creditors on their heels; some were eloping lovers; some were no more than children, for it was almost a tradition among the lively apprentices of Edo occasionally to slip away in bands for a *nuke-mairi* (secret pilgrimage). On their return from such a sacred mission employers usually found it hard to discipline them too severely. They were not alone in sneaking off informally, for nuke-mairi meant avoiding the expensive farewell parties and giving of souvenirs upon return of the ''official'' pilgrim.

About every sixty years in the Tokugawa period another sort of pilgrimage to Ise took place. This was the great and mysterious *okage-mairi,* a pilgrimage under divine grace. As though by the wave of some almighty hand a restlessness would sweep the land and thousands upon thousands would leave for Ise without warning, often with no more than the clothes on their back and a dipper for water. Poems of the day said:

> *How grateful we are*
> *That we can visit Ise*
> *With only a dipper in hand.*
>
> *By dint of divine grace*
> *We visit Ise*
> *Carrying no money.*

They would sleep under bridges, subsist on alms, and march down the road in great companies. Tired, emaciated, moving as though half-hypnotized, they would yet sing hymns, dance, and hold aloft banners and wands all day long. As much as three-quarters of the population of a town would disappear overnight. Bands of children as young as five, six, or seven would vanish toward Ise. Commonly the mass pilgrimage would begin with rumors that Ise's magical charms had fallen from heaven. Once started, the pilgrimage fever spread like wildfire. The numbers sound awesome; contemporary observers compared them to endless streams of ants flowing toward the holy shrines. Between April 9 and May 29, 1705, for example, 3,620,000 were said to have worshiped at the Grand Shrine. The figure may be exaggerated, but by all accounts the crowds were immense.

The great pilgrimages to Ise came to a spectacular end in 1867, the same year the Tokugawa regime was giving way to imperial rule. Once more word went out of signs and wonders connected with the Grand Shrine, though now in the context of a recent famine and economic decline and of an obviously collapsing, revolutionary political situation. The hungry poor would snake through the homes and businesses of the well-to-do in frenzied dance, a variation on the okage-mairi frenzy, taking whatever they needed.

At Ise itself the turmoil of October and November of that year clearly reflected the topsy-turvy world in revolutionary change. Men wore women's attire and vice versa. People threw money away on the street as though it had no meaning. And all the time ceaseless processions, music, and dancing continued in a scene beyond description.[25]

The sylvan shrines of Ise have therefore seen much of both the calm beauty and the tumultuous history of Japan. The preceding vignettes from the Buddhist and Shinto past represent only fragments of its religious history, yet they suggest something of its diversity and its power in the lives of countless Japanese at all levels of society.

## EXEMPLARY PERSONS

Like any religion, Japanese religion is ultimately made up of individual human beings who live it out in the context of their lives. Within the panorama of Japanese religious history certain individuals stand out as exemplary—both of Japanese religion itself and of the degree to which individuals can mark high points in the ebb and flow of religious history.

To focus on key individuals in Japanese religious history, however, is almost ironic, especially when the individuals stand out for altering the flow of that history. Much of Japanese religion discovers its "salvation" within *community* rather than in or for individuals. Moreover, Japan is resistant to the innovative individual and appreciative of conserving traditional, communal conventions and patterns. It may be fair to say, in short, that in Japan the individual is less a self-subsisting, independent, innovating agent than the loyal member of communal groupings, and identity belongs more to the group than to the self. The exemplary persons discussed below, Shinran Shonin and Motoori Norinaga, both denied, for example, that they have added anything not already said by their teachers. Both of them showed, at crucial moments, willingness to sacrifice their own interests and identity to those of a communal group.

### Shinran Shonin (1173–1262)

Shinran was born into an aristocratic family in twelfth-century Kyoto. He was ordained a Tendai Buddhist monk at the early age of nine and lived for the next twenty years in the Tendai monastery on Mt. Hiei near Kyoto. Like other important Buddhist reformers of the thirteenth century Shinran thus spent his formative years within the monastic world of a traditional and well-established Buddhism.

Although the details of his life on Mt. Hiei are not available, one can presume a number of things. Monks were disciplined in traditional Buddhist practice and thought, with heavy emphasis on a celibate and strict morality, as well

---

25. Material on the late Tokugawa pilgrimage is based on Hitoo Marukawa, "Religious Circumstances of the late Tokugawa and Early Meiji Periods," *Tenri Journal of Religion*, no. 11 (December 1970), 43–78.

as in meditation practices and scriptural study. Specifically for Shinran, however, this involved early exposure to nembutsu practice (calling on the name of Amida Buddha, or namu Amida butsu) and to the various Mahayana scriptures that teach of Amida and his Pure Land.

It also involved exposure to political intrigue and perhaps a certain religious hypocrisy, for Tendai had come upon a period of degeneration from within and undue influence from the political powers of Kyoto. It had also entered a period of increasing esoteric practices under the influence of Shingon Buddhism.

Whatever Shinran faced, however, by the age of twenty-nine (1201) he was clearly motivated to leave Tendai and seek other paths of Buddhism. Motivating factors included a powerful vision he had while on a private religious retreat, and his discovery of the Pure Land master Honen (1133–1212), the founder of the Jodo sect.

The exact details of the vision are not at all clear, though it seems to have been a strong influence on Shinran's subsequent life and teaching. The weight of evidence indicates that in this vision the bodhisattva Kannon appeared to him in the form of Prince Shotoku (573–621) and made the following vow: If Shinran's karma were to bring him into contact with women, Kannon would take the form of a beautiful woman with whom Shinran might have a conjugal relationship and through whom Shinran might be helped both in his vocation and in his ultimate rebirth into Amida's Pure Land. Kannon then charged Shinran to make this promise and its significance known to others.[26]

The meaning of this vision is subject to speculation. Nowhere does Shinran elaborate on it. Given what is known about his life and thought, however, speculation may be fruitful.

First of all, though not necessarily most important, the vision suggests an interest in the opposite sex. This would not be unlikely since Shinran had already alluded to his "sinfulness" as a Tendai monk, and indeed he later married a woman who remained with him throughout his life. This interest, and the subsequent marriage, could be seen as sanctified by the vision insofar as Shinran saw it as the will of the bodhisattva.

Related to this, however, is the important idea that Buddhist life and Pure Land salvation can be fulfilled outside monastic life. In effect the vision tells Shinran that the religious vocation may be led even in married life. This is significant, for Shinran became the first major Buddhist figure to marry. As such he valorized a whole new direction for Buddhist practice and seriously called into question centuries of both the orthodoxy and orthopraxis of normative (monastic) Buddhism.

In the second place, the vision could be seen as confirming his interest in Amida Buddha and the Pure Land teachings that implied. Kannon is, after all,

---

26. See Shinran's vision as repeated in his *Godensho* as translated in D. T. Suzuki, *Collected Writings on Shin Buddhism* (Kyoto: Shinshu Otaniku, 1973), p. 170 and as discussed in Alica and Daigan Matsunaga, *Foundation of Japanese Buddhism,* vol. II (Los Angeles & Tokyo: Buddhist Books International, 1976), 86–88.

the "right hand" of Amida, the compassionate activity of Amida Buddha. In addition, the vision suggests Amida's Pure Land as the ultimate salvation.

In the third place, the vision charges Shinran to spread the good news of Amida's compassionate mercy, and his promise to all beings of salvation in his Pure Land, regardless of their station in life. Like Prince Shotoku, with whom Shinran identified, a layman is chosen to bring the message of Amida's saving grace to all those who have ears to hear, eyes to see, hearts/minds of entrusting faith (*shinjin*), and lips to call on Amida through nembutsu.

Such speculations may offer a glimpse into Shinran's deepest motivations and into his unique contributions to Buddhist thought, practice, and history. Already in his vision we can see the germ of his most significant contributions. This germ, however, needed some nurturing even though the soil was fertile and the seed planted. For this, we turn to the other major factor in Shinran's earlier life—the Pure Land master Honen.

Honen had already begun what Shinran eventually brought to full flower, the transmission and establishment of separate Pure Land sects within Japan. Pure Land teachings and nembutsu practice had long been present but always as a part of the other established sects or as nonofficial popular practices outside the fold of official Buddhism. Now, Honen had brought over from China an official line of transmission in the Pure Land Buddhism of China and was propagating that in Japan right under the eyes of established Buddhism in Kyoto.

Shinran had heard of Honen and, with the inspiration of his vision behind him, quickly left Tendai to become his disciple. Under Honen, he steeped himself in Pure Land practice and thought, nurturing the seed of his interest to germination and early budding. By 1207 Shinran had become one of Honen's chief disciples and was increasingly singled out as a religious genius.

The Kyoto years with Honen, however, came to an abrupt end in 1207 when, for a variety of reasons, Honen's group came into disfavor with the religious and political authorities, and an attempt to break up the group followed quickly. The reasons for this are twofold. Lay disciples may have abused some of the privileges given them to be both laymen and yet "monks," and the Buddhist authorities of the day may have been jealous (or at least disturbed) about both Honen's dramatic successes and his deviations from traditional Buddhist discipline and practice.

Whatever the reasons, Honen and Shinran, together with other leading figures in the movement, were exiled to separate places in the Japanese islands— Honen to Tosa province and Shinran to Echigo province. Though both were pardoned and released from exile in 1211, they never met again, and Shinran carried on alone.

Shinran's years of exile were important to him. It was during this period that he experienced himself as "neither layman nor monk." It was an "in-between time" both for his own vocational identity and in his life story. After all, the exile had brought with it the official denial of his right to wear monastic robes and had separated him dramatically from the environment of Honen and of Kyoto Buddhism. He was now—in many ways—on his own.

Second, though there is some question about this, Shinran seems to have met and married his wife during these years and begun a family which eventually came to six children.

All these factors together formed a dramatic turning point in Shinran's life. Having lived in one form or another of Buddhist orders until this point, he was now living the lay life and was thrust into a context he had not known before. No wonder he saw himself as "neither layman nor monk"! Shinran came out of this period of his life in 1211, having established for himself and subsequently for others a new model for the Buddhist religious life—a life totally devoted to Buddhist practice and thought on the one hand yet immersed in the ordinary lay life as well.

For Shinran this life was justified as not only appropriate but perhaps even necessary given human needs and Amida's vow of salvation. According to Shinran, since salvation depends absolutely on pure entrusting mind (shinjin) and on the calling on Amida in that state (nembutsu), we can do nothing of our own volition to effect salvation. All forms of "self-power" (**jiriki**) must therefore be abandoned—even the pretense of celibacy and the monastic life. In whatever life style we live we need only depend on the "power of the other" (**tariki**)—the power of Amida's vow, wisdom, and compassion—for rebirth in the Pure Land. This became Shinran's major theme and he subsequently took this teaching out to the ordinary people of Japan: first in Echigo, then in the eastern provinces known as the Kanto area, and finally back to Kyoto.

In each of these areas and periods of his life he continued his practice, his study, his writing, his preaching and teaching, and his organization of disciples into congregations (*monto*) of Pure Land practitioners. For example, he finished the first draft of his major written work, the *Kyogyoshinso,* in 1224. Especially in the Kanto area, but also in Kyoto, he helped establish autonomous groups who later (after his death in 1262) became the basis for an independent Pure Land sect, called the Jodoshin (True Pure Land) sect which looked to him as its founder.

His later years in Kyoto brought some difficulties as well. The problem with autonomous groups and a kind of lay "priesthood of all believers," as well as with the heredity of power through family blood lines, was that disputes over authority and doctrine were even more likely to arise than in a strong traditional hierarchy where orthodoxy and orthopraxis were clearer. Shinran spent much of his later years in Kyoto trying to iron out such difficulties, even at one point having to disown and deny his own son for attempting to usurp power.

Regardless of difficulties and internal disputes, however, the power of Shinran's life and vision lived on through the Jodoshin sect. Shinran lived and remained even after death an "exemplary person": He not only represents one major orientation within Japanese religion generally and Japanese Buddhism specifically, but he "moved" history by establishing a new direction and a new form of Buddhist practice and thought—one that has subsequently affected millions of Japanese religiously as a major factor in their lives.

For the intellectual and theological elite, Shinran also provided a profound and radical reinterpretation of Buddhist thought and practice—one that spoke of a radical form of faith (shinjin) as turning the self over (eko) to Amida, and one that disavowed any particular actions or beliefs as necessary to the goal. Similarly, he provided a reinterpretation of rebirth in the Pure Land by suggesting that the Pure Land might be realized or discovered in this life if we would but call on the Amida of our own mind through true entrusting mind (shinjin).

As with all exemplary persons, Shinran's life seems to have been consistent with his views. Take, for example, his own name for himself, Gutoku ("foolish/shaven-headed"). Of this name, and no doubt of Shinran's life and thought, the Japanese philosopher Nishida Kitaro (1870–1945) has said:

> Wisdom in religion is to know wisdom itself; virtue in religion is to enact virtue itself. . . . The truth is, however, that . . . the person who is adrift within human wisdom and virtue cannot know that wisdom, that virtue. Every person, no matter who he is, must return to the original body of his own naked self; he must once let go from the cliff's edge and come back to life after perishing, or he cannot know them. In other words, only the person who has been able to experience deeply what it is to be "foolish/shaven" can know wisdom and virtue.[27]

Shinran simply had another language and a specific discipline for accomplishing this death and rebirth. As he himself summarizes it, "Saved by the inconceivable working of Amida's Vow, I shall realize birth into the Pure Land: the moment you entrust yourself thus, so that the mind set upon saying the Name arises within you, you are brought to share in the benefit of being grasped by Amida, never to be abandoned."[28]

## Motoori Norinaga (1730–1801)

Motoori Norinaga is yet another exemplary person, though for different reasons than Shinran. First of all, he represents a close relationship to Shinto, though he honored Buddhism and Confucianism as well. Second, his Shinto interests were related to a search for a unique Japanese spirit and cultural tradition. Third, he was neither priest nor monk but a layman with close ties to several strands of Japanese religion; yet he was trained in nonreligious occupations as a physician and a scholar-teacher. Fourth, he was historically important for both looking backward to reassess the value of a native religious and cultural (literary) tradition and looking forward to help reestablish in Japan some of the values

---

27. As translated in Dennis Hirota, *Tannisho: A Primer* (Kyoto: Ryukoku University, 1982), p. 12.
28. Ibid., p. 22.

and forms of that tradition, especially through the founding of the ''national learning'' (kokugaku) movement or school of thought.

Motoori was born in Ise province in 1730 as Ozu Norinaga, the second son of a modest merchant-class family. His father, Ozu Sadatoshi, died by the time Norinaga was ten years old, and the family business was turned over to Norinaga's older (adopted) brother, Ozu Sadaharu. Norinaga and his sisters were raised by their mother in their home of birth while the fortunes of the family business moved to Edo (Tokyo) with Sadaharu. Norinaga was left free, in short, to pursue his own interests in his education and early life—free of the obligation of taking over the family business himself.

In this early period Norinaga showed great interest in education and reading the Chinese Confucian (and Buddhist) classics. Not long after, before he was twenty years old, he was also reading Japanese literature and poetry, particularly of the Heian period. Thus did he show, at an early age, a great interest in learning—an interest that would later dominate his life as a scholar and teacher.

Norinaga's religious upbringing and environment were much like that of other Japanese children. Confucianism was the dominant political-social philosophy of the time; Buddhism was the family practice that aimed for rebirth in Amida's Pure Land after death; the Shinto kami were worshiped on special occasions; and the ancestral spirits were honored on the anniversaries of their death. Most of the major strands of Japanese religion were, in short, present at one point or another in this typically eclectic religious home.

One factor stands out, however, as especially significant for young Norinaga and his parents. Though officially he was the second son (after his adopted older brother), he was in fact the firstborn son and child of his father and mother—one they had prayed for to the kami of childbirth and child protection, Mikumari no kami of Yoshino Shrine in Yamato province. His birth was considered a gift of the kami, and his parents vowed that Norinaga would visit the shrine to pay homage to the kami on his thirteenth birthday. When he did so at age thirteen, the visit made a deep impression on him and may well have been one of the major factors in his eventual interest in Shinto.

In the meantime he was absorbed more in Pure Land Buddhist practice and in Confucian thought than in anything else. As his education continued, however, he became more and more absorbed in Heian literature, especially the formal *waka* poetry of the Heian aristocracy and Murasaki Shikibu's great twelfth-century novel, *The Tale of Genji*. This Heian literary interest became dominant later on and formed one significant element in his viewpoint.

By his late teenage years it had become clear that Norinaga was no ordinary young man. In fact, had he been an ordinary young man of that day, he would have been satisfied either to form a branch family of the Ozu clan and take up a trade or to let himself be adopted by a childless couple as the male heir to a merchant family and occupation.

In fact, at an obvious crisis point in his life, he turned down just such an opportunity in order to seek his spiritual, intellectual, and vocational identity elsewhere. No doubt his mother was upset, since it was her responsibility (the father being dead and the older brother in far-off Edo) to see that Norinaga fared well in life as befitted the son of a proper merchant-class family. Norinaga, however, had other ideas, and when his mother suggested he become a physician, he reluctantly agreed, saying: "It is base and uncongenial to make medicine my occupation; it is against the real intentions which I have as a man. However, it would be even more opposed to the (Confucian, social) way if I were to denigrate intentionally the examples of my parents and ancestors simply to vindicate my own uprightness."[29]

By this time Norinaga was torn intellectually, spiritually, and vocationally. As a young medical student in Kyoto, however, he could train for an occupation yet pursue his other interests at the same time. Thus did he pursue his studies of Neo-Confucian thought, Heian literature, and ancient Shinto texts.

That he was beginning to find himself while in Kyoto seems evident in his adoption of a new name, substituting Motoori for Ozu. The name Motoori had belonged to one of the Ozu's more luminous ancestors, Motoori Takehide (d. 1591), who had been of the samurai, not merchant, class. To Norinaga he was a more fitting role model than the more recent merchant ancestors, especially since he was supposed to have been a strong, creative, and innovative person.

Whatever his motives, however, Norinaga now identified with a more professional and learned part of society, though he never forgot his roots in the merchant class. He now felt free to pursue his own path under the Motoori name and became increasingly knowledgeable and active in the intellectual circles of Kyoto, especially the *kogaku* ("study of antiquity") movement inspired by such people as Keichen (1640–1701) and Ogyu Sorai (1666–1728) who were interested in Heian literature and ancient Shinto writings.

Before his interest in such matters came to full flower, however, Motoori returned to his native area to practice medicine and begin a family of his own. While there he not only practiced medicine but continued to pursue his studies, now increasingly in demand as a lecturer on Heian literature and a participant in a local poetry club.

At this point the direction of his life and the nature of his interests were strongly influenced by the works of Kamo Mabuchi (1697–1769), a Shinto scholar who had begun work on the ancient, sacred Shinto writing, the *Kojiki,* and on the earliest Japanese collection of poetry, the *Manyoshu.* Under the influence of Mabuchi's work, Motoori turned his attention more directly to ancient Shinto as the source of a unique Japanese spirit, and to the ancient way (kodo) exemplified in these writings. Under Mabuchi's influence Motoori entered into his lifelong vocation—the study of the ancient way, the restoration of a pure (or "natural") Shinto (*shizen-no-shinto*), and the establishment of a new interest in national learning (kokugaku).

---

29. As translated in Shigeru Matsumoto, *Motoori Norinaga* (Cambridge: Harvard University Press, 1970), p. 27.

This new focus of Motoori's interest did not, however, mean an abandonment of his previous interests in Heian literature and poetry. It only put those interests in a clearer framework and directed them toward a unique Japanese spirit. For Motoori Heian literature and poetry continued as a focus of interest; they expressed for him one absolutely important ingredient: **mono-no-aware** ("sensitivity to things"). This ingredient of a unique Japanese spirit undercut, for Motoori, all the Chinese—especially Neo-Confucian—theories about reality, social conventions, and moral behavior. It indicated that, at bottom, the uniqueness of the Japanese view lay not in rational abstraction and artificial social conventions but in emotional, aesthetic sensitivity to both the beauty and the pathos of life. A Japanese hero, for example Genji in *The Tale of Gengi*, is not a hero for his political, social, or moral power and behavior; rather, he is a hero of mono-no-aware—one who is easily moved to tears, for example, at the falling of a cherry blossom or who can easily dash off a poetic response to a hint of feminine interest.

For Motoori poetic reality and "feminine" values were more important than intellectual/descriptive reality and "masculine" values. Heian literature and waka poetry provided a model for this, one that Motoori sought to make live again in Japan. Anything else, for example Confucian thought or even Buddhist ideas, worked against that in their attempts to construct and manage human life, or in their attempts to be detached from emotion (aware) and things (mono). As Motoori says:

> In general, the real heart of a human being is effeminate and tender like a woman or child. To be manly, resolute, and wise is a mere superficial appearance. As far as the depth of man's real heart is concerned, the wisest men do not differ from a woman or a child. The difference between them lies merely in that the former conceal the real heart for shame, whereas the latter do not.[30]

With this important ingredient already established, Motoori turned to his growing interest in the *Kojiki* and, within that, the mythology reflected in the first major section called the "Age of the Kami," that is, the sacred Shinto stories of the creation of the world, the birth of myriad kami (including Amaterasu), the creation of the Japanese islands, the creation of human beings, and the establishment of rule on earth through the divine imperial line. It was in these stories, so Motoori thought, that the ancient way (kodo) was revealed and a unique Japanese religious outlook on life was to be found. This ancient way was, in turn, the same as his "natural Shinto"—the "principal way" (taido) of Japan.

> What is called a principal Way is something as follows: Buddhists believe the Way of the Buddha to be the principal Way; Confucians hold the Way of the Sages to be the principal Way; for Taoists, it is conformity to nature. As for our country, the principal Way is *shizen no shinto* or natural Shinto. . . . Natural Shinto is the

---

30. Ibid., p. 49.

Way that existed since the beginning of heaven and earth and the age of *kami*. It differs from the so-called Shinto of the present day.[31]

For Motoori the *Kojiki* was the ancient way's chief scripture, and it provided the evidence, the framework, and the religious basis for a unique Japanese spirit and a superior Japanese status among all humans. Motoori's studies convinced him that kami power stands before, with, and after the world and that the ways of the kami are not to be known or explained by humans—their power and actions are "inscrutable mystery."

The way of humans, in light of this, is to worship kami, attain a pure/sincere heart (*magokoro*), and honor the emperor as the manifestation of the divine will on earth and in history. The sincere heart is especially important because it represents the human potential for goodness and the spark of the divine in the human. It is the human possibility to know and follow the ancient way, and the *Kojiki* reveals its earliest manifestation in Japan (though it was subsequently covered over, says Motoori, by Chinese influences).

Magokoro is also important because it is the place in Motoori's thought where mono-no-aware in Heian literature could make best contact with the ancient way revealed in the *Kojiki*. Though Motoori seems to tie them together rather explicitly by tracing the etymology of aware to the emotional response of the heavenly kami to Amaterasu's return from a cave, the following commentary on Motoori's magokoro also does so:

> It was in "rejection" of this "rational" (Neo-Confucian) explanation that Motoori proposed the basis of true understanding, the *magokoro,* which is the pure mind that apprehends reality in its essential uniqueness and comprehends it sentiently and emotionally. Such an act of comprehension, represented by the discovery of *mono no aware,* leads to a truly mythic (thus metaphoric) understanding of the world—grasping the essential meaning of phenomena intuitively and identifying with it sympathetically. Sympathy and intuition replace rational comprehension; particularity and uniqueness replace principle, category, and typification; and the tangible replaces the intangible.[32]

This is precisely Motoori's "poetic reality" out of mono-no-aware sensitivity, and magokoro is the expression of that in the teachings of the ancient way. Together, these form yet another instance in Japanese history of a religio-aesthetic sensitivity as the ground and ideal of life. This particular one is simply grounded religiously in Shinto rather than in Buddhism, and looks more to the *Kojiki* than to Heian literature as the crucial sacred text. In fact, it is almost as though by deciphering the *Kojiki* Motoori seeks to reenter a golden, mythic time of the gods and overcome the distancing of history and language. His work on

---

31. Ibid., p. 63.

32. H. D. Harootunian, "The Consciousness of Archaic Form in the New Realism of Kokugaku." In *Japanese Thought in the Tokugawa Period,* by T. Najita and I. Scheiner, (Chicago: University of Chicago Press, 1978), p. 82.

the *Kojiki* could be said to be an attempt to recover the poetic "voice" of the paradisal past—unseparated by words, abstractions, theories, and history itself—and more directly (poetically) to experience the pure heart itself.

For the rest of his life, Motoori made his work on the *Kojiki* his project and, indeed, he published his major work, the *Kojiki-den,* in 1798, just a few years before his death.

His work was not, however, merely backward looking. For him the *Kojiki* and ancient way, not to mention the budding national learning movement, had immediate, practical implications, to show how people should behave and how political/social structures should operate. This came not only from his own motivation but by virtue of his growing importance as a scholar, teacher, and adviser to leaders and disciples alike. The former were especially interested in his teachings as they related to the nation. The major themes of his teachings are as follows.

First, and perhaps most fundamentally, Motoori saw history itself—especially Japanese history—as the unfolding of the kami will in and through people with inborn kami potential (magokoro) and in and through the divine imperial rule. Specifically, the emperors of Japan were seen as divine descendants of the great ancestral sun goddess, Amaterasu, as well as the person and political/religious institution through which the kami's will primarily operates. Closely related was the importance of absolute devotion to the emperor.

Second, since the universal kami nature is known only in Japan, and since Amaterasu is understood to have been "born" in Japan, the Japanese islands and the nation are both unique and sacred. They are also, necessarily, superior in some way, as this comment from Motoori suggests:

> From the central truth that the Emperor is the direct descendant of the gods, the tenet that Japan ranks far above all other countries is a natural consequence. No other nation is entitled to equality with her, and all are bound to do homage to the Japanese sovereign and pay tribute to him.[33]

Such a theocratic view had important ramifications for later followers of Motoori and for later developments in Japanese religio-political history. In the meantime, however, it was a natural outgrowth of Motoori's reading of the *Kojiki* and of subsequent history: the great kami were universal deities yet uniquely related to and known in Japan. Therefore, there was a special relationship and implied promise—indeed, almost a notion of a covenant community, a "chosen people." Although at some level all history and all life are (for Motoori) in the hands of kami, only in Japan has this been understood and acknowledged, and only in Japan have the gods descended to rule in the form of the imperial line.

Motoori died in 1801, having lived a full and fulfilling life, and having completed his major written contribution to Japanese scholarship, literature, religion, and society. Like Shinran, however, he left behind not only written work

---

33. D. C. Holtom, *The National Faith of Japan* (New York: Paragon Corp., 1965), p. 49.

but admirers and disciples as well. His influence, in fact, continued to grow beyond his death.

Like Shinran, also, he seems to have lived a life consistent with his ideals. Perhaps this is best seen not only in his continuing avocation as a poet but also in the poem he asked to have placed on his gravestone—a gravestone that, to this day, stands next to a cherry tree and presents a poem that is full of mono-no-aware.

> *Should someone ask me*
> *About the Japanese spirit,*
> *It is the wild cherry blossoms*
> *Blooming in the morning sun.*[34]

---

34. As translated in Matsumoto, *Motoori Norinaga*, p. 69.

# countercultures

## OUTSIDE THE MAINSTREAM

Dissent against orthodoxy, or alternatives to the religious mainstream, is a relative matter. What is inside and what is outside looks different from the perspective of different social classes, settings, and periods. The situation is especially confusing in a religious tradition like Japan's where there is no one orthodoxy and the mainstream consists of many different "ways" or strands. Nonetheless, important alternative patterns can be found in the social role of religious personalities and groups especially.

Here differences are marked. The collection of religious institutions that can be labeled "mainstream" are those that have close ties to national or provincial governments and to the always-powerful family system. At the heart of that collection is a network of key Shinto shrines and Buddhist temples that have traditionally been patronized by the government with gifts or offerings and with the appointment of priests, blessings these key shrines and temples have in turn passed on to their often-numerous dependent shrines and temples. The members of those centers of worship usually owe their allegiances by virtue of family tradition; they are *ujiko* (familial members) of a shrine, and their ancestors were enrolled in a temple at a time when everyone was required to do so, namely, in the early Tokugawa era. In brief, mainstream religious institutions are those one belongs to if one has not made a self-conscious, deliberate choice to be something else.

That choice is a difficult one to make in a society as deeply imbued with

Confucian values of loyalty to family and rulers as traditional Japan. Alternative "dissident" movements have arisen, however, though one hastens to add that their "protest" against family and state has usually been oblique at best. Japanese new religious movements have often been embraced by families as units that have, themselves, characteristically given prominent place to Confucian morality. For all that, Japan in some periods has been a virtual hotbed of new and alternative ("outside") religious movements, and they have a distinctive style that sets them apart from the mainstream networks.

The difference between mainstream and outsider styles goes back to prehistoric times. Ichiro Hori has argued that even then two kinds of kami were known: the ujigami (kami of a clan and community) and the hitogami (deities who appeared as "mysterious visitors"). The former were upholders of the regular and the familiar and were worshiped by customary rites at the community shrine. The latter were gods from distant places who would break through at uncanny times, such as the turn of the year, and were associated with shamanism. Those who wished to become great shamans or shamanesses might seek out such gods by dwelling in the woods or mountains and practicing austerities until their favor was won.

For Buddhism during the Nara period, as we have seen, the distinction between ujigami and hitogami took the form of a distinction between the mainstream temples of official Buddhism in the capital and an "unofficial," highly shamanistic Buddhism popular in the countryside. The leaders of the latter forms of Buddhism made up for what they lacked in theological education and government support with powers of healing and divination acquired through mountain asceticism and with the support of the common people.

A real if tenuous link joins this unofficial Buddhism of the Nara era, called *obasoku* or bosatsu-do (bodhisattva-way) Buddhism, with the popular shamanistic Buddhism of later periods called shugendo. Practiced by mountain priests called yamabushi, it emphasized austerities by which the adept gained powers of magic and healing. Shamanesses, often called miko, have always been part of popular religion, too. Though sometimes employed by yamabushi, their tradition is closer to Shinto than to the Buddhism of the mountain priests.

These various popular traditions have not generally been persecuted by the government and official religion, and indeed they have often had certain links to the latter and received covert encouragement. But they are implicitly and potentially dissident; they say by their very existence that there are religious needs—especially for the kind of ecstatic immediacy of religious experience offered by shamanism, and for such concrete benefits as healing—that are not met by the religious mainstream. In addition they say that there are certain classes of society whose needs are not being met. In any event, they are important alternatives to the mainstream and exist outside of it.

Such movements took a new form in the Kamakura period. The great prophet Nichiren, as well as the Pure Land evangelists Honen and Shinran, were dissidents in a more obvious way and suffered some persecution as a result, even though their movements soon became part of the mainstream. All three represented the simplification and popularization of religion, common characteristics of alternative movements outside the mainstream, and all were in the shamanistic tradition insofar as they featured powerfully charismatic figures operating out of immediate religious experience gained through initiatory processes. Nichiren, especially, epitomizes the leader of such movements: He protested against the evils of the religion and government of his day and was virtually divinized by his followers, being considered a bodhisattva or buddha. Like others since his time he was a dissident precisely in his extreme emphasis on morality and nationalism and in his clear claim to represent "true religion."

The "dissent" expressed by the New Religions of nineteenth- and twentieth-century Japan shows a return to some of the most fundamental shamanistic features. These religious movements are offshoots of the popular religion of the Tokugawa period. In that age, no doubt in part because of the government's attempts to use religion to regulate society and because of its general disinterest in ordinary religion, popular cults flourished. Pilgrimages such as the Ise mairi, exhibitions of especially miracular images in temples, and street activities of various wandering preachers, diviners, healers, and so on, drew thousands if not millions eager for color and excitement and perhaps also a glint of the transcendent. The government attempted to control those manifestations without much success, judging from the repeated enactment of repressive ordinances. Much of popular Tokugawa religion can properly be considered dissent for it expresses frustration at the official ideology and its results. Minimally, however, it represents a clear example of alternative, "outside" movements. Some of its themes—pilgrimage, the charismatic personality, healing, and divination—surface in clarified form in the New Religions of later times. The clarity is enhanced by the tendency of the New Religions to narrow the focus and simplify the activity. For example, the shamanistic, charismatic personality is the founder; the one place of pilgrimage is to the religion's sacred center; healing and divination are typically performed by the one sure, simple technique taught by the faith. Simplification is found in these religions with their simple doctrine and easy entry. As we shall see in more detail, Tenrikyo exemplifies these qualities in several ways, namely, in its foundress, Nakayama Miki, who received her first divine message while in shamanistic trance; in its pilgrimages to Tenri City and the *kanrodai,* the sacred pillar marking the spot of the creation of the world; in its healing practices based on a simple rite of hand gestures; and in its simple and definite steps of initiation.

Here are some basic characteristics of many such outside religious movements in Japan.[1]

1. Most movements have a charismatic founder who has shamanistic qual-

---

1. This list of features is suggested by Harry Thomsen, *The New Religions of Japan* (Tokyo and Rutland, Vt: Charles E. Tuttle Co., 1963), pp. 20–29.

ities, that is, who received his or her power through an initiatory experience involving immediate contact with a god or a divine force, and who continues this relationship to divinity as the central reality of the movement. Usually this charismatic leader has power to heal and to deliver divine messages. By centering the authority of the movement on personal, immediate, divine contact of the shamanistic sort, the religion may remain aloof from, outside and critical of, the ordinary religious and social mainstream and thus appeal to the disaffected or those whose lives have been shaken by rapid social change.

2. Most movements have a single, simple, sure key to power and liberation. These new religious movements generally offer a single technique, accessible to everyone, such as a simple chant or ritual practice that heals and saves. Closely related to this is the tendency of almost all Japanese alternative movements to affirm monotheism in theory, practice, or both—centering on a single god, single buddha, or unified cosmic reality rather than the innumerable kami and buddhas of mainstream religion.

3. Most movements focus on a sacred center. Continuing with some modification the ancient Japanese religious motifs of sacred mountains and pilgrimage, these religious movements frequently have their own central shrine—sometimes an entire holy city as in the case of Tenrikyo—that is a place of pilgrimage for the scattered adherents. This has been a feature especially of modern movements, but earlier parallels can be found.

4. Many of these movements place emphasis on the healing of mind and body. Healing rather than sociological and other-worldly benefits are typical of movements that, lacking the family and community supports of conventional faiths, must provide intensity of experience and concrete benefits impressive enough to compensate for this loss and to attract members.

5. Most movements offer an eschatological hope for religious fulfillment in this world. Related to the previous characteristic of interest in more immediate benefits, these movements show a strong orientation toward the near future—not so much life in paradise after death but a better future in this world through new prosperity, reincarnation, or a transformation of this world. Again, this is especially a characteristic of modern New Religions, but it has earlier parallels as well. Eschatological hope is, naturally, a consolation of the poor and oppressed, but it is also a common religious response of those who see their world changing for the better, though in a confusing and uncertain way, and who expect an earthly paradise. Thus, for example, in a time of ambivalent change back in the seventh century, a prophet said that a certain divine insect would bring fabulous riches to those who worshiped him, whereas, in the tumultuous nineteenth and twentieth centuries, prophets like Okada Mokichi of World Messianity have said that the light and power of God are now growing in the world at an unprecedented rate, shaking its foundations but bringing with it imminent paradise.

We shall now turn to some specific examples of such alternative religious movements in Japan.

# EXEMPLARY MOVEMENTS

## The Caterpillar Cult

According to the *Nihonshoki*[2] a curious incident occurred in the third year of the reign of Empress Kogyoku (644 C.E.). This was just before the coup that overthrew Soga rule and saw the Nakatomi house return to a position of power. Political discontent and a foreboding that change was in the air was widespread. The dictator Soga Emishi and his arrogant, violent son Iruka, who had killed a popular heir to the throne in 643, were generally hated by all but their closest followers, including Chinese and Korean immigrant traders and craftsmen who were technologically more advanced than the indigenous Japanese population. This dislike was engendered, in part, because the Soga regarded themselves as progressives seeking to advance Buddhism and the higher culture of the continent among their backward people.

The *Nihonshoki* calls this an era of supernatural portents when the activities of *kannagi* (shamanistic "witches and wizards") and cryptic popular songs abounded. An atmosphere of discontent and impending change was also evidenced in the whirl of whispered plots and counterplots that characterized Japan in the year 644.

During these times a certain Ofube no Oshi of Azuma promoted the worship of a kind of large green caterpillar, saying it was a kami of *tokoyo,* the other world. He said that devotion to this deity would bring one prosperity and long life. The kannagi joined in the cause uttering oracles and confirming that the power of this god would make the poor rich and the old young. People threw away food and possessions, placing them by the side of the road and shouting, "The new riches are coming!" They proceeded to enshrine the caterpillar of the heavenly world with song and dance. But one chieftain, Kawakatsu of the Kadano clan among the Chinese immigrants, angered that the people should be so deluded, struck down Ofube no Oshi and thereby made him a martyr to his faith. The kannagi, now intimidated, ceased their propagation of the cult. A popular song went around saying that Uzumasa (Kawakatsu or his agent) "has struck down the kami of the other world, whom we had heard was god of gods."

Several features of this story show some common characteristics of religions outside the mainstream, in Japan and elsewhere. First, it was started by a private individual apparently on the basis of personal revelation. Although we know nothing about Ofube's personality, he apparently played the role of the charismatic religious leader able to draw a following. The pattern of private revelations and charismatic leadership drawing an enthusiastic following is typical of alternate religious movements.

---

2. See W. G. Aston, *Nihongi* (London: George Allen & Unwin, reprint, 1956), pt. 2, pp. 188–189; Robert Ellwood, "A Cargo Cult in Seventh-Century Japan," *History of Religions*, 23, 3 (February 1984), pp. 222–239.

Second, the caterpillar cult gained the support of the kannagi, custodians of the old pre-Buddhist, shamanistic tradition, whose adherence must have made the caterpillar cult seem more legitimate in the eyes of many. Every new religious movement profits by having a tie, through people or symbols, to previous elements of the culture so it can be seen as a new form of something older and already accepted. When the kannagi threw their weight behind the cult, it seemed that the cult was simply a current product of an old form of shamanistic revelation. The reference to the other world, Tokoyo, an old non-Buddhist paradise sometimes conceived as a land lying far out at sea, performed a similar function. As we shall see, other similar movements, too, have feigned legitimacy by linkage to such symbols of ancient Japanese spirituality as sacred mountains, pilgrimages, paradisal hopes, and shamanistic revelations.

Third, we must note that this movement had all the characteristics of what are called cargo cults.[3] This is the term given modern religious movements (strongest in New Guinea and Melanesia in the 1930s and 1940s) in which native prophets claimed that, after a coming upheaval, material wealth like that seen in the cargo ships of white colonial rulers would come to the natives from gods or ancestors. Such Native American movements as the Ghost Dance of the late nineteenth century were comparable.

These movements clearly arise from a sense of the powerlessness of an oppressed indigenous population that feels that only divine intervention can reverse the situation. Often, as in the caterpillar cult of ancient Japan, throwing out one's existing worldly goods is a part of the process: It says more clearly than words that the power those goods once represented is no longer there; it clears the way for the new cargo and is a desperate gesture to force the hand of the gods in bringing in the new riches, for without them the people, having disposed of all else, will now die.

The outbreak of this movement in 644 suggests that two qualities associated with modern cargo cults might have been felt by these early Japanese as well: First, there was the oppressive, insensitive rule of colonial masters (or of the later Soga) with their foreign ways and foreign goods. Second, there was a sense of rapid change that was turning away old values and social structures based on kami, clan, and shaman in favor of buddhas, a centralized state, and a rationalized Confucian social order. To people who felt at home only in the old patterns, these changes must have brought a feeling of chaos and senselessness, of a fast-changing world with which they could not keep up. Out of such feelings arise apocalyptic, millennial movements such as cargo cults and the caterpillar cult we have described. Later movements, including the contemporary New Religions, have a comparable background among people who feel they have been left behind in times of rapid change.

---

3. On cargo cults, see Peter Worsley, *The Trumpet Shall Sound* (New York: Schocken Books, 1968), and Kenelm Burridge, *New Heaven, New Earth* (New York: Schocken Books, 1967).

This leads to a final consideration—the political meaning of the caterpillar cult. Like many religious movements it was ostensibly nonpolitical, but for reasons already suggested it was actually a religious, cultural, and political protest all wrapped up together. Its ties to the indigenous shamanistic tradition and its foundation by a leader of the immigrant community that was well placed under Soga rule says as much. Although we have no evidence that this movement was directly linked to the coup led by a Nakatomi and an imperial prince (later the Emperor Tenchi) that overthrew the Soga, it was clearly something blown up by the gathering winds of revolution.

## Nichiren and Nichiren Buddhism

For our next exemplary movement outside the mainstream we move many centuries ahead to the Kamakura period. As we have seen this was not only a period of far-reaching political and cultural change but also an era when Japanese Buddhism was shaken by changes so great they have been compared with the Protestant reformation in Europe. Several major new forms of Buddhism took popular hold in that time; namely, Pure Land, Nichiren, and Zen. Each was marked by strong leadership, like that of Honen and Shinran in Pure Land, Dogen and Eisai in Zen, and Nichiren. Each moved to simplify, and some to popularize, Japanese Buddhism, especially in contrast to the elaborate Shingon and Tendai forms. The Kamakura reformers were above all concerned with questions of personal salvation, as were their counterparts in the European reformation, and they sought simpler, surer religious ways that were accessible to everyone, whether priest or peasant. In Pure Land and Nichiren teachings, for example, this meant an emphasis on faith and simplified ritual: faith in Amida and chanting the nembutsu in the case of Pure Land, faith in the *Lotus Sutra* and chanting the title of that sutra in Nichiren.

Of all the Kamakura movements, Nichiren's was the most radical in the sense of being most dissident or "protest-ant" (politically, socially, and religiously) and the most intolerant. In its day it was very much an outside, "counterculture" movement. Even in its subsequent history Nichiren Buddhism—although "domesticated" considerably—has never entirely lost its sectarian "protestantism." It has continually insisted on its unique truth, its special revelation through Nichiren, its this-worldly power and coming paradise, its evangelistic zeal, and its combative attitude. To study it is to see how a dissident, alternative movement can become a major religious force with a long history, and how such movements tend to "spin-off" the mainstream.

Nichiren (1222–1282) was born of humble parents; his father was a fisherman.[4] His original name was Zennichimaro, but the name Nichiren (meaning

---

4. See Masaharu Anesaki, *Nichiren the Buddhist Prophet* (Cambridge: Harvard University Press, 1916).

"sun-lotus," the symbol of Japan and of the sutra he exalted above all others) was later taken as his religious name. Growing up in times of conflict, civil war, and change, this intelligent boy was, as he said, deeply disturbed by two questions: "How can I be sure of salvation?" and "Why were imperial forces defeated by the Kamakura regime in 1221 despite the prayers and incantations offered by Shingon and Tendai priests on their behalf?" These two great religious problems—personal salvation and the meaning of history—were his lifelong concerns, and they led him to the monastic life. Ordained in his home village at sixteen, he subsequently studied the tenets of various schools of Buddhism in their temples. At Mt. Hiei he became convinced that the answers to his spiritual problems lay in the *Lotus Sutra* alone, but he was expelled by his radical view that there might be only one truth (or one true expression of it).

Nonetheless, Nichiren began his prophetic mission in the 1250s, urging that the whole nation embrace the supreme doctrine of the *Lotus Sutra* and follow its teaching by saying: "*namu myoho renge kyo*" ("hail to the marvelous teaching of the *Lotus Sutra*"). Nichiren blamed both natural and social calamities on the nation's imperfect or nonexistent faith in the *Lotus Sutra*. Furthermore, he accused other forms of Buddhism of spreading false teachings. (Nichiren's attitude toward teachings other than his own is well expressed in his famous phrase, "The nembutsu is hell, Zen is a devil, Shingon is the ruin of the nation, Ritsu is treason.") In 1260 Nichiren presented a document, the *Rissho ankoku ron,* to the government, vehemently making these claims and prophesying also that if Japan did not repent it would be invaded by foreigners. (Nichiren later claimed the vindication of his prophecy when the Mongols attempted to take Japan in 1274 and 1281.) Nichiren was exiled to remote districts in 1261 and 1271 for this audacious act. Each of these exiles were short lived, and Nichiren continued his activities in and around the Kyoto area. Adding to his fame was a near-assassination in 1264 and an order of execution in 1271 from which he was miraculously saved at the last minute.

Nichiren's interpretation of the *Lotus Sutra* led him to grasp as central the absolute unity of reality; all distinctions of time and space, inner and outer, spirit and matter, were illusory. (This is a common Buddhist concept, of course, but Nichiren carried it to characteristic extremes.) A key principle in his thought is *ichinen sanzen* ("one thought—three thousand"), that is, that all realms of reality exist simultaneously in a single moment of meditation. All things, including all states of reincarnation from hell to the bodhisattvas are really in the mind, here and now. According to Nichiren, in a half hour one can pass through the worlds of hell, the hungry ghosts, animals, titans, humans, gods, and beings far along the path to buddhahood—not as places but as states of consciousness. Enlightenment, in other words, is here and now, right in the midst of ordinary life. Related to this grand unification of all things in the present moment of consciousness is *esho funi* ("inner and outer not two"), the principle that affirms that one's inner, subjective life and the outer environment around it are profoundly interwoven. Thus a subjective cause, such as strong faith in the *Lotus Sutra* and the chanting of its title, can affect outer realities, and one's external environment can affect one's inner life. These ideas have been strongly emphasized by modern followers of Nichiren who have taught that right faith ought to produce good material results as well as spiritual consolation, and that right religion ought to be a cultural and political force to produce a positive environment for spiritual maturation.

As still another expression of the same unifying impulse, Nichiren emphasized that the three aspects (or "bodies") of buddha-nature, as taught by conventional Mahayana (the *dharmakaya* or essence body, the *sambhogakaya* or bliss body, and the *nirmanakaya* or manifest body), must all be seen as one, and the believer must experience and incarnate all three simultaneously. Other forms of Buddhism, he said, had gone astray by emphasizing one over the others.

A more unusual teaching of Nichiren was that he himself was a bodhisattva—an incarnation of one of the bodhisattvas who, according to the *Lotus Sutra,* heard the Buddha deliver the teachings of the sutra. Called Jogyo in Japanese, this bodhisattva was destined to great suffering, but out of his ordeal he would be able to deliver true faith, especially the *Lotus* chant, to the world at a time when it was needed. Thus Nichiren had an explanation for the persecutions that he endured. (Contemporary Nichiren Shoshu Buddhism claims he was the new historical Buddha for our age whose teaching supersedes that of the earlier historical Buddha.)

Nichiren centered his faith and practice on the "three great hidden truths." These were the *gohonzon,* an object of worship made by Nichiren himself, the *daimoku* or *Lotus* chant inscribed on the gohonzon, and the *kaidan,* or ordination platform that Nichiren wished to establish on the slopes of Mt. Fuji. Of these three, the kaidan functions to indicate a sacred place, and many Nichiren groups have their major temples there. More metaphorically, however, it means the establishment of true faith throughout Japan and the world.

Nichiren was a Japanese patriot at a time when loyalty was conceived more in terms of obligation to village, family, and feudal lord than to the nation. Nichiren called himself, for example, "the pillar, the eyes, and the great vessel of Japan." He was convinced that Japan had a very special destiny as a land in which the new and truest form of Buddhism would appear and from which it would spread to the rest of the earth. He said, however, that the success of Japan would depend on the extent to which it revered the true form of Buddhism as he understood it.

After the death of Nichiren his followers grew, despite persecution and division, into two competing groups—Nichiren-shu and Nichiren-shoshu. Nichiren missionaries were zealous and rough, even interrupting the worship of other sects to argue and harangue. During the fourteenth and fifteenth centuries Nichiren followers took up arms and precipitated an uprising. During the Tokugawa era, however, the Nichiren denominations were relatively quiet. In modern Japan, Nichiren faith has spawned several new religious movements. The best known is Soka Gakkai, technically a lay organization within Nichiren-sho-shu. Together, Nichiren-shoshu and Soka Gakkai are by far the largest of the Nichiren groups today.

Soka Gakkai was founded in 1930 by a schoolteacher named Makiguchi Tsunesaburo, a convert to Nichiren-shoshu. At first it was no more than a mod-est discussion group interested by ideas Makiguchi had expounded in several educational and philosophical works—ideas in which Nichiren teachings were combined with Western pragmatism. Makiguchi held that the traditional phil-osophical triad of supreme values—goodness, beauty, and truth—ought to be replaced by goodness, beauty, and benefit, for absolute truth cannot be known, and not all that is true is of any human use anyway. Benefit, on the other hand, can be known and is, by definition, of use. Therefore people should seek that which is pragmatically helpful in order to live fuller, happier lives here and now. This philosophy of life actually correlates well (says Soka Gakkai) with the deep insights of Nichiren Buddhism, for as we have seen the latter also tells us that all the wonders of reality exist in the present moment and there is nothing to be sought outside the here and now. This can be realized and fulfilled, of course, only through the faith and techniques of Nichiren-shoshu, especially chanting the daimoku, the *Lotus Sutra*'s title.

The lively spirit of Soka Gakkai suggests a modern, streamlined version of the ancient Buddhist faith. Here are no ascetic monks in meditation and no tea ceremonies or esoteric rites. It is essentially a movement of laypeople who feel they have little time or aptitude for the contemplative ways, though the rapid chanting of Nichiren services has a strange other-worldly energy of its own. Rather, Soka Gakkai presents an image of lively young people not only chanting but intensely involved in marching bands, popular music concerts, and exuber-ant conventions, all well-known activities of the movement.

Nichiren Buddhism, both historically and in modern Japan, reveals itself as a dissident and alternative movement despite its numbers and popularity. In its militancy, its struggle for individual conversions, its political activity, and its service to the lower classes it shows at least a sociological if not a religious dissent. Similarly, by its emphasis on themes not usually found in the mainline teachings of Buddhism, it reflects a movement outside the mainstream.

## Nakayama Miki and Tenrikyo

Among the first of the major contemporary New Religions of Japan is Tenrikyo, the Religion of Heavenly Wisdom. Tenrikyo traces its inception to 1838 when its foundress, a farmwoman named Nakayama Miki (1798–1887), was believed to have been possessed by the creator high god Tenri no Mikoto, God of Heav-enly Wisdom; or Tsukihi, Moon/Sun; or Oyagami, God the Parent.

The foundress and her family present an interesting picture of the roots of a New Religion. Miki grew up in a village near Nara. Her father was of minor samurai rank, and her husband came from a local landowning family. In the hard times that plagued Japan near the end of the Tokugawa regime, they found life increasingly difficult, and their social status did not spare them the back-breaking work in the rice paddies and the fields that was the peasant's lot.

Then, in 1837, Miki's eldest son Shuji suffered a severe pain in the leg and was unable to work. The family summoned a yamabushi healer whose min-istrations involved the use of a female assistant who, in trance, would be pos-sessed by a kami adept at diagnosis and cure. These seances seemed to provide temporary relief. On one occasion, in December 1838, the regular assistant was unable to be present, and Miki volunteered to take her place. An amazing thing happened. According to Tenrikyo accounts the kami who entered Miki identified himself through her lips as the "true and original God" and said that, as was predestined, he would use Miki as his shrine. After long consultations the family was compelled to acquiesce. From then on Miki was the voice and form of God in this world.

At first the exalted vocation seemed to bring little benefit. Giving away the household's possessions, she led the family into the direst poverty and was thought by many to have gone mad. But in the 1850s things began to change. Miki began constructive work, and under divine guidance she began to practice spiritual healing, especially in cases of childbirth and smallpox. Before long she was offering simple worship, consisting mostly of chants, to the Tenri deity.

The dramatic events of the Meiji restoration in the late 1860s seemed to Miki to suggest that God was striving with tremendous eagerness to transform and save the world and, in the process, to exalt the poor and bring down the mighty. Then in her seventies, she wrote verses, taught the sacred dance that is the religion's basic liturgy, and began revealing its sacred scripture—the *Ofude-saki*.

Tenrikyo taught that God the Parent, the creator who had made human-kind through an elaborate process described in the scriptures, was now eagerly trying to call humanity back to the original right relationship between creator and creation. God inspired the foundress to have a sacred pillar, the kanrodai, erected at the spot in her yard where the creation was believed to have begun. To this day a sacred dance symbolic of that creation is performed around it as the principal Tenrikyo rite. The main Tenrikyo temple, to which pilgrims come from around the world, is constructed over the kanrodai.

Tenrikyo represents a religion of peasant background that grew up amid the shocks of modernization. It carries over many motifs of folk religion but with an important difference: though grounded in popular and pluralistic shamanism, it teaches that there is only one authoritative mediator of one supreme God and only one ultimate sacred place and sacred rite. This bespeaks a growing need, as the traditional matrix of village shrine and temple slowly faded before new ways of life, for religion to offer simple, new, and positive teachings to a confused generation that also wanted to believe that God's hand was involved in the radical changes the nation was undergoing. In its institutional life Tenrikyo also combined the old with the new by preserving family-based authority but promoting modern schools, hospitals, mass-media communication, and personal testimonials. Like other New Religions, Tenrikyo has helped ordinary people to come to terms with rapid change.[5] Like other alternative or dissident movements, it has provided a religious "way" outside the mainstream.

5. See Robert S. Ellwood, *Tenrikyo: A Pilgrimage Faith* (Tenri, Japan: Tenri University, 1982).

# 5

## religion
## and the arts

### FOUNDATIONS

In the following section we will discuss four important and distinctive bases for the unique relationship between religion and the arts in Japan.

1. A short documentary film was once in circulation called "Japan's Art: From the Land." Its message was clear and essentially correct: Japan's art reveals a love of the land, and most of the Japanese arts are ultimately inspired by nature. To leave it at that, of course, would be an oversimplification in the extreme. Nonetheless, the land is an appropriate place to begin a discussion of Japanese religion and the arts, for the Japanese perception of nature is a crucial element in the unique relation that religion and the arts have had in Japan. For the Japanese, from ancient times until now, this perception has included both religious and aesthetic dimensions—both a sense that nature reveals sacrality and that aesthetic sensitivity to its beauty has religious significance.

For evidence of nature's sacrality one need only point to an ancient Shinto tradition about the creation of the islands: The Japanese islands were created, so the story goes, by the ancient, heavenly kami who dipped their long spears down out of the high plain of heaven into the depths of the primal waters. The mud that dripped off their spears as they pulled them back out formed the Japanese islands. Thus are the islands a creation of the gods.

The tradition and story, however, go further: The islands were a creation of the heavenly kami as well as a mirror image of the heavenly abode and thus, in effect, an earthly paradise. Moreover, this paradise was not only eventually peopled by humans but also from a very early time "peopled" by both earthly kami and heavenly kami for the benefit of the land and its population. Nature was seen, in short, as hierophany—as something in and through which sacred power was revealed.

The sacrality of the land, however, is only to be matched by its beauty and purity in the eyes of the Japanese. From the point of view of ancient Shinto, the Japanese islands were not only objectively beautiful, but it was precisely in the intuitive and aesthetic sensitivity to this beauty that sacrality could be felt and known. Sacred reality was revealed not so much through words and scripture but in religio-aesthetic intuition, experience, and sensitivity, especially in the context of ritual.

The shrines of Japanese Shinto indicate this. They often stand in sacred natural surroundings that are also beautiful and pure; they are places of natural awe and sacrality. Religious and aesthetic awareness go hand in hand.

2. If religio-aesthetic sensitivity in an earthly paradise is one important foundation for religion and art in Japan, another is the importance of ritual and religious practices. Much of the religious art of Japan finds its roots in religious

Uda Mikumari Shrine, Nara Prefecture. John Weatherhill, Inc.

practices of one sort or another, including shamanism, ritual dance and music, and the ritual handling of such natural materials as stone and wood.

Several of these elements are reflected in one of the central myth cycles of ancient Japan. In this particular story the sun goddess Amaterasu, being upset with certain actions of another kami, withdraws into a cave and pulls a huge rock across the entrance to close it. The result is immediate darkness and the threat of eventual death as the sun retreats. The heavenly kami, concerned deeply about this turn of events, gather together to form a plan to call her back out. What the plan amounts to is a ritual for calling forth the kami, a ritual that becomes a paradigm for all Shinto ritual subsequent to it.

The ritual recounted in the myth entailed gathering sacred symbols together, lighting a fire before the cave door, and having the shamaness kami, Ame no Uzume, become possessed and dance on an overturned tub, uttering magical words and baring her breasts as she did so. The rest of the kami, quite taken with this event, clapped and laughed loudly. Hearing the noise, Amaterasu became curious and peeked out of the cave. As she became more curious she ventured further out until at last she again shone throughout the world bringing life and renewal with her.

This myth is significant for several reasons, but for our purposes it is important to notice the relation of performing art (dance, music, drama) to shamanic ritual, and a possible relation of literary art (story, song, poetry) to shamanic utterance. The shaman is the religious functionary who invites possession by kami and spirits of the dead and communicates their will or tells their story. The shaman is the one with special powers to combat evil and exorcise malevolent spirits by ritual means. In Japan, the shaman is the one who, through ritual dance and music (kagura), calls forth the kami to be present and to bring its benefits to the world.

Still another aspect of this foundation in religious practice focuses less on the relation of performing or literary arts to shamans and ritual than on the ancient artist or craftsman as having semi-priestly functions. This aspect brings us back to the sacred land but suggests how the artists in Japan may have made use of natural materials of inherent sacrality.

A rather recent documentary film may help explain this connection between artistic and religious practice. In a film on Zen Buddhism, "Zen in Ryoko-in,"[1] one can see traditional carpenters working on the rebuilding of a Zen temple. At one crucial point in that process—the raising and placing of the main roof-support timber—a ceremony is performed. In the ceremony, and in addition to the Buddhist elements, the carpenters appear in Shinto robes to read ancient Shinto prayers. Although a bit surprising to the outsider, this makes

---

1. For further information on this and other films on Japan see Robert McDermott, ed. *Focus on Buddhism: A Guide to Audio-Visual Resources for Teaching Religion* (Chambersburg, Penn.: Anima Publications, 1981), and Richard Pilgrim, *Buddhism and the Arts of Japan* (Chambersburg, Penn.: Anima Publications, 1981), pp. 61–67.

perfect sense within a tradition where Shinto and Buddhism have worked together and where carpentry itself has had religious overtones. The craftsman and artist in traditional and ancient Japan could only approach and use inherently sacred, natural materials (wood, stone, water, etc.) in a semi-priestly manner, so their vocations carried an inherent religious meaning. As the art historian Langdon Warner says: "Dealing, as this body of beliefs does, with the essence of life and with the spirits inhabiting all natural and many artificial objects, it came about that no tree could be marked for felling, no bush tapped for lacquer juice, no oven built for smelting or for pottery, and no forge fire lit without appeal to the kami resident in each."[2]

3. Buddhism has had, of course, a major impact on the religious life of the Japanese, but nowhere is that more evident than in its art. Buddhism brought with it a sophisticated tradition of iconography (sculptures and paintings of various figures in the Buddhist "pantheon"), symbolic architecture (for example, the pagoda), its own "literature" in the form of scripture, and its own ritual performing arts (music, chant, dance dramas, etc.).

The impact of these arts was immediate and long-ranging. Up to that point Japan had had little or no iconography of its own, and it was particularly in this area that Buddhism was impressively endowed. Not only was the iconography artistically impressive, but the early Japanese quickly realized that it embodied potent sacred forces and expressed profound truths. To a people already attuned to the close relation of the religious to the aesthetic this iconography and new religion broadened and deepened artistic representation of sacred reality and the ritual uses of art. Temples were built enshrining this art and its religious power, and rather quickly Buddhist art was present throughout the country.

4. A fourth and final factor for understanding the relationship between religion and the arts in Japan lies in the literary world of the twelfth-century Heian aristocratic culture. The courtly circles of ancient Kyoto maintained a literary and poetic sophistication that was crucial to subsequent developments. In these developments, however, there was less a concern with how religion makes use of art than with how art carries religious meaning. Here, a deepened aesthetic sensitivity expressed itself poetically; artistic pursuit and aesthetic sensitivity were themselves a religious way. One can begin to see this development in *The Tale of Genji,* by Murasaki Shikibu. In this novel of courtly manners and intrigue in the late Heian period it becomes very clear that the fundamental values of life lie in a heightened aesthetic sensitivity to things, and poetry is the primary means of expression and discourse. In fact, the Japanese refer to this sensitivity as mono-no-aware, "sensitivity to things," and this novel is one of its major expressions.

This intuitive, emotional, aesthetic sensitivity is related to notions of the true, pure heart (*makoto-no-kokoro*) found in early Japan. As such, it describes a

---

2. Langdon Warner, *The Enduring Art of Japan* (New York: Grove Press, 1952), pp. 18–19.

particular orientation of the Japanese to intuitive experience rather than to objective description or reason as the major mode of knowing or apprehending reality. Mono-no-aware is a way of perceiving reality and a mode of being in the world that emphasizes aesthetic intuition, experiential sensitivity to the invisible and unspoken, openness to depth and mystery, and appreciation of the pathos of passing beauty.

Such an orientation, in the hands of the sophisticated court poets of Heian Japan and increasingly under the influence of Buddhist ideals, took on clearly religious meaning. Aesthetic sensitivity entailed experience of the underlying essence and depth (*hon'i*) of things—the sublime, profound stillness beneath the multiple and transient world of things—and poetry became the disciplined way of attaining and expressing that experience. In fact, poetry began to be considered a way—a "way of poetry" (kado)—having its own meditative disciplines and its own spiritual meanings.

Several important aesthetic terms indicating these factors are first used in this "way." The term sabi ("solitariness"), for example, indicated the feeling of quiet aloneness and slight melancholy amidst the ephemeral beauty of nature. The term yugen ("sublime beauty") indicated a form of beauty (in nature and in poetry) that evoked an experience of the profound, the deep, the ineffable.

This literary or poetic way of Heian Japan creatively brought together several elements we have already discussed: the sense of nature as sacred and beautiful, the importance of religio-aesthetic sensitivity, and the centrality of poetic expression. It subsequently became the foundation for much of what we shall discuss later as "religion in the service of art." In the meantime, however, it only suggests how these distinct though complementary factors in the foundations of Japanese religion and art formed a unique religio-aesthetic tradition—a tradition that may be discussed around two different foci: art in the service of religion and religion in the service of art.

## ART IN THE SERVICE OF RELIGION

The religions of Japan have all had art, in some form or another, as an important ingredient. In such cases art has served an important function within those various religions. The following discussion focuses on the religions of Japan and the ways in which art has functioned within them.

One of the most obvious and important places where art has served religion is in the iconography of Buddhism, especially within the schools of early Buddhism such as Tendai and Shingon. The great founder of Shingon Buddhism, Kobo Daishi (774–835), said, for example:

> The Dharma is beyond speech, but without speech it cannot be revealed. Suchness transcends forms, but without depending on forms it cannot be realized. Though one may at times err by taking the finger pointing to the moon to be the

moon itself, the Buddha's teachings which guide people are limitless. . . . Since the Esoteric Buddhist teachings are so profound as to defy expression in writing, they are revealed through the medium of painting to those who are yet to be enlightened. The various postures and mudras (depicted in mandalas) are products of the great compassion of the Buddha; the sight of them may well enable one to attain Buddhahood. The secrets of the sutras and commentaries are for the most part depicted in the paintings, and all the essentials of the Esoteric Buddhist doctrines are, in reality, set forth therein.[3]

This statement just about says it all! In it one can find expressed the various functions Buddhist iconography has had within Buddhist practice: as symbols pointing to ideals and truths beyond themselves, as didactic teaching devices, and as parts of the vehicle or process by which one seeks enlightenment. Not only are these three functions implied, but the statement even includes the risk involved—especially from a Buddhist point of view—in using form (here, art) as a formulation of the essentially formless reality of truth (suchness/emptiness). Hence Kobo Daishi is here concerned about mistaking the "fingers for the moon."

Senju Kannon Bodhisattva, Heian Period. (John Weatherhill, Inc.)

3. Yoshita Hakeda, trans., *Kukai: Major Works* (New York: Columbia University Press, 1972), p. 145.

As one example of this art, the thousand-armed (*senju*) Kannon represents the bodhisattva's compassion and willingness to help others and, in this particular version of Kannon, the offering hands are infinite. The statue, however, is not Kannon, nor is Kannon the statue. "Kannon" is the element of compassion intrinsic to enlightenment, whether thought of as some external force working in the cosmos on one's behalf or as the internal compassion of anyone who may become enlightened. The "moon" to which Kannon points is living compassion, and the "finger" points to that moon as both symbol and teacher. Moreover, using this as an object of meditation, the Shingon monk can realize union and integration with that compassion; he can "internalize" the statue, as it were, through meditative practice. Thus the statue, just like the mandala, can be not only an important pointer to the truth (dharma) but itself an important part of the process of realizing that truth.

The art of Zen Buddhism, on the other hand, is quite different. Iconography can be found in Zen, but it serves a less central function in religious practice. In Zen it is other kinds of art that serve: calligraphy, gardens, tea ceremony, and even some of the martial arts (for example, archery). Moreover, the use and function of these arts are rather different. In Zen, art is less a symbol with obvious religious content designed to teach or point beyond itself than a natural expression of and adjunct discipline for seated meditation (zazen).

Of course, Zen's important connection to art is historically determined, too, by virtue of Zen as a patron of the arts and as the vehicle through which certain styles of Chinese art came into Japan in the thirteenth century. Zen's connection to art, however, is deeper and more intrinsic to Zen itself than mere historical accident could account for. Zen experience itself, as cultivated and understood within Japanese culture and Japanese religio-aesthetic sensitivity, has had an intrinsic aesthetic character.

Again, the film "Zen in Ryoko-in" shows this nicely when the Abbot of the temple says, after meditating, "fresh very fresh;" or when he paints an orchid and suggests this as a most appropriate immediate expression of meditative experience, or when he says "flower is buddha;" or, finally, when he calls this beautiful temple with all its fine art an "observatory of inner space."[4] All these comments reveal the natural and intrinsically aesthetic character of Zen experience as many Japanese have understood it. If this aesthetically rich environment of the temple is an observatory of inner space, then obviously the "inner space" here referred to has an important aesthetic content.

One prominent, impressive work of Zen art that exemplifies this is the famous rock garden at Ryoanji Temple in Kyoto. Made of scattered large rocks on a raked sand base, the garden both creates a Zen religio-aesthetic atmosphere of quietude and stillness and expresses the Zen ideal that "form is emptiness, emptiness is form." As one part of an observatory of inner space it expresses the importance of an inner emptiness from which the scattered thoughts and

---

4. See n. 2. (Cf. Pilgrim, pp. 38f).

Stone Garden, Ryoanji Temple, Kyoto.

objects of the mind and world can arise. This emptiness itself, at least in much of Japanese Zen, has carried more than a hint of tranquility amidst its aesthetic surroundings and has thus expressed itself most naturally in artistic/poetic form.

A very different place where the arts have served religion is to be found in Shinto. Closely related to earlier discussion of the arts in religious practice and ritual, this art has to do with sacred music and dance as a central element in Shinto practice.

Unlike Buddhism, Shinto has had very little iconography to form its artistic base; rather, the focus of Shinto practice in general, and of Shinto art specifically, is ritual. As suggested above, at the core of this ritual is the dance and music called kagura—dance and music designed to call forth the kami, to entertain the kami, and to ensure the benefits of the kami presence.

Though the form of kagura has changed over the centuries, and though there are variations in it from one area to another in Japan, in fundamental form and meaning it is consistent with its mythic prototype: Young girls called miko— remnants of ancient female shamanism—dance while carrying sacred symbols, and the kami is honored and brought into presence. Some particularly ancient forms of kagura (called *mikagura*) are even performed at night before a fire placed in front of a shrine in almost exact replica of the mythic model of Uzume's dance. Through such ritual performance the intrinsic purity, goodness, and creativity of life are renewed and continued.

The continuing importance and power of the arts serving religion can be seen in many of the New Religions of twentieth-century Japan. In Tenrikyo, for example, the dance is used for purification. Other New Religions, such as Om-oto and PL Kyodan, make even greater use of the arts and weave several of the strands of the Japanese religio-aesthetic tradition into their own unique fabric of twentieth-century religious life.

## RELIGION IN THE SERVICE OF ART

There is a less obvious but no less important manner in which religion and the arts are related in Japan. This has to do with the degree to which aesthetic sensitivity, artistic creativity, and art itself have been understood as of religious or spiritual importance. The roots of this go deep into Japan's past, but the earliest and clearest manifestation is in Heian period poetry. It was with Heian poetry and poetics that self-consciousness arose concerning art as a distinctive "way" of religious searching and power. As one commentator on the Heian poets says:

> To succeed in expressing the essential quality of a topic it was not enough merely to handle it according to the decorum of conventional treatment. It was necessary in their view that the poet undergo the most rigorous preparation—that he achieve a kind of mystical identification with the topic by means of intense concentration and meditation. . . . The adaptation of a religious ideal [here, meditation influenced by Tendai Buddhism] to poetic practice may seem remarkable, yet it is hardly surprising in this strongly religious age when the art of poetry was regarded as a Way of life and just as surely a means to ultimate truth as the sermons of the Buddha.[5]

A way of poetry is not only a meditative process but also a poetic expression of such experience—experience that clearly has religio-aesthetic character and involves a sense of direct participation in the immediately sensed world. Terms such as yugen or sabi were popular poetic ideals that the poetry carried in its images and evoked in the reader. For example:

> *As evening falls,*
> *From along the moors the autumn wind*
> *Blows chill into the heart,*
> *And the quails raise their plaintive cry*
> *In the deep grass of secluded Fukakusa*[6]
> *Shunzei (1114–1204)*

The Heian poetic way became a model and a basis for many other arts in Japan, and the popularity of various forms of art as a "way" continues to this

---

5. Robert Brower and Earl Miner, *Japanese Court Poetry* (Stanford: Stanford University Press, 1961), p. 257.
6. As translated in ibid., p. 266.

day. Of course, not all these ways lived up to the religious ideals, nor have all of them understood the religious character in the same way as the Heian poets did. The Japanese tradition, however, is full of such things as the way of painting (gado), the way of calligraphy (*shodo*), the way of tea (chado), and the way of the sword (*kendo*). Similarly, many of the greatest artists of Japan have represented these ways in their ideal form: for example, Yoshida Kenko (1283–1350) in literature, Zeami Motokiyo (1363–1443) in noh drama, Sogi (1421–1502) in linked verse, Soami (d. 1525) in gardens and painting, Sesshu (1420–1506) in landscape painting, Sen Rikyu (1521–1591) in tea, Matsuo Basho (1644–1694) in haiku poetry, and many more.

Perhaps the most well known of these artists was Basho, who reflects in his most famous poem this continuing tradition in which Buddhist-influenced religio-aesthetic experience was seen as the basis for true creativity in the arts, and art—like the scattered rocks of Ryoanji's garden—was the form and formulation of emptiness or no-mind (**mushin**) experience:

> *On a withered branch*
> *A crow settles—*
> *Autumn nightfall.*

Basho, however, speaks of the continuity of the tradition in a different way when he remarks that the "one spirit" he seeks to follow in his art is the same line followed by the Heian poet Saigyo, the renga poet Sogi, the landscape painter Sesshu, and the tea master Rikyu. "One spirit activates all their works. It is the spirit of *fuga* [lit. 'wind elegance']; he who cherishes it accepts Nature and becomes a friend of the four seasons. Whatever objects he sees are referred to the flowers; whatever thoughts he conceives are related to the moon."[7]

Basho's poem and his comment indicate the religio-aesthetic point: Aesthetic form (the *ga* of fuga) arises out of the mind of the "wind-blown hermit" (*fu* or Basho as *furabo*), the mind or no-mind (mushin) slips easily in between subject and object and "accepts" nature as it is immediately and directly experienced. Out of such experience the world of objects and thoughts is aesthetically and religiously transformed; everything is a flower, and all thoughts arise on the basis of the "moon" of enlightenment. The splash of a frog appears out of and disappears back into the silence of an old pond.

A different "way" of art, however, may be worth discussing, and that is the noh drama of medieval and later Japan. Created in the fourteenth century out of a variety of dance, drama, and musical forms of that time, the noh came into its own as an independent, sophisticated form of drama and music under the able hand of the great noh master Zeami Motokiyo (1363–1443). Subsequently it became a form of drama integral to the elite culture of the Japanese

---

7. As translated in D. T. Suzuki, *Zen and Japanese Culture* (New York: Pantheon Books, 1959), p. 157.

ruling class and continues today as a highly sophisticated art form representing ideals, stories, and tastes of the medieval period when most of the plays were written and most of the ideals of acting established.

Although there are certainly aspects of noh that are not religious, one important ingredient in its history and nature is its religious meaning since, historically, it is connected both to the Japanese ritual tradition of sacred music and dance, and to the literary/aesthetic tradition based in the Heian period.

Its roots in ritual are especially tied to kagura but also to such forms of folk ritual as *dengaku* (field dance and music) and other such religious forms of entertainment as *bugaku* and *gagaku*. Even today, the influence of these forms is still evident. Especially sacred noh plays, like "Okina," are performed only on special festival or ritual occasions, whether at shrines and temples or in noh theaters. Even when not performed on ritual occasions, the very style of performance and the characters represented in the plots give the performance of noh a ritual-like atmosphere.

The roots of noh in Heian aesthetics and in the ideals of the artistic way represent noh's participation in a highly refined and increasingly Zen-influenced medieval culture. Aside from the plots, the nature of acting was seen as religious or spiritual. The ideal actor did not simply mime the character but used his "spiritual strength" (*shinriki*), says Zeami, to point beyond the noh's external appearance in order to reveal its essence and depth. Yugen appears again, here, as the key aesthetic category and form of beauty that points beyond external beauty to the beauty of sublimity, mystery, and stillness. The essence of noh, says Zeami, "is to be seen with the mind, while the performance is seen with the eyes. . . . Before the yugen of a master actor, all praise fails, admiration transcends the comprehension of the mind, and all attempts at classification and grading are made impossible. The art which excites such a reaction on the part of the audience may be called the art of the miraculous."[8]

In saying these things Zeami is, in part, influenced by the ideals of the artistic way of the Heian poets, now deepened by influence from Zen. This influence can be seen in the following statement by Zeami:

> The universe is a vessel producing the various things, each in its own season; the flowers and leaves, the snow and the moon, the mountains and seas, the seedlings and trees, the animate and the inanimate. By making these things the essence of your artistic vision, by becoming one with the universal vessel, and by securing your vessel in the great *mu* [Nothingness] style of the Way of Emptiness [*kudo*], you will attain the ineffable flowers [*myoka*] of this art.[9]

Such an understanding of artistic pursuit and creativity carries with it clear religious implications. Even today these ideals are held out as goals. Noh continues to seek yugen and the "ineffable flowers" that reflect the spiritual depths.

---

8. As translated in William DeBary, *Sources of Japanese Tradition,* vol. 1 (New York: Columbia University Press, 1964), pp. 296, 285, 287.

9. As translated in Pilgrim, *Buddhism and the Arts,* pp. 48–49.

Noh's religious meaning, however, is not limited to its ritual origins or its expression of the ideals of an artistic way. It is also religious to the extent that its plots are filled with religious characters, themes, views, and so on. These plays, written for the most part in the fifteenth and sixteenth centuries, represent the worldview of the times and as such their religiosity is manifest. Throughout the plays one can find kami, buddhas, bodhisattvas, ghosts, demons, priests, monks, and animal spirits, as well as recurring themes of spirit possession, demon exorcism, pilgrimage to holy sites, Amida pietism, and views of reincarnation. One is presented on stage with the mythos and the ethos of a religious world.

In fact, it could be argued that the very structure of many of the plots can of themselves be shown to be religious. For example, a typical plot structure is the appearance, in the first act of the two-act play, of a troubled ghost who haunts some particular place because of remaining attachments to the world or remaining passions left over from life. As the play moves on, the ghost is led to retell the story of his or her life as it relates to these attachments and passions. Often this retelling is accompanied by a reenactment of the crucial parts of that life story as well, and—in and through the retelling and reenactment—there is catharsis and release from the very attachments and passions holding the ghost from his or her "salvation."

The structure of the play itself thus implies a central religious theme: Confession and ritual reenactment may themselves "exorcise" the demons of attachment and passion and help effect one's release into a peaceful afterlife or rebirth.

Even today, long beyond the medieval world of noh, many of these traditional artistic ways continue. Newer forms of this phenomenon can be found as well, however. One place where religion serves art in modern Japan is in various works of contemporary literature. Explicit and implicit religious themes, for example, run through the works of Mishima Yukio as well as the works of other contemporary novelists. Similarly, the artistic vocation itself, and the aesthetic sensitivity it necessitates, implies a spiritual depth and insight into the nature of humanity and the world.

Contemporary Japanese architecture is another interesting place where religious themes are appearing in modern Japan. Certain contemporary architects (for example, Arata Isozaki and Kisho Kurokawa) have shown great interest in ma (intervals in space and time) as a criterion for design. This is a term that carries religious meaning from ancient Shinto and Buddhism. As a feature of design it makes prominent use of space and bridges across such space. As carrying religious meaning it suggests an important and recurring motif in Japanese religion that the sacred is perhaps better revealed or experienced in the emptiness or space in between things than in the existence or thingness of things. In Shinto terms it suggests the dynamic coming and going of invisible kami energy as it moves into and out of the interstices of being—slipping, as it were, in and out of things but never captured statically by things.

This architectural interest suggests the motif we have been following here, namely that there is a unique relationship in Japan between the aesthetic and the religious—whether seen in the various "foundations" discussed above or in terms of art serving religion and religion serving art. So important is this motif in Japan that two contemporary commentators, in writing about the "Japanese mind," point to the centrality of the aesthetic element in understanding religion and even social relationships.[10] The editor in this same source then suggests that aesthetics may be Japan's uniquely spiritual expression and contribution to world cultures.[11]

Some would no doubt caution against overestimating the centrality of aesthetic sensitivity in Japanese culture and religion, yet its importance cannot be denied. Although art has served religion in every culture, perhaps only in Japan has aesthetic experience been so overtly related to religious experience and artistic pursuits themselves been so self-consciously thought of as "ways" of religious significance.

10. Kishimoto Hideo and Kosaka Masaaki, respectively, in *The Japanese Mind,* ed. Charles A. Moore, (Honolulu: University of Hawaii Press, 1967), pp. 118, 245 (cf. 296).

11. Ibid., pp. 296–297.

*conceptual worlds*

## INTRODUCTION

There is a certain irony associated with discussing "conceptual worlds" in Japan. Reality or "life," religiously understood, is for the Japanese less a function of concept, belief system, and rational theories than an occasion for living as fully and as well as possible. It is a truism, though nonetheless truthful, that Japan has never produced a strong tradition of religious philosophy, since such a tradition would emphasize the conceptual articulation of individual and collective worldviews or constructs of reality. Japan does, of course, have its explicit and implicit views of reality, but these do not dominate the religious life, and many central issues (for example, the nature of death and evil) remain relatively vague in much of the tradition.

Other ways of understanding "reality" have upstaged the rational, conceptual way and, for this reason, the following discussion is divided in a special manner. First, we shall discuss "descriptive realities and worldviews" as those explicit and implicit beliefs that the Japanese have held about the nature of reality. Second, we shall discuss "poetic realities" as those notions of reality that resist descriptive articulation and objective definition. In the former we will find conceptual worlds as primary but in the latter we will find immediately experienced reality as primary—a sense of reality in which truth is not so much a collection of truths as it is a certain quality or mode of experience.

To feature the distinction between descriptive and poetic realities this way carries a certain risk, namely that of overemphasizing and overromanticizing the poetic element in the Japanese tradition. To overlook such distinctions, however, would be a disservice to that same tradition, since the distinction is valid and the poetic element uniquely strong in Japan.

## DESCRIPTIVE REALITIES AND WORLDVIEWS

In attempting to discuss Japanese religious worldviews one is immediately up against religio-cultural complexity and the problems of generalization. One way to accomplish the task would be to attempt a generalized summary of each of the major religious traditions that have influenced Japan: Shinto, Taoism, Confucianism, and Buddhism.* Such discrete summaries would tend, however, to avoid the complex mix of views from these traditions and to emphasize the notion that descriptive realities are a product of institutional and official "theologies." Moreover, this method would tend to leave out the "unofficial" views implicit in folk religion.

Another way would be to discuss relatively distinct religious paradigms (ways of seeing or understanding reality) as they relate to these various traditions—or, indeed, to the culture more broadly defined. Such paradigms cut across the religions of Japan as well as across the distinction between religion and culture. They allow for the mixing of religious views in one person or group and suggest that these religious views are actually lived out in human life to help provide a meaningful world.

The two distinct paradigms discussed below are referred to as "vertical" and "horizontal." Care must be taken, however, to avoid a too-literal understanding of these words as merely directional indicators. Although both of these, as cosmologies, have a certain directional element, in general the terms vertical and horizontal must be understood with quotation marks around them; that is, to refer to something more than their literal meaning.

Beyond their directional element, these terms refer here to ontological hierarchy and ontological distance, that is, the degree to which any given view posits a distinctive hierarchy and separation in the very nature of being, especially between the realms of the sacred as distinct from the realms of the human and natural world. Also involved here is the degree to which a view posits the objective, literal existence of sacred forces.

### Vertical Worlds and Paradigms

The earliest written records of the Japanese, the *Kojiki* and *Nihonshoki,* represent mytho-historical views primarily of the early Yamato peoples who dominated Japan in the early centuries of our era. Though not actually written down until the eighth century, they reflect oral traditions of considerable antiquity—certainly predating the arrival of Buddhism in the sixth century. Although exceptions can certainly be found in these sources, the predominant religious view of

---

*For example, see Appendix.

reality that emerges takes the following shape: (a) The heavenly kami, residing on the "high plane of heaven" (takama-no-hara), are the progenitors and on-going creative powers of this world. (b) The "manifested middle world" (u-tsushi-yo, the world of nature and the human) is created by the gods and is sacred, good, and beautiful. (c) This same world is permeated by earthly kami and spirits (**tama**) as well, not to mention spirits of the dead. (d) Humans are created by the gods as essentially good and pure, defiled only by external pollutions (e.g. death or blood) and internal states (e.g. a selfish heart). (e) The religious life is a process of ritual purity and supplication by which one calls the kami into presence, seeks the kami's blessings, and sends it off. (f) The land of death and darkness (yomotsu kuni) awaits the souls of the dead, though beyond that place the souls may become ancestral spirits or even kami. (This land is variously considered to be in the mountains or under this present world, but is a "nether" world.)

These views, which dominate both the ancient sources and the classical Shinto tradition throughout Japanese history, reflect what is being called here a "vertical" cosmology and paradigm. A three-storied hierarchical universe is depicted in which the heavenly kami are both distinct and separate and are thought to exist literally as independent beings. Although the three realms can be bridged, the predominant impression is one of hierarchy and distance—distinct and ontologically separate realms within the nature of being.

In this view, the goodness and creativity of life are based on the goodness, sincerity, or truth (**makoto**) of kami, as well as in their creative power (*musubi*). Death and evil are not positive forces working against life as much as natural parts of life that can be dealt with in one way or another.

People such as Motoori Norinaga, discussed in Chapter 3, represented this view in later Japanese history. He clearly expressed the centrality of the heavenly kami as transcendent, mysterious forces ruling by their inscrutable will through the vehicle of the imperial line and institutions. The differentiation between the divine and human realms was clear in his notion that humanity cannot know or understand this transcendent, inscrutable realm.

One can find the vertical cosmology and paradigm present in Buddhism as well, particularly within popular Buddhism outside the normative orthodoxies of monastic thought and practice. In these more popular forms, it is clearer that "celestial" buddhas and bodhisattvas are understood to be distinct existent forces operating in various sectors of the cosmos for the benefit of others. To pray to such beings, or to call on their name, can produce wondrous results. The classical location of this idea, but by no means the only one, is the Pure Land tradition. As popularly understood, this tradition reflects both ontological hierarchy and distance in notions of the Amida Buddha residing in his Pure Land in the western sector of the cosmos—a paradisal place one hopes to attain after death.

A Japanese precursor of Pure Land Buddhism, Genshin (942–1017), makes these views particularly vivid in his *Ojoyoshu.* In that writing, and in illustrations inspired by it that circulated widely in Japan, the contrast between Amida's Pure

Land and the Buddhist hells is graphically drawn.[1] The buddha realms are clearly and literally distant from this and other worlds and reflect both ontological gaps and hierarchies in the nature of being.

These gaps are not to be bridged easily or in this life. They are bridged ultimately by the power of Amida or other celestial buddhas and bodhisattvas. Quite literally, in fact, the Pure Land tradition—especially in medieval Japan— pictured Amida coming down from his Pure Land to this world to rescue the souls of faithful believers at the time of their death and bring them into his Pure Land.

Human inability to bridge these gaps was heightened by ideas that time itself was working against human possibility. Beliefs about the degeneration of time (mappo), grounded in ancient Indian ideas of time, were very widespread in the Heian and Kamakura periods. The Pure Land and other buddha realms now seemed even more impossible and distant goals, hence the need to rely on the ''other power'' (tariki) of the buddhas.

Although such forms of popular Buddhism are more obvious examples, the vertical paradigm can be found in other places as well. Perhaps the clearest of these are beliefs in the *rokudo,* or ''six realms'' of existence: hells, hungry ghosts, animals, titans, humans, and gods. Such divisions in the nature of being represent ontological hierarchy both cosmologically and soteriologically; not only is there ''verticality'' in the nature of possible modes of existence, but also in ideas of superior and inferior rebirths. Other related ideas came into Japan with Buddhism: One is that cosmic geography extends from the lowest hells to the transcendent buddha realms, and at the center of all stands the cosmic Mt. Sumeru extending upward toward the heavenly realms. In this system a vertical and horizontal cosmology is clearly spelled out with places in it for the six realms and more.[2]

Although it is not clear just how pervasive such ideas were in early Japan, they reflect ancient Indian Buddhist ideas. The rokudo, especially, may have carried some weight in the Japanese tradition and can be found expressed or reflected particularly in early and medieval literature.[3] Notions of rebirth along a Buddhist ''great chain of being'', although present in the orthodox sources of Buddhism, were probably more pervasive in the popular mind than in the monastic schools. Similarly, the Japanese adapted an Indian vertical cosmology in relating some of their own mountains to the Sumeru motif.[4]

---

1. See excerpts of this work in Ryusaku Tsunoda, ed, *Sources of Japanese Tradition,* 2 vols., vol. 1 (New York: Columbia University Press, 1964), pp. 192–197.

2. Rare eighth-century maps reflecting this religious and cosmic geography can be seen in John Rosenfield, et al., *The Courtly Tradition in Japanese Art and Literature* (Cambridge: The Fogg Art Museum of Harvard University, 1973), pp. 104–109.

3. This system has recently been discussed in William LaFleur, *The Karma of Words* (Berkeley: University of California Press, 1983), chaps. 2 and 6.

4. Alan Grapard, ''Flying Mountains and Walkers of Emptiness,'' *History of Religions,* 21/3 (February 1982), pp. 218–219.

Sanno Shrine Mandala, Muromachi
Period. (John Weatherhill, Inc.)

Although the vertical worldview can be found elsewhere in Buddhism, it
is perhaps better to note how the paradigm is expressed in the mix of Buddhism
with Shinto. That way we will clearly see that it is neither merely a Shinto nor
merely a Buddhist paradigm but rather one that cuts across the religions of Japan.

This appears most graphically in the Shinto/Buddhist mandalas reflecting
ideas of honji suijaku, or "original essence, manifest traces." Many such mandalas reflect ontological hierarchy and distance. At the top (above the clouds)
are the sacred realms of kami and buddhas; below them one might find a sacred
mountain reaching up into the clouds; at the mountain's base will be shrines
and/or temples as the locus of human efforts to meet the sacred; beyond that,
and not even pictured, is the realm of normal human activity.

Such mandalas stand as graphic evidence of a Japanized (Shintoized) Buddhist vertical cosmology and paradigm. Unlike more purely Buddhist examples of the paradigm, however, here the sacred and human realms are closer together, and the mediation of a sacralized nature (especially mountains) becomes central. In this view "pure lands" are not external to this world since this very world is pure as a realm of the kami's activity.

In summary, the vertical cosmology, whether seen as Shinto or Buddhist, remains a major paradigm within descriptive realities and worldviews in Japan. The central, common characteristic of this paradigm is belief in literally existent sacred forces that, although able to mingle in this world, belong to a separate, superior realm thought to be "above" and clearly transcendent of this world. It has most often been expressed in a two- , three- , or even six-storied universe in which humans seek to work with the divine for the betterment of life.

## Horizontal Worlds and Paradigms

Unlike the vertical paradigm, the horizontal paradigm tends to deemphasize any distance or distinction between realms of being and to deemphasize hierarchical structures. It collapses ontological distance and hierarchy and emphasizes a closeness between the human and the sacred realms. It emphasizes the sacrality of *this* world and time rather than the sacrality of other worlds and times on some great chain of being.

In Shinto and Japanese folk religion, this paradigm is shown in a deemphasis on the heavenly kami of classical Shinto and an emphasis on earthly kami, various kinds of nature spirits (tama), and the spirits of the dead. Such forces are thought to reside in the mountains or beyond the sea in the "other" world (tokoyo) and to permeate nature. In addition, such forces are rather easily called into presence and sent off again for whatever specific purposes there may be. The human realm easily merges into the sacred by virtue of either becoming ancestral spirits at death or eventually becoming a kami (as in the hitogami tradition discussed in Chapter 3).

In short, although the sacred is a distinct "realm" (i.e. tokoyo) and not to be treated idly, the line dividing the sacred, the human, and the natural worlds is vague at best, as the following elements indicate: (a) One can easily feel the presence of kami at particularly sacred (especially natural) settings. (b) Ancient shamanism called on spirits or kami to possess them and speak through them. (c) Kami come as "mysterious visitors" (marebito) to be entertained and sent off. (d) A mere clap of the hands at a Shinto shrine may summon them. As Shintoists themselves have said:

> The world of the *kami* does not transcend that of man, and man does not need to seek to enter a divine, transcendental world to attain salvation. He seeks salvation by bringing *kami* into the human [and natural] world—into the daily life of the home, the market place, and the cooperation of the people. Man experiences

*kami* in this world and salvation is attained in the harmonious development of the world.[5]

In Shinto, there is a word [called] *naka-ima* [lit. "middle-now"] which means the present, in the middle between past and future; this expression contains a meaning of blessing on the present. The word *naka* [middle, center, inside] also denotes a relation to place. . . . These words [therefore] express to perfection the Shinto idea that this world is a world full of blessing. . . . [This] present time and this present dwelling place [are] a blessed [sacred] time and a blessed [sacred] place.[6]

This does not, of course, deny elements of the vertical paradigm, for example the existence of heavenly kami, notions of an afterworld, or ideas of a distinctive realm for the sacred. The horizontal paradigm qualifies these elements and provides a rather different emphasis. (The two paradigms are, at some extreme point, mutually exclusive, but in normal practice they are found together as a matter of shifting emphases.)

Shinto is not the only place where one can find this paradigm. Taoism and Confucianism (in Japan) have represented it as well, though in very different ways. Taoist notions, for example, of an organic, dynamic, integrated, harmonious cosmos operating by the principles of yin and yang tend to collapse both ontological distance and hierarchy, in spite of the notion of Tao as some transcendent power or force. Taoism tends to emphasize harmony and balance between and among relatively equal forces and aspects of reality both visible and invisible. Whether in the "religious Taoism" represented by the Japanese "way of yin and yang" (onmyodo), or in the "philosophic Taoism" that influenced Zen, these tendencies predominate in the Japanese forms of Taoism.

Confucianism and Neo-Confucianism could also be seen from the point of view of the horizontal paradigm. Both emphasize human, social intercourse as a harmonious structure grounded in either the "will of heaven," inner principles of reality (ri), sincerity and other Confucian virtues, or appropriate rules of decorum. Although different, none of these latter ideas represent an ontologically distinct or literally transcendent realm. They range from metaphysical to natural/human bases upon which reality (especially human reality) operates.

Moreover, regardless of the religious or metaphysical bases that function in Confucianism, its consistent focus has been the realm of human morality, ethics, and social harmony—very much a this-worldly (even "practical") concern. The following sketch of the functions of the Neo-Confucian scholar (*jusha*) in Tokugawa Japan clearly indicates these issues:

Secure in the conviction that the books of the [Confucian] Sages revealed the ultimate truth, the jusha entered the realm of their prime concern—the realm of

5. Sokyo Ono, *Shinto: The Kami Way* (Rutland, Vt.: Charles E. Tuttle Co., 1962), p. 107.

6. Shinto Committee for the IXth International Congress for the History of Religions, *An Outline of Shinto Teachings* (Tokyo: Kokugakuin University, 1958), p. 23.

human relations, of state and society. Their contributions in this field were, for the Japan of their day, vital and creative. The pioneers of the movement saw in the [Confucian] Classics Heaven's laws for human society. . . . [for] its structural and moral basis.[7]

Although some may question whether Confucianism represents a *religious* view of reality, it has been a central value system and organizational scheme for Japanese society. Its importance in Japan has often been underestimated (though one can see further discussion of it, here, in Chapters 3 and 8). The horizontal reality system it envisions is a moral/social one for human society. In Japan, it quietly came in with other Chinese elements at a very early time and has consistently played a part in Japanese education and values. Culminating as the dominant philosophy of the Tokugawa regime and society, Confucianism produced a *social* hierarchy, but its underlying paradigm is horizontal and non-hierarchical.

The final major expression of the horizontal paradigm is Buddhism. Although much of popular Buddhism (as discussed above) reflects a vertical paradigm, the central thrust of normative, orthodox, monastic Buddhism has been precisely to collapse all ontological (or other) distinctions by a process of "emptying" the objective thingness of things and awaken (**bodhi**) to the fullness of this very moment. In fact, Mahayana Buddhism has rather consistently claimed that in such awakening there is no distinction between *samsara* (this life of birth-death-rebirth) and nirvana (salvation, liberation). As such, Buddhism is the extreme and radical example of the horizontal paradigm.

This central Mahayana motif is expressed in a variety of ways and with a variety of different nuances, not only in Indian Buddhism but in Chinese and Japanese Buddhism as well. In Japan, the motif was at least philosophically present in the six Nara sects, but where it became distinctly Japanese and dominant in both thought and practice was in the Tendai, Shingon, and Zen sects.

In theoretical terms this teaching is nowhere better exemplified than in Tendai. Keeping in mind that Tendai saw itself as an all-inclusive "umbrella" over Mahayana Buddhism, it is instructive to realize that its central teaching of the "three truths" (*sandai*) is precisely a reflection of the horizontal description of reality we are concerned with here. As we have seen, these three truths state that: (a) the phenomenal world is empty (ku), (b) yet provisionally existent (*ke*); and (c) the realization of this is the mean (*chu*) or middle way between the other two. This realization (or "awakening to") of the "middle way" is precisely what the Buddha spoke of centuries before and what early Mahayana in India referred to as *madhyamika* (middle way). It indicates awakened awareness in the midst of this very life by which the world is being continually emptied (sunyata, ku) yet filled by the realization of the suchness (*tathata*, **shinnyo**) of things.

---

7. John W. Hall, "The Confucian Teacher in Tokugawa Japan" in *Confucianism in Action*, ed. D. S. Nivison and A. F. Wright (Stanford: Stanford University Press, 1959), p. 273.

The Shingon sect is another important locale for this teaching. Its founder in Japan, Kukai, focused his teaching on sokushin jobutsu, or realization of buddhahood in this very body. Also, Shingon in general was a major source of the idea that enlightenment is originally or fundamentally present all the time (**hongaku**). In fact, Shingon (and Tendai esoteric Buddhism as well) fostered understandings of sacred geography and pilgrimage, for example, as processes for internal spiritual awakening. In short, the external world became, through ritual and meditation practices, "internalized" and thereby sacralized. Buddhist practices were means by which the apparently "sacred other" was realized as part of oneself and one's own world; all distinctions of self and other, profane and sacred, higher and lower realms, and so forth, were overcome and collapsed.

> It is clear from this that in Kukai's thought Awakening could bring about a trans-formation of polluted profane space into pure space, a Pure Land, the original residence of the Buddha's heart-mind. Kukai defined the process as one of in-teriorization, since the Buddha's residence is originally within us. It is an illusion that the Pure Land of Buddha is exterior to man, so totally transcendent that going beyond the realm of forms is necessary. But Kukai warned: "In the middle of my mind, there is the principle of the mind of the pure Bodhi." This amounts to saying that we have always been there before entering the sacred space, that the transmutation is not really a change but is merely becoming what one already was.[8]

Such views are not only in perfect keeping with a Buddhist horizontal paradigm but they also indicate a difference of opinion or emphasis within Japanese Buddhism over the nature (and location) of the Pure Land. Buddhists who emphasize the vertical paradigm understand the Pure Land to be a distinct and distant realm in some other world, attained after death. The horizontal perspective emphasizes, as the seventeenth-century Zen master Hakuin says, that "the Pure Land is nowhere but right here."

To mention Zen here is of course to indicate another major branch of Japanese Buddhism that has taught a distinctly horizontal paradigm. Though one can find many expressions of this in Zen, perhaps the simplest and easiest is the analogy that Zen likes to repeat about itself: "Before one studies Zen, mountains are mountains and rivers are rivers. When one becomes a serious practitioner, however, mountains are no longer mountains and rivers are no longer rivers. Yet, when one truly understands and awakens to the truth, mountains are mountains and rivers are rivers."

We might paraphrase this analogy for our own purposes as follows: Initially one lives in a literal, subject-object, descriptive world. Under the influence of meditation practice, however, one empties the world of its objective, literal character. Yet, true awakening or enlightenment "returns" one to the phenomenal world in its suchness, as based on an abiding emptiness.

---

8. Grapard, "Flying Mountains," p. 208.

Zen takes the horizontal paradigm to its logical end in not only insisting on the collapse of all ontological separateness but in being even reluctant to use words of description to teach or express its views. It is "iconoclastic" about descriptive language precisely because it fears we might mistake a description of reality for reality itself. With that in mind, Zen can be seen as a bridge to "poetic realities," since we now move beyond "reality" or worldview as a function of description in the search for Japanese conceptual worlds.


## POETIC REALITIES

Unlike descriptive realities, poetic realities are realities of immediate experience and feeling that resist any objective description. They are "reality" sensed and lived rather than "reality" described.

We have already encountered hints of this move to poetic reality: In Shinto, for example, the emphasis on living in the purity of this moment (*naka-ima*) begins to suggest an emphasis on the poetic reality of immediate experience and action as the primary locale of reality. In Buddhism we have noted a similar emphasis, especially in Zen, that explicitly resists descriptive realities. Now, in fact, we can look further at both these religious modes of being as they emphasize the centrality of immediate, aesthetic experience as crucial to the religious life. Here we will find that immediately lived reality takes precedence over ideas about reality.


### Shinto

The key to understanding Shinto's relation to poetic reality lies in understanding the importance it gives to purity, aesthetic sensitivity, and emotional sensitivity or "heart" (**kokoro**). The former was discussed in Chapter 5, and we now turn to a discussion of the latter.

A pure heart and deep sincerity characterize what Shinto refers to as "truth" (makoto). "Truth," here, is distinctly *not* some right or wrong view about the nature of things; it is a state of the mind/heart. Truth *is* as truth is lived in purity and emotional sensitivity.

> Truth in Shinto is dependent on the individual values in the activities, circumstances, and actions attached to definite, concrete beings; and as such it cannot be manifested in laws and lists. For this reason, in the field of morality, it was necessary, rather than to compile a list of sins and virtues, to bring the soul [heart] into union with the Divine. . . . Thus it was important to preserve, by *harae* [ritual purification], a pure, unpolluted soul, and unclouded mind, and always to be free from prejudice as a newly-born baby. The expressions *akaki kokoro* ("bright heart"), *kiyoki kokoro* ("pure heart"), *tadashiki kokoro* ("correct heart"), and *naoki*

*kokoro* ("straight heart") express this condition of unity with the Divine. . . . [These were] demanded in Shinto as the basis of all action.[9]

A related idea is expressed in Shinto as *meijo shugi,* or reverance for bright-ness and purity in all matters—external and internal, both in life and in the heart. These values carry with them an aesthetic dimension in their concern for freshness, cleanliness, external purity, and ritual order.[10]

We wish to emphasize here the centrality of pure feeling, experience, and sensitivity—of the quality of the lived moment—in this Shinto notion of truth and reality. From this viewpoint in Shinto, it is less the *Kojiki* or *Nihonshoki* that express the truth than poetry collections such as the *Manyoshu,* an eighth-century collection representing pre-Buddhist, Shinto sensitivities. (Indeed, poetry from the *Manyoshu* on has been a central literary form in Japan that has expressed this and other poetic realities. A study of Japanese poetry is, in part, a study of Shinto and Buddhist contributions to these poetic realities.)

The poetic reality of Shinto has perhaps been best expressed by the great eighteenth-century Shinto scholar Motoori Norinaga (discussed in Chapter 3). Combining makoto and kokoro, he speaks of magokoro as the "sincere heart" that is both the essence of kami and the essence of the divine nature in humans. He makes very clear that magokoro is no mere idea to be believed but a quality of experience to be lived. Finally, he relates magokoro to Heian aesthetic ideas of mono-no-aware that suggest an aesthetic sensitivity to the wonder and beauty of things. For Motoori, these qualities form the very core of Shinto life and are best exemplified in ancient Japanese poetry and literature, as well as in the *Kojiki* and *Nihonshoki* texts.[11]

Still another way to suggest poetic reality in Shinto is to consider the cen-trality of ritual action and the importance of direct experience of the presence of kami in and through ritual. Shinto ritual is not only a process of purification (internal and external) but also a process of waiting for and waiting on the pres-ence of kami in the tranquil stillness of nature; it demands an experiential sen-sitivity to see, hear, or feel the coming and going of kami. As one Shinto priest told me [Pilgrim], Shinto ritual (especially individual worship) is primarily a matter of waiting in the right state of mind for the coming of kami and then being a proper host for the sacred guest. Such moments are moments of direct experience of kami and—insofar as they are crucial to the renewal of life and the self—are central moments in a poetic reality.

---

9. Shinto Committee, *An Outline,* p. 31.

10. Tsunetsugu Muraoka, *Studies in Shinto Thought* (Tokyo: Ministry of Education, 1964), pp. 29–46.

11. Shigeru Matsumoto, *Motoori Norinaga* (Cambridge: Harvard University Press, 1970), p. 156.

## Buddhism

As we have already seen, the horizontal paradigm in Buddhism gets taken to its logical end—the absolute, radical collapse of all distinctions and separations in emptiness, and yet the absolute and radical affirmation of the world in its suchness. In these cases, reality is distinctly *not* an issue or a function of description; the only reality worth speaking about is the immediately lived reality of awakened consciousness, a reality of radical intimacy with all things. The great Zen master Dogen Zenji (1200–1253) had this in mind when he said:

> To study the way of the Buddha is to study your own self. To study your own self is to forget yourself. To forget yourself is to have the objective [phenomenal] world prevail [intimately] in you. To have the objective world prevail in you is to let go of your "own" body and mind as well as the body and mind of "others". The enlightenment thus attained may seem to come to an end, but . . . [it] should be prolonged and prolonged.

> The exertion [of constantly "letting go" or "forgetting"] that brings the exertion of others into realization is our exertion right at this moment. This exertion of the moment is not innate or inherent in us, nor does it come and go, visiting or departing. What we call the "moment" does not precede exertion. The "moment" is when exertion is actually being performed. That is to say, the exertion of a day is the seed of all Buddhas, it is the exertion of all Buddhas. By this exertion Buddhahood is realized [and lived]. . . . At this moment a flower blossoms, a leaf falls—it is the manifestation of sustained exertion. A mirror is brightened, a mirror is broken—it is the manifestation of sustained exertion. Everything is exertion.[12]

Reality in such a view is no descriptive, objective something. Rather, it is each moment authentically lived (out of emptiness/suchness). Such moments are SUCH moments, and Dogen calls them the absolute fullness of being and time, as well as the totality of buddha-reality. The varying content of these moments— whether flowers blossoming or mirrors breaking, whether eating food or helping others—is relatively unimportant since each is a moment of enlightened existence and each a moment of radical poetic reality.

Dogen and Zen are not the only instances in Japanese Buddhism where this idea is expressed. As we have seen above, wherever the horizontal paradigm begins to function strongly the move toward poetic reality begins to take place. Therefore, this same tendency exists in the other normative, orthodox sectarian groups (especially Tendai and Shingon), not to mention the literature and arts of Japan that have been influenced by Buddhism.

The poetic (or aesthetic) dimension fits into all this very importantly. William LaFleur, in a book on Buddhism and literature, suggests that a Buddhist

---

12. Tsunoda, *Sources,* vol. I, pp. 245–246 and 244–245, respectively.

sense of reality took on a clearly aesthetic character very early in Japan. In discussing the Buddhist critique of symbols (that is that symbols risk creating distinctions and separations in the otherwise seamless fabric of reality, and tend to point away from immediately lived reality for their meaning), he says:

> This critique of symbols brought it [Buddhism] into a very specific aesthetic mode—one we customarily associate with Zen; but it appeared in Japan even prior to the great growth of Zen in the thirteenth century and is in many ways the consequence of *hongaku*. It requires the return of a poet's perceptions and mind to the simple recognition of phenomena. This recognition is powerful because it represents a *renewed* simplicity rather than a naive simplicity. This aesthetic mode lives off the way it *redirects* our focused attention to phenomena for their own sake. It does so with stunning effect by reversing the symbolizing habit of the mind. The poetry that results from and expresses this aesthetic mode invites us to see things in and for themselves; it deliberately rejects the attempt to discover "meanings," implications hidden or coded into a poem.[13]

This is a crucial point for it not only indicates an important, intrinsic connection between Buddhist ''reality'' and aesthetic, poetic reality, but it also suggests one foundation for an artistic tradition in Japan that—deeply influenced by Buddhism—gave expression to nonsymbolic, nonnarrative, immediately apprehended reality. This artistic tradition has understood itself as constituted by distinctive ''ways'' of spiritual significance, and it has found that both path and goal involve a poetic reality of some depth and sophistication. Although this tradition is discussed in Chapter 5, it is elucidated by the following passage from a travel diary of the great haiku poet Basho (1644–1694) that reflects a poetic reality—even in its prose. (The strange, literal translation offered here allows a pregnant silence to seep through the gaps and cracks in the narrative flow, and to create a poetic reality even in English.)

> In the demesne of Yamagata the mountain temple called Ryūshakuji. Founded by Jikaku Daishi, unusually well-kept quiet place. "You must go and see it," people urged; from here, off back towards Obanazawa, about seven *li*. Sun not yet down. Reserved space at dormitory at bottom, then climbed to temple on ridge. This mountain, one of rocky steeps, ancient pines and cypresses, old earth and stone and smooth moss, and on the rocks temple-doors locked, no sound. Climbed along edges of and crept over boulders, worshiped at temples, penetrating scene, profound quietness, heart/mind open clear.

> *quiet*
> *into rock absorbing*
> *cicada sounds*[14]

---

13. LaFleur, *Karma*, p. 23–24.

14. From Basho's *Back Roads to Far Towns*, [*Oku-no-hosomichi*], trans. Cid Carman and Kamaike Susumu (New York: Grossman Publishers, 1968), p. 99.

# ritual
# and the practice
# of religion

## THE PERFORMANCE OF RELIGION

Japanese religion is world-famous for its vivid, colorful ceremonies. Whether the stately sacred dance and exuberant procession of a Shinto festival or the quiet customs of a Zen meditation hall, these activities—often centuries old—may draw throngs of visitors from across the country and around the world. Often these practices will be of concern only to the inhabitants of a particular village, neighborhood, or monastery, but they will nonetheless express their deepest feeling of roots and religious awe.

On the other hand visitors frequently leave Japan both fascinated and puzzled by its religious rites. They find them beautifully enacted and full of drama and fascination, yet their precise religious meaning seems strangely elusive. Westerners tend to want to know exactly why something is done, what religious beliefs lie behind it and rationalize it, and what spiritual or worldly benefits are expected to come from it. They are perplexed that credible answers to natural queries like these are so hard to come by. Sometimes the questioner is given a mythic kind of explanation that seems so naive that one wonders how people so obviously intelligent as modern Japanese could still believe it (if they do). Sometimes there is simply a look of surprise that anyone would ask such a question.

Even more mystifying to one who comes equipped with Western preconceptions about religion is the lack of belief that so often seems to underlie the most elaborate rites. Western visitors have found it odd that the Japanese should go to such ornate extremes to honor gods whose actual existence no one appeared to take seriously. If one adds to this the observation that Japanese religious ceremonies frequently seem also to be theater, civic pageant, and raucous carnival, then one can understand the outsider's puzzlement. Indeed, one may even suspect that religion here is merely serving as a performing art or entertainment.

This judgment overlooks such Western parallels as Mardi Gras and, in many instances, Christmas. Even more important, it overlooks some considerations that go to the very heart of Japanese religion. For the very fact that in Japanese religion belief appears to be fairly unimportant, whereas rituals and festivals are put on with meticulous care and expense, indicates that it is to the latter that we must look for significant clues to meaning.

Important elements of Japanese religion can be traced back to the shamanic performances of archaic times. The dramatist and critic Richard Schechner, depending considerably on studies of shamanism and related rites, has advanced theories of theater focusing on performance and environment.[1] He holds that the theatrical experience should become a total environment transformed by performance. For there to be total environment, of course, the audience must become not just spectators but participants in the drama just as did the shaman's audience; the audience should help make it happen and expect to be blessed and healed. Environmental theater is theater in that it deliberately uses the theatrical conventions to make audience and actor do unusual things to induce a very special experience; in its totalism it also creates powerful reality.

This perspective suits Japanese ritual as it does traditional Japanese theater, the noh and kabuki. All are centered on a performance that, far from being merely realistic, heightens reality by giving an intense, stylized expression to human feeling so powerful (especially in noh) as to induce transcendent wonder. These theatrical arts have roots in the shaman who, possessed by a god, danced and gave oracles in trance. Such nonordinary behavior would itself be a sign of its divine character, and watchers would be struck with awe, believing they were consorting with a god.

In the same way a Japanese religious rite does not conceal the fact that what is being done is nonordinary and therefore requires special dress, special settings, and unusual gestures and intonation to set it apart. The notion, prevalent in some though not all Western religions, that a religious service ought to be as plain-spoken and as "natural" as possible would be quite alien to the Japanese mind.

In part, of course, this is because Japanese behavior as a whole is more formal than modern Western behavior. That is, it shows a greater concern for wearing the right clothes, saying the right things, and performing the right courtesies on any given occasion. In short, it expects people to adapt themselves thoroughly to every situation; even the Japanese language goes much further than English in providing a distinctive grammar and vocabulary for different

---

1. See Richard Schechner, *Environmental Theater* (New York: Hawthorne Books, 1973).

social circumstances. In one sense, then, the religious ritual is simply one more formalized role into which people move with ease.

But Japanese religion is not simply a charade any more than Japanese society is. The different language and stance the Japanese adapt at work and with relatives, or with those seen as social superiors and those seen as equals, does not mean that a person is nothing but a chameleon with no individuality. Sensitive, skillful adaptability to varying social and ritual forms is seen as a supreme virtue, sublimely exemplified by as great a literary paragon as Prince Genji, and its perfection makes one as memorable an individual as he. The ultimate message is not that any one form of behavior is truer than another, but that the true reality is society. Its forms, with all their intricate manifestations, control of individual destinies. The famous allusiveness and vagueness of Japanese conversation, full of unspoken agreements and wordless understandings, bears this out: it bespeaks on a secular level the Buddhist/Taoist realization that words and concepts are but poor conveyors of what is really important. The relative position of people, as reflected by the way they talk and act upon meeting, may be more important than what they say; words are really important only insofar as they define the nature of the relationship.

The same assumptions apply to religion, particularly religious rites. They too are less important for what they say than for what they show, not only about gods but also about human society and human sensitivity to situations old and new. Japanese religious practice is not fundamentally talk *about* the sacred nor even entirely prayers *to* the sacred; above all it is hierophany—in Mircea Eliade's term a showing of the sacred, both in itself and in the ultimately sacred structures of human life.[2] To be sure, it is a showing of the sacred through human beings and human art, but that is wholly in line with the deepest experience of both shamanistic Shinto and Buddhism; it is the human who gives word and form to the god or to the universal principle of enlightenment.

Now let us look at more specific characteristics of Japanese ritual: Shinto worship is essentially a recognition and celebration of the presence of the kami believed to dwell in the shrine. In ancient times kami were often thought to come and go, and a rite might begin by summoning the deity from heaven or from across the sea; his or her presence might be manifested in the spirit-possession of a shaman or shamaness. Though present rites are highly stylized, traces of these beliefs remain. The brisk clapping with which public and private Shinto worship begins is a token of calling or catching the attention of the god, and the exuberance of a Shinto festival's climax suggests the dynamic divine presence among the people. The sacred dance, kagura or bugaku, that is often part of that climax is thought of both as entertainment for the kami and, like shamanistic dance, a manifestation of his or her presence, for the gods themselves are dancers, as we know from the story of Ame no Uzume, the goddess who danced at

---

2. Mircea Eliade, *The Sacred and the Profane* (New York: Harcourt Brace Jovanovich, 1959), p. 11.

the time of the heavenly cave-hiding of Amaterasu. The oldest noh play (and the most frequently performed, even today) is "Okina" (The Old Man). It is said to derive from an occasion when an old man (the kami of the shrine) was observed dancing under a great evergreen tree at the Kasuga Shrine in Nara. (That tree, the Yogo pine, is painted on the backdrop of every noh stage, revealing the link between Shinto sacred dance and the classic theater.)

Shinto worship also has an important sociological dimension in that most shrine kami are ujigami, deities of particular clans or, today, families, trades, or communities. In this connection its purpose is to bind together the god with his or her people. The food offerings that characterize most Shinto worship are essentially first fruits for which the kami is thanked, and they represent an exchange of life between human and divine planes. Worshipers later often receive a token amount of the offered food and drink almost as a sort of holy communion; this suggests further the interplay of life between the two realms through the medium of food.

In all this the special, nonordinary nature of the activity is indicated in numerous ways. Priests and their assistants, as well as dancers, wear special vestments; those of the participants are based on the dress of Heian courtiers. Even more revealing is a special tempo to the Shinto rite: At the start of the service, when the offerings are being presented and removed and the prayer or *norito* recited, the priests move with a ponderous slowness, much slower than the pace of normal walking or activity, as though matching the pace of beings who dwell in another dimension of time. Much of the sacred dance is also slow, or begins so. But then in later stages, when the deity's presence is well established and its first needs have been met, the festival may change to a mood of excitement and quickness greater than the usual human rate. When the *mikoshi* or palanquin containing the deity is carried through the streets where its people live, it is borne on the shoulders of young men who run as fast as they can, zigzagging through the streets and shouting *"Washo! Washo!"* This is the mood of all the lively, carnival-like activities with which the festival is likely to end.

Broadly speaking Shinto worship is of three types: Most conspicuous are the colorful matsuri or festivals. Many shrines have an annual festival in which solemn offerings and prayers are followed by lively popular activities of the sort described above; major shrines may have more than one such event a year. Second, shrines will have periodic offerings presented by priests, but with little public participation. These range in frequency from the twice-daily presentations at the Grand Shrine of Ise to small places of worship whose kami must be content with attention once or twice a month or less. Finally, as every observant visitor to Japan knows, all important shrines receive a regular stream of private worshipers who pause before the sanctuary to clap hands twice, drop a coin in the offering grill, and say a short prayer before turning again to the business of daily life. Private shrine visits are especially popular at the New Year.

Buddhist ritual and religious practices have a different focus. In the Mahayana Buddhism of Japan, the supreme purpose of religious practice is to realize within oneself the ultimate, unconditioned reality—the emptiness, the buddha-nature, or the bodhisattva wisdom and compassion called enlightenment. To be sure, Buddhist rites in Japan as elsewhere have often been characterized as prayer and incantation, or they have often been thought to achieve other ends such as the protection of the nation, the healing of the sick, or the repose of the dead. Some figures in the Buddhist pantheon, especially the healing buddha Yakushi and the great bodhisattva Kannon, have been treated by the unsophisiticated as little different from gods and goddesses who can be persuaded to answer prayers and grant this-worldly boons. But this power ultimately derives from the power of overcoming illusion and realizing oneness with unconditioned reality, for that is the message of sutras chanted in the rites, and that is the source of the strength wielded by buddhas and bodhisattvas whose compassion, derived from the same source, might lead them to grant a devotee's petition.

Thus in the esoteric Buddhism of Shingon and Tendai the point was to achieve buddhahood "in this lifetime, in this body" by the "three secrets" of mudras or hand gestures, dharani or chants, and mandala meditations by which one visualizes buddhas and various aspects of buddha-realization. Through these means one uses the external structures to realize the internal structures of buddhahood, aligning the energies of one's own mind to them and finally becoming what one performs.

In the case of the Kamakura Buddhist schools, the single, simple, sure key to salvation that each of them offered was a means both of attaining buddhahood through oneness with the absolute and of generating its power. Pure Land Buddhists say namu Amida Butsu ("hail Amida Buddha") as an act of faith in Amida's vow to bring into his Pure Land those who call upon his name; yet informed disciples of Honen or Shinran tell us that Amida really represents the absolute itself and thus one's own buddha-nature. To say the nembutsu, then, is finally to affirm and realize one's own buddha-nature.

Nichiren Buddhism has always stressed the oneness of subjective and objective reality, of inner and outer. Its chant, the daimoku, or "namu myoho renge kyo," has been widely interpreted to mean, esoterically, "dedication to the wondrous essence (myoho, "marvelous dharma") and the phenomenal world (renge, "lotus," a common symbol of expressed, phenomenal reality) united." But at the same time the power of this chant to achieve such specific ends as health and prosperity, a new car or a new friend, has not been overlooked and indeed has been proclaimed as possible by the modern Nichiren mass movement, Soka Gakkai.

The basic practice of Zen is zazen, or seated meditation. During good zazen one is a buddha and at one with emptiness. Zen has not been as directed toward secondary ends as have other forms of Kamakura Buddhism, chiefly because of its more monastic and upper-class character, although Zen monks who serve as temple priests perform the same funeral and other pastoral rites as any Buddhist clergy.

Buddhist ritual in Japan, then, can be thought of as directed toward enabling one to become a buddha and to share in the power attained by oneness with unconditioned reality, and yet as providing alternate sources of power for meeting human needs and desires of a more limited sort.

## EXEMPLARY MODELS OF JAPANESE RITUAL

### Shinto

Now we shall look at the progression of a typical Shinto matsuri or festival, one that most shrines hold once a year and that amounts to a neighborhood or community holiday as well as a religious rite.

Days before the great occasion observers will know that something is afoot, not only from the festive purple bunting and banners around the shrine bearing the character for "matsuri" but also from the bustle of activity on the grounds: cleaning, polishing, and setting up booths. Representatives of the shrine will be making their way through the community soliciting donations to help cover expenses, and participants will be studying their parts. The shrine and its parish tingle with an air of anticipation and excitement.[3]

The solemn portions of the rite in the shrine itself will probably begin fairly early in the morning, both to allow more time for the merriment that follows and to accord with a widespread human feeling that the gods are entitled to the first thoughts and activities of the day.

A Shinto shrine is composed of three basic parts: At the back, set higher than the rest, is a chamber reached only by exceedingly steep steps and a massive door; it is called the *honden*. In it will be an object, a **shintai**, that represents the presence of the kami—an ancient mirror or sword, even a scroll inscribed with the deity's name. This room is entered very seldom and only by priests; offerings may be placed here at the major annual matsuri. Before the great steps and door is the hall of offerings, where stands the eight-legged table (four on each end) upon which offerings are placed, together with such symbols of the presence of deity as mirrors, gohei (zigzag-cut strips of paper on an upright stick), and a large drum. Before this stage-like area is a larger pavilion called the hall of prayers. Here prominent members of the shrine community may be seated during the matsuri.

The Shinto matsuri can be thought of as consisting of four parts, each beginning with the letter "p" in English: purification, presentation of offerings, prayer or petition, and participation.

Purification is extremely important for, as we have seen, the contrast of purity and pollution is basic to Shinto, and the matsuri is intended to create an

---

3. For an introduction to the world of Japanese festivals and other aspects of traditional popular religion, see Geoffrey Bownas, *Japanese Rainmaking and Other Folk Practices* (London: George Allen & Unwin, 1963).

atmosphere of great purity hallowed by the presence of kami. The ceremony will usually begin with a priest appearing all vested in a white silk or cotton robe, or the colored vestment known as a *kariginu,* together with *hakama,* wide pants, and *eboshi,* the high black hat worn by Shinto priests. (The colors worn depend on the season and the seniority of the priest.) These vestments, usually completed with the *shaku,* a wide flat stick held in the hand, are derived from court dress of the Heian period. The priest will open the rite by a gesture of purification such as making sweeping arm movements with an evergreen branch, sprinkling salt, or waving the *harai-gushi,* a stick bearing thick linen or paper streamers.

Next comes the presentation of offerings, a very slow and solemn matter. The offerings are brought from a side chamber or building on trays held high by the participants, who proceed with careful, deliberate steps; if several participants serve, they will be handed just as deliberately from one to another. The chief priest then sets them on the eight-legged table in the hall of prayers.

The offerings themselves typically consist of vegetables, fruit, seafood, and salt, together with rice and rice wine. Red meat and fowl are rarely, if ever, presented. Items that are not food, such as cloth and ornamental swords, are occasionally offered in accordance with shrine tradition; they are characteristic of offerings presented by imperial envoys at national shrines such as Ise. Invariably the offerings are arranged on the trays with exquisite decorative taste, since the Japanese believe generally that food ought to be attractively presented.

When the offerings are set on the table the chief priest steps forward to recite the prayer or norito. He holds the text against the shaku, gripped by both hands before his chest. The norito will be in dignified, somewhat archaic language. These prayers will usually thank the kami for benefits over the past year and ask for continued bountiful harvests, health, and prosperity. The priest, bowing slightly, says the prayer in a high, strained, chanting voice, or else he offers it silently. After the prayer the offerings are removed. They will later be consumed by the priests and their families, or otherwise disposed of reverently.

Then comes the part of the festival we may call participation, when the whole community becomes actively involved. It begins decorously enough. The leading laity seated in the hall may come forward one by one, each presenting, slowly and with dignity, a green branch at the offering table and each receiving a sip of rice wine offered previously as a kind of communion. Other laypeople present may also receive it. Kagura or sacred dance may be performed at this time, either in the shrine or on a special *kagura-den* or stage reserved for these performances. The dancers are most frequently female miko, or young maidens vividly clothed in red and white who assist about the shrine as receptionists, dancers, and even presenters of offerings in private services. Though colorful, the dances have a solemn air about them, too; they are, after all, entertainment for the kami and expressions of the divine presence. The most famous male dances are the bugaku—ancient Chinese court dances that have been preserved in the Japanese imperial court and a few old shrines in Japan as a priceless cultural heritage. They are danced with splendid costumes and slow stomping steps in the open air to the accompaniment of ancient court music called gagaku.

Kagura, Fushimi Inari Shrine, Kyoto.

We also see more vigorous activity. It is common for a small shrine to be carried through the streets on the shoulders of boisterous young men. There may be a world-famous procession, like the *Gion Matsuri* or *Jidai Matsuri* in Kyoto. The former, said to derive from the ninth century when it was performed to counter an epidemic, involves the movement of floats carrying whole trees down the streets of the city. As always, the evergreen of these boughs brings health and purity. The Jidai Matsuri is a modern Kyoto festival in which participants in the long parade wear costumes from the Heian period, when Kyoto was the imperial capital. Other matsuri culminate in such events as horse races, boat races, running with torches to the top of a mountain, or folk dancing. The specific content of such matsuri are as varied as the individual customs of the shrines themselves, but they will actively engage all present, either as participants or as avid spectators, and bring the heart of the matsuri—the kami presence—out of the shrine and into public access.

The matsuri may also include a carnival set up on the shrine grounds. Today much of it will consist of booths offering the sort of games and snacks typical of carnivals the world over. But it would not be surprising to find a display of *sumo* wrestling among its attractions. Sumo has ancient connections to Shinto, suggested by the gohei-like strips that are part of the wrestler's formal costume. In olden times this form of hand-to-hand combat was used both at the imperial court and in shrine festivals to divine how the harvest would be, or at the New Year to discern whether the coming year would bring good or ill. (Other competitive activities during matsuri, such as the horse and boat races already mentioned, are likely to have a similar background.)

Shinto worship, characterized by reverence to the kami through the solemn presentation of prayer and offerings and by widespread participation of the community, accentuates the deeply local and agricultural roots of Japanese religion.

## Zen Meditation

Zen and Shinto have certain common features in Japanese religious forms. Comparisons have often been made between the clear, natural lines of the oldest Shinto shrines, such as Ise, and the Zen meditation hall or temple buildings. Both the insides and the outsides of a Zen temple are exemplified by Zen landscape design, and the rock garden with an expanse of raked white gravel set only with rocks and a few tufts of moss is oddly reminiscent of those *shiki* or demarcated sacred spaces under the open sky used for Shinto worship before shrines were built. In both there is a sense that through simplicity and close rapport with nature one encounters the sacred.

Yet obviously there are differences. Shinto is polytheistic, indigenous, and closely tied sociologically to local community and clan. Its practice focuses on ritual worship of the kami rather than on meditation for the realization of buddhahood, and it has relatively little philosophical or theological expression. Zen, being Buddhist, is an imported religion, though one that has put down very deep roots in Japan. Especially in the Kamakura and Muromachi periods, its great institutions had important national, social, and cultural influence. Intrinsically, however, Zen focuses on meditation as the royal road to nondualistic experience. Let us look, then, at the life of the Zen Buddhist monk or nun and at the practice of Zen meditation (zazen).

The practice of Zen in temples or monasteries varies from one place to another, but here is a typical regimen based on the usage at the Sokokuji Temple in Kyoto.[4] Monks rise as early as 3 a.m., wash, and immediately enter the temple hall for recitation of the sutras, done formally in chanting tones to the accompaniment of drums, gongs, and clappers. This is an impressive practice in which, as in all such Buddhist recitations, the emphasis is not so much on the meaning of the words as on the sounds themselves as a focus for the mind, allowing it to center itself. Then comes a period of zazen, or seated Zen meditation, in the *zendo* or meditation hall. During zazen monks may enter the chamber of the *roshi* or Zen master for a private interview, called *dokusan* or *sanzen*. Next comes breakfast, served and eaten in the zendo itself at the monk's place of meditation. Characteristically the food is served in silence with simple ceremony; the monk lifts his bowl high as though receiving sustenance from the universe itself. Zen food is typically austere, vegetarian fare but carefully prepared.

After breakfast comes more zazen and then daily cleaning. On some days a sermon or lecture will follow. On other days, immediately after cleaning comes the practice of mendicancy, when the monks file out of the temple chanting sutras

---

4. The daily schedule is based on Koji Sato, *The Zen Life* (New York and Tokyo: John Weatherhill, 1972), p. 142.

and go into the community to receive alms. Each monk stands silently at the door of a house until something is placed in his upheld bowl; afterwards he bows in thanks and moves on to the next house. (Such practices are considered beneficial for the giver in earning good karma and promoting a spirit of selflessness, and for the monk-recipient they engender humility. In all, the deed enacts the mutual inter-dependency of all beings in the universe.)

The midday meal comes at 10 or 11 a.m., followed by zazen. Manual labor, perhaps in the garden or kitchen, lasts from 1 to 3 or 4 p.m. After work there is another recitation of the sutras, the evening meal, and evening zazen with an opportunity again for an interview with the roshi. Lights are out as early as 8 p.m. in the winter and 9 p.m. in the summer.

During the periods known as *sesshin* or intensive training, the regimen will be even stricter, with more time devoted to zazen and interviews. The hardest of all is the *rohatsu dai sesshin,* from the first to the eighth of December, commemorating the Buddha's enlightenment. In spite of these austerities, Zen monastic life is often not as harsh in practice as it appears on paper. There are days off, parties, and excursions. Most Zen monks are in fact youths who are spending a few years in training to become temple priests, often in succession to their fathers, and who, like schoolboys everywhere, may find ways to circumvent the rules. Today, many people from both Japan and the West also make retreats to Zen monasteries for limited periods of time.

Zazen, the fundamental Zen practice, is an important method of meditation pursued by many people both within and outside formal Zen. It is ideally practiced in the full lotus position (that is, with legs crossed and feet raised so that the soles of both feet face upward), but it may also be practiced in one of several easier ways, even seated in a chair. Generally a round cushion is used. The hands are laid left on top of the right, thumbs pressed together. The back is straight without being rigid, the eyes half-closed. In the Soto tradition the meditator faces a wall; in Rinzai, one focuses on the floor some four feet in front.[5]

Meditation is a process of stilling and concentrating the mind, and several methods are taught by Zen masters. These include counting the breaths from one to ten over and over, simple mindfulness of breathing, and working on *koans.* Koans, used especially in the Rinzai tradition, are enigmatic riddles or sayings that convey a profound Buddhist message and are intended to bring the mind up against the limits of ordinary rational thought. Examples are "What was your face before you were born?" "What is the sound of one hand?" or simply the word *"mu!"* which means emptiness or nothingness. (All of these refer to the undivided "suchness" from which we and all things originate, but they are posed in such a way as to precipitate an experience rather than impart an idea. Koans are not to be thought about intellectually but "worked on" in the mind—re-

---

5. A good practical guide to the practice of Zen, especially for Westerners, is Philip Kapleau, *The Three Pillars of Zen* (Boston: Beacon Press, 1967).

peated until they sink to deeper and deeper levels of consciousness, doing their own work in their own way to break through our ordinary subject/object awareness.)

During zazen a proctor or *jikijitsu* will probably walk slowly back and forth in front of the rows of seated meditators carrying a long flat stick called a *keishaku*. He may use it to strike someone smartly but not severely on the shoulder if that person appears drowsy or inattentive, or if the meditator himself indicates the need to be recalled to alertness by bowing as the proctor passes by. Zazen periods will usually last half an hour. At the end of that period meditators may rise for a short walking meditation, called *kinhin,* perhaps accompanied by chanting.

For the serious practitioner of Zen the interview with the roshi goes hand in hand with zazen, for then his or her practice is tested and strengthened. A roshi is supposed to have exceptional insight into the spiritual state of the disciple and to be able to give advice or tests according to one's needs. There may be gentle words of encouragement or even a simple smile and dismissal in silence. At other times a person's progress might be tested through forms of shock therapy or intense interrogation. This is particularly the case with koan students who will be asked to demonstrate their understanding of the koan on which they are working. Ordinarily what is expected is a nonintellectual, nonverbal ''answer'' that shows that the meaning has been wholly absorbed. The ''one-hand'' koan, for example, may be answered by simply thrusting forward a hand in a single unified gesture. These procedures often lead to very lively exchanges, though the only final ''answer'' is enlightenment itself.[6]

Zen meditation is a quiet yet steep path to enlightenment as the wordless realization of one's true nature—often called satori, or awakening realization. It can come quietly and unexpectedly during deep zazen, while working in the garden or kitchen, or when slapped during an interview by a harsh yet wise roshi. But the same realization also produces a state of mind that can express itself in exquisite art and poetry and in a singularly tranquil and compassionate life. It is a mind that, like a meditator in zazen, is emptied of subject/object consciousness and yet abides in nondualistic awareness of the universe; it simply sees things as they are in themselves (suchness) without the interference of ego and subject/object distinctions. To Zen, the enlightened mind is the truly natural mind, the mind allowed to be itself apart from all delusion or desire. It is awakened in meditation but is ultimately demonstrated in all arenas of life: work, caring for others, artistic creativity, or exercising the insight of a roshi.

## Nichiren Buddhist Practice

Nichiren Buddhism is beyond doubt the most powerful form of Buddhism in Japan today, whether considered in terms of numbers, strength of commitment,

---

6. See Yoel Hoffman, *The Sound of the One Hand: 281 Zen Koans with Answers* (New York: Basic Books, 1975).

or institutional activity. This is in large part because of the remarkable growth of the Soka Gakkai movement in the postwar years—an organization branching off from the older Nichiren Shoshu denomination and related to two smaller but likewise vital and important Nichiren-related New Religions: Rissho Kosei Kai and Reiyukai. But, as we have seen, all this is nothing new. Nichiren Buddhism has from the start possessed remarkable power to stir up popular fervor, inspire sectarian movements, and present itself as a radically contemporary version of the ancient Buddhist faith.

These features, and other facets of the Nichiren appeal as well, are crystallized and communicated in Nichiren's dynamic forms of ritual. According to Nichiren himself, this religious practice emphasizes three features: the gohonzon or object of worship, the daimoku or chant, and the kaidan or ordination platform. These he called the "three great hidden principles."

The gohonzon is the chief focus of worship. It is an inscribed, rectangular scroll containing the daimoku (to be described in a moment) in the center and the names of leading buddhas and bodhisattvas of the *Lotus Sutra* elsewhere. It is thus a sort of mandala of the cosmos as seen inwardly by Nichiren, with the daimoku as the sounds or words of power aligned to its central reality and the *Lotus Sutra* as the consummate spiritual text. Containing no pictorial image, the gohonzon suggests the overriding importance of word and sound in Nichiren Buddhism. Whether in front of the altars at home or in temples, the devotees worship whenever possible before the gohonzon, for it is said to be like a mirror of the innermost reality of a human being and to possess greater power to bring out that reality.

The daimoku consists of the words "namu myoho renge kyo." Literally they mean "hail to the wonderful dharma *Lotus Sutra*," and thus they point to the central importance of that text to Nichiren. In interpreting the daimoku, however, Nichiren believers usually prefer more exoteric meanings. In Buddhist thought, dharma can refer to the buddha-wisdom that is the essence of truth itself, the changeless absolute, and the many-petaled lotus of the phenomenal world of appearance, change, and multiplicity. The chant can then mean "dedication to the wondrous essence and the phenomenal world united!" or "devotion to the mystic law of cause and effect through sound!" The latter expression emphasizes the power of the daimoku to effect changes in a universe in which subject and object, and all planes of reality, are collapsed into one.

The kaidan or "ordination platform" may seem somewhat more puzzling as a basic principle. First, it must be understood that the right of a Buddhist temple or movement to ordain priests on its own had long been a point of contention, since it symbolized whether such an institution was truly independent or just a branch of some other temple or group. Since Nichiren believed that his was not just a new branch off an older tree but rather the fruit of a whole new Buddhist dispensation and revelation, this matter was naturally of great concern to him. Indeed, the kaidan took on a mystical, apocalyptic meaning. It was not only his ecclesiastical center at Mt. Minobu but was also sometimes identified

The Daimoku Chant, Soka Gakkai. (Soka Gakkai.)

with Nichiren himself. At other times it is identified with Vulture Peak, from which the Buddha had allegedly delivered the *Lotus Sutra.*

Congregational Nichiren worship, like worship at home altars, fundamentally consists of reciting the daimoku. It is said rapidly, in unison, to the accompaniment of loud drums. Often worshipers hold the peculiar Nichiren rosary, 108 beads arranged in a circle with extensions to resemble vaguely the human form, and rub it rapidly with a rustling sound during chanting. The intense, dynamic atmosphere of such Nichiren worship is remarkable; the observer as well as the participants can hardly help but sense a tremendous concentration of energy. After perhaps fifteen or twenty minutes of such chanting the chant may change to *gongyo,* the recitation of a passage from the *Lotus Sutra.* This is done in a lighter but even more rapid tone with bells. In both cases it is clear that the verbal meaning of the chant is not as important as the psychological or spiritual state induced by its intensive sounds and actions.

Apart from the processions, sermons, and traditions of special festivals and pilgrimages, the daimoku and other chants are really the heart of traditional Nichiren practice. Modern Nichiren groups may include more informal sessions in which the energy of the rite is related to the needs of the people, but even there the central rituals have not changed. Meetings of Soka Gakkai chapters, for example, devote adequate time to discussion, and their gatherings and literature are full of testimonials of people whose lives were transformed by the daimoku. At American Nichiren-Shoshu meetings one can hear testimonials of people who have stopped a drug habit, had a house sold, obtained a good job, and above all else found radiant happiness once they started chanting the daimoku, and the same kind of testimonial can be heard in Japan.

The other modern Nichiren groups, Reiyukai and Rissho Kosei Kai, include in their practice a group activity called the *hoza*—group discussions that, with their overtones of group therapy, undoubtedly account for much of the popularity of these movements, for they convey a concern for the problems of ordinary individuals not shown by much of traditional Japanese religion. In a hoza group, ten to twenty persons, both male and female, sit in a circle with a counselor. The participants ask the counselor questions on personal matters that he or she will answer with Buddhist insight. Here are two actual examples: A teacher of flower arrangement asked what should be done about a student who had stolen a vase. The reply was to be very kind to the student and give her another vase. Then, the counselor predicted, the student would repent, return both vases, and be saved. Another person seemed always to have a bad cold and asked for advice. The answer was that the disease was ultimately the result of egotism; if the person would think less of herself, believe more in the Buddha, and work harder to try to bring others to the religion, the cause of sickness would disappear and so would the sickness.[7]

Nichiren Buddhism, then, displays considerable power in the modern world because it conjoins the mystique and force of ancient chants and texts with a practical concern for people's problems.

## Yamabushi Rites

Few elements of Japanese religion are more colorful than the yamabushi—the mountain priests who practice elaborate austerities and initiations in the mountains to acquire sacred power, then exercise that power among the common people to heal and divine. As we have seen, the yamabushi sect, shugendo, has its roots in the Nara period or even earlier. Japanese Buddhism has long found itself divided between orthodox, institutional forms and popular forms in which Buddhist concepts, usually esoteric or tantric, are thoroughly blended with Taoist magic and Shinto shamanism, with its ancient traditions of mountains as centers of sacred power. Shugendo has been the most visible expression of that side of Japanese Buddhism. Most yamabushi groups have had tenuous ties with Shingon or Tendai monasteries since the Middle Ages, though they largely went their own way until the movement was suppressed by the Meiji government in 1872. It has, however, experienced a modest revival since the achievement of complete religious freedom in 1945, and so the vivid yamabushi rituals can now be seen in some places.

---

7. From Harry Thomsen, *The New Religions of Japan* (Rutland, Vt: Charles E. Tuttle Co., 1963), p. 121.

Among the most active of those places is Mt. Haguro, one of three sacred mountains in the far north of Honshu, Japan's main island.[8] The Tendai-related yamabushi order located there goes up into the mountain four times a year for four seasonal rituals, known as *mine* or "peaks." The spring peak, no longer observed separately, was a collection of rites related to New Year's ceremonies and heavily influenced by Taoism. The summer peak, involving all three mountains, centers around the ritual opening and closing of various places of pilgrimage in the sacred territory. This is a time when lay pilgrims throng the area. The autumn peak, which is the most important because participation in it is essential to the initiation and promotion of members of the yamabushi order, consists mainly of a series of ritual confinements and initiatory experiences representing death, descent into hell, rebirth, and culminates in a ritual fire (*goma*). The winter peak is a lively New Year's Eve celebration of the end of ascetic confinement and of divination for the coming new year. This writer (Ellwood) observed the winter peak on the night of December 31, 1966 to January 1, 1967. The following paragraphs describe that event as an example of yamabushi ritual.

Mt. Haguro is in the snow country of Japan, and the sacred mountain was deeply covered at that time of year. The rites were held on a large snowy field in front of a commodious Shinto shrine. Around the clearing were the fringes of dark pine forests. The activities began about 2 p.m. as the yamabushi priests entered the area noisily blowing their conch shells. They were dressed in black-and-white-checked blouses, white pantaloons, and high black eboshi as headgear. Around their necks were curious cases and mirrors as breastplates. At 3 o'clock a Shinto service was held in the shrine. In front of the shrine were two large straw "insects," said to ward off harm to the coming year's rice crop. Standing on top of them, yamabushi threw down sacred straw ropes to pilgrims who would put them over their house doors to keep evil away; the scramble for these was often rough.

The ensuing rituals all had a twofold character, for the Haguro yamabushi order is divided into two parts, and ritual contention between them plays the universal role of such sacred combat at New Year's time: it symbolizes the struggle between the old and the new year and divines whether the new year will be good or bad. The order was divided into two sections, each with identical lodges built back-to-back in the ritual area. Within each lodge was a lower part filled with milling people and a higher floor containing an altar and the seat of that section's *matsu-hijiri*—the yamabushi who had that night completed one hundred days of residence in the mountain as a hermit-ascetic.

What followed were several rites of combat between the two sides. Men faced each other shouting insults. This was done in good fun, abetted by the

---

8. See H. Byron Earhart, *A Religious Study of the Mount Haguro Sect of Shugendo* (Tokyo: Sophia University Press, 1970). On the autumn peak, see the interesting description in Carmen Blacker, *The Catalpa Bow: A Study of Shamanistic Practices in Japan* (London: George Allen & Unwin, 1975), chap. 2.

sake that had been flowing freely in the lodges. Then in the main shrine hall two lines of yamabushi alternated in circling about in a dance step said to imitate the crow sacred to Mt. Haguro. Next, a man disguised as a giant rabbit entered; he was reportedly an envoy of Gassan or "Moon Mountain," one of the other sacred mountains. He sat between two low tables while yamabushi came up to the table in pairs, one from each line. Once there, they put their hands on the table and the "rabbit" would lean quickly this way and that trying to hit each with a folded fan while the visitors tried to pull their hands back before he did. This is said to divine the coming year. Each yamabushi represents a month; apparently, if his hand is hit, that month will be bad for the surrounding area.

Meanwhile, outside, a contest had developed between the two sides as they sought to pull their respective giant straw "insects" over and into a fire. Judges were present to determine the winner.

Since it was now about midnight, another contest developed for lighting a new, pure fire for the new year. Representatives of each of the two parties had a plate holding gunpowder and old-fashioned flint and steel implements. Whoever managed to light the powder first was the winner. As in other contests the winner was said to be from the group whose matsu-hijiri had accumulated the most spiritual power during his period of confinement, although the ascetic himself did not participate. In these contests it was reported that if one side won, the coming year would be good for farming; if the other was triumphant, the year would be good for fishing.

The last ceremony was a curious one, the *kuni-wake,* or division of the country. It represented an ancient jurisdictional dispute between the Haguro order and the yamabushi order of Kumano and Mt. Hiko, the other major shugendo headquarters. A priest representing the Haguro group stood beside a round, varnished beam set in the snow at a 45-degree angle and spoke in a low, menacing voice to four yamabushi—representing the other side—standing about twenty feet away. The latter came up one by one, with a kind of dancing step, to challenge the priest. The latter put his hand across the beam and repeated his low and angry tones; the others retreated. This was said to reaffirm Haguro's right to its claims, that is, to have exclusive rights to serve all northern and eastern Japan.

By now the rites were over and the night was dark and cold. Most participants and visitors retired to the shrine hall to sleep in blanket-rolls or sleeping bags; no doubt like mine, their minds were full of wonder at this glimpse into the world of archaic practices. All too soon, however, we were awakened by the drums and music of the 5 a.m. Shinto New Year's service in the main shrine. It had no direct connection with the yamabushi rites of the night before, but many straggled in to participate in it. The crowd of Shinto pilgrims was large; many were members of the widespread *ko* or devotional fraternity of this shrine, which organizes tours from various towns to its major festivals. After the usual offering and norito, the names of hundreds of persons—ko members—were read aloud by a priest while the chief priest chanted over and over *"kanai anzen, shintai kenzai, shobai kanzen, shosan joju"* (''peace in the home, physical health, success in business, praise and accomplishment''). Since names as well as prayers were recited in a singing voice, with the dropping and swallowing of inflection at the end of each phrase, the effect was not displeasing but rather like a round. After the prayers, hymns unique to the area were sung and the mysterious-sounding Shinto music played.

People began cautiously and wearily to make their way home over snowy roads and down mountain slopes, slowly returning to the world of the twentieth century after a turning of the year that seemed like the opening of a door to a timeless realm of sacred myth and ritual.

8

# religion and society

## RELIGION IN SOCIOLOGICAL PERSPECTIVE

The sociology of religion deals with the religious life of human beings living in interaction with one another, in dependence on one another, in hierarchical structures of authority, and in communally based patterns of behavior. In the study of religion, sociology continually reminds us that religion without such social factors would be unimaginable. We learn religious concepts, including the very language we must use to talk and think about religion, from others: parents, community, school. Whether we accept or reject the religion of our upbringing, an interaction with society is involved. Rebels or hermits who repudiate the social environment are, in the last analysis, simply putting themselves in a different relation to society than do conformists. The words and visions that express that protest were originally learned and are therefore social. Whether or not there is such a thing as a purely personal religion, it could have no direct impact on human history until the individual puts it into words and symbols and communicates it at least to one other person, and then it becomes a social phenomenon, if for no other reason than that it assumes a shared mode of communication.

Yet religion is constantly moving back and forth between the deeply inward and the "outer" social expression. That is its nature: to give public expression to human inwardness and to internalize individually a society's values and visions of ultimate reality. This twofold locus of religion—in a society's public temples and rituals and in the depths of people's hearts—serves to bring individual and society together so that individuals think and feel with social, communal confirmation. But it can also create tension, for once in a while the individual will see a different vision, "march to a different drum," or dream a different dream from that of society. The result may then be division, confrontation, or the start of a new sect or religion. Through these dynamics the history of religion moves forward, never staying the same and never repeating itself.

All these features can be seen in Japan. Indeed, Japan illustrates some of them to an exceptional degree. The communal character of religion has rarely been adhered to with more fidelity, and longstanding traditions better kept alive, than in many deeply rooted Shinto and Buddhist customs. Yet such exponents of visionary, charismatic faith as the Kamakura Buddhist reformers and the founders of the modern New Religions are models of the more individualistic vision.

These two polar characteristics go back to the very beginning, to the already mentioned ujigami or clan-protecting kami, and the hitogami or alien humanlike gods who may come as marebito (mysterious visitors) to possess shamans and impart strange signs and wonders.[1] In these two types of kami can be seen the two roles of religion: the sacred as expressive of communal identity and the sacred as that which breaks in from the outside community. These poles have both persisted. Most families still think of a particular shrine as housing their traditional ujigami, whether it is the community shrine or one maintained by the clan at its ancestral homestead. The custom still exists of paying respects to the ujigami at the New Year, on festival days, and after important family events. Newborn children are customarily presented to their ujigami about a month after birth. Most Japanese are also aware of a family relationship to a particular Buddhist temple and so to the denomination it represents; they will look to this temple for funeral and memorial services or at other crucial times when the services of Buddhism are necessary.

On the other hand, these persons will not hesitate to look outside the local communal tradition in seeking other divine powers by, for example, praying to other kami or buddhas and going on pilgrimages to other shrines. At times such "outside" deities may even eclipse older ujigami types.

A former ujigami shrine in Shinohata, north of Tokyo, was faithfully attended until World War II, but has since the war been neglected except for minimal upkeep and perfunctory rituals on the annual festival day. More popular now is the Hachiman Shrine on a lovely wooded rise outside of town. Villagers enjoy strolling to it from time to time, and its matsuri is the major community event of the year.[2]

Shinohata reflects other practices as well. It is common to pray for health and blessings to Fudo, the fierce-looking, fire-encircled Buddhist figure so pop-

---

1. See Ichiro Hori, "Mysterious Visitors from the Harvest to the New Year," in *Studies in Japanese Folklore*, ed. Richard M. Dorson (Bloomington: Indiana University Press, 1963), pp. 76–103.

2. Ronald P. Dore, *Shinohata* (New York: Pantheon Books, 1978), chaps. 13–15.

ular in Japan, and to Kobo-sama (Kobo Daishi), the sainted founder of Shingon who is venerated as much in popular religion as in his own denomination. *Hotoke*—the word means both a buddha and the spirits of the departed—are still honored at some household altars with simple offerings of water and incense. All such practices evidence alternatives to the ujigami structure and an interest in hitogami.

The relation between communal identity and outside supernatural assistance is typical of Japan. Local shrines like the Hachiman Shrine at Shinohata and all ujigami shrines help establish identity by showing that one is a member of family and community as one participates in shrine worship and festival. So also, in its own way, does attending family or community funerals and memorials in familiar Buddhist temples or offering service to hotoke at household altars. Even pilgrimage and praying to such nonlocal figures as Fudo or Kobo-sama, however, have communal characteristics and community support, though they seek outside supernatural assistance.

These two aspects of the religious life, the communal and the individual, express two kinds of religious communities, natural and intentional. These two are found everywhere in the religious world and are well evidenced in Japan. The natural religious community is the one that a person is born into: family, village, or neighborhood. Thus, insofar as a family or a community is united around the ujigami and traditional temple, that grouping and practice form a natural religious community. Intentional religious communities, on the other hand, are those that people create or join by individual choice. The Japanese New Religions are excellent examples. People usually first seek them out as a source of outside supernatural assistance, but the next step could well be joining in order to receive further blessings. Such decisions can cut through family ties and align one religiously much more closely with fellow believers who are far away than with one's own unconverted neighbors.

Of course gray areas exist between these two types of religious communities. In Japan it would be very common for a family to join a New Religion as a whole, thus preserving a natural unit in an intentional community. By now there are second- and third-generation families in such religions as Tenrikyo, and when they live in Tenrikyo villages one finds the intentional community really functioning as a natural community. Similarly the great denominational temples of Zen, Jodo Shinshu, or Shingon Buddhism serve for the most part as centers of natural religious communities, yet they maintain something of the distinctive ideologies and universality more characteristic of intentional communities. These two types of community, and in turn the two aspects of religion we are discussing, might also be reflected in two types of religious leadership: the institutional and the charismatic.

Institutional leadership is present when a person carries religious rank and authority primarily because of his or her office or title rather than because of personal charisma or innate spiritual power. Institutional leadership can be prepared for by formal education in the religious tradition and bestowed by appointment, election, or heredity. Hereditary succession to the priesthood of a Shinto shrine or Buddhist temple is exceedingly common. Even when the appointment is nominally made by some higher authority the choice will in fact ordinarily go to the heir of the incumbent. Similarly, even when there is no suitable candidate by natural heredity, a close approximation is pursued: the incumbent institutional leader selects a favorite disciple who becomes in effect his adopted son and is subsequently trained for the position. This pattern is deeply ingrained in Japanese patterns of culture and society, too; one finds hereditary leaders in the arts, in business, in education, and in family life.

Even the New Religions, founded by highly charismatic leaders in recent times, have been quick to adopt the successor principle. The leaders of these religions today are generally the natural or adoptive heirs of the original charismatic founder. (This has meant, incidentally, that although the founders and early evangelists of many New Religions were women, successive leadership has tended to pass into the hands of men. Even though women sometimes retain a figurehead role or function behind the scenes, outward appearances call for hereditary succession based on a patriarchal father/son model.)

On the other hand, our survey of Japanese religious history has made it clear that Japanese religion has been punctuated by the activities of strongly charismatic leaders, from Kobo Daishi to Nakayama Miki. They have been people who communicated to others a deep sense of individual spiritual gifts and charismatic power. Marvelous tales have grown up around them, and disciples have sat at their feet. Some have had only local reputations, whereas others have been founders of major denominations, but they clearly offset the tendency of Japanese religion to adopt the more highly conservative, institutional leadership pattern.

Of course it is not impossible for charismatic leaders to appear within traditional, institutional structures. The charismatic yamabushi priests, with other institutional orders and tenuous links to Shingon and Tendai, can be regarded in this light. Zen has produced its celebrated eccentrics and iconoclasts such as Ikkyu or Hakuin, but even there the institutional links remain.

Beyond the typologies and tensions of communal versus individual, however, a sociological perspective must also encompass the larger picture of religion in Japanese society in general and the relations of religion to the state. Here the problem becomes one of interpreting pluralistic religion in a cohesive society. To this may be added, at least in modern times, the comparative strength and stability of the Japanese state and economy despite that same religious pluralism.

Here, however, we can ask whether the pluralism is quite what it seems to be. The great historian Edward Gibbon, thinking of the riotous profusion of creeds and cults that flourished in the late Roman Empire, remarked that to the common people all such creeds were equally true, and to the magistrates all were equally useful. Much the same statement could be made of the Japanese situation, and it should be made with no overtones of cynicism. Japanese people, as we have seen, tend to think of ultimate truth as inexpressible, so all visible spiritual paths represent only relative and conditioned ways toward it. In this sense all ways are equally true since they can all lead to the inexpressible. The government, for its part, has in various periods seen religious diversity as offering convenient devices for manipulating and indirectly administering people. In the Tokugawa period families were registered with the government by mandatory membership in government-controlled Buddhist temples; from 1868 to 1945 the same was done through Shinto shrines. More opportunistically, governments have often fostered religious institutional splits in order to keep any one institution from becoming too strong and so challenging the government's own power.

Religious diversity has limits. In America many who can accept the panorama of mainstream American religion as a legitimate expression of liberty bridle at "cults" that allegedly introduce alien teachings and do not "play by the rules" in such matters as recruitment and fund raising. Similarly, in Japan, religions perceived as foreign to the Japanese heritage and as operating outside expected patterns have found the going rough. One thinks of the persecution of Christianity after its initial sixteenth-century success and of the hostility that many of the more recent New Religions have faced, especially from the authorities, as they sought a legal status that brought them into the system and subordinated them to the state. (Since 1945, of course, full religious freedom has been obtained, and there is no direct government supervision of religion; before, religious groups had to be licensed through a procedure that included government approval of their doctrinal statements, worship, and administration.)

The "rules" by which religions are tacitly expected to operate in Japan are, more than anything else, Confucian. As so often in Japan, Confucianism plays the role of a moral and ethical substratum that, its preconditions being met, allows a harmless surface diversity. Indeed, one could argue, as many have, that these principles go back beyond Confucian influences on early Japan to the values inherent in ancient clan structures and an agricultural society with their demands for loyalty and cooperative effort; Confucianism did not so much create as articulate the values by which Japanese society works.

Fundamental to Confucian principles is the family. Thus, one "rule" or expectation of religion in Japan is that it inculcate the value of loyalty to family. Families in turn see themselves as part of extended families and as rooted in a village or district. Religious practices that express solidarity with those units are well regarded. The basic Confucian model is the patriarchal family. Religions that express that in their own structure, as in the concept of hereditary succession of leadership, would on that score be regarded as conforming to expectation.

Likewise, Confucianism regards the state, at whose apex is the emperor, as an extension of the patriarchal family, thus requiring similar loyalty and service as an extension of family/village cooperation for the common good. Within this family framework Confucianism views religion as subordinate to the state, not necessarily in the modern totalitarian sense all too apparent in the Japan of the 1930s and 1940s, but in the sense that religion like everything else ought to be a part of family and community life, inculcating loyalty to superiors and benevolence to all, and linking sovereign and subject. It was not only the right but also the duty of the ruler to patronize religion, as it is religion's duty to instruct and exemplify the aforementioned virtues. The supreme good in Confucianism is an efficient society peopled by wise men and women devoted to active service on behalf of the welfare of all, and guided by selfless sovereigns and ministers whose only thought is to demonstrate that ideal in all their life and work. For a religion to fail to provide symbols of cohesion in such a society, and to stand against it in implicit criticism or in sole devotion to private spiritual quests, would not be regarded as a proper use of personal freedom, much less a heroic protest against conformity. It would be seen as antisocial and perverse, the work of selfish and possibly dangerous persons. It is understandable, then, that those religions that clearly play their proper role within the Confucian social organism are best accepted. Virtually all religions that have endured in Japan have adapted external forms agreeable to the patriarchal family model and have made their peace with the state.

Just as Japan is not a lotus pond of unlimited religious tolerance, however, so is it not the walled-off Confucian utopia that its Tokugawa overlords once wanted to make it. There is another well-known side to the Japanese character: an intense curiosity about the outside world, and sometimes avid eagerness to take up with the latest new idea from abroad. Although Christianity breaks the mold of conventional Japanese religion, it has long elicited a great deal of interest and some converts. So, more recently, have such entries as Islam and the Hare Krishna movement.

Furthermore, Confucian ideology notwithstanding, the celebrated Japanese capacity for social conformity has limits beyond which it cannot be pushed. Oppression has often produced strikes, riots, and peasant rebellions. The religious side of that response has been movements, often more or less shamanistic, that have implicity or openly criticized the existing order and offered hope for a better world to come. We have seen examples from the Nara period down to the New Religions of today. Although most such movements have eventually come to terms, at least outwardly, with state and society, they have also usually retained an aura about them of protest and dissent, of going against the stream. This has added to their appeal for some, while calling forth the disdain of others. Thus, though it dates as far back as the Kamakura period, Nichiren Buddhism with its legacy of prophetic intransigence has never been completely digested by Japanese society, and its progeny remain somewhat controversial to this day. The emergence of such groups keeps the underlying communal Confucian values in Japanese religion under healthy tension, forcing them to remain flexible and open to new possibilities.

The relation of the state to religion has varied. In premodern times the relation was usually expressed through ceremonial offerings and patronage to selected shrines and temples on the part of the imperial and shogunal courts and some degree of control over shrines and temples through control of temple/shrine ranking systems and the appointment of the priestly hierarchies. At the same time, religious movements that presumed too much or that seemed to mock state control experienced occasional persecution—either because (like Christianity) they were too foreign or because (like the assorted wandering shamans and sacred dancers of the Tokugawa era) they were too populist and might somehow arouse working-class irresponsibility or discontent.

During the period between the Meiji Restoration (1868) and 1945, as we have seen, the state sought increasingly to control religious life directly as a part of its effort to centralize the entire nation and put it under totalitarian discipline. But since 1945 Japan has enjoyed complete freedom of religion, despite the fact that religious bodies are still officially registered. Needless to say, occasional controversial areas remain, such as the status of the Ise Grand Shrine and the propriety of Soka Gakkai's sponsoring what is in effect its own political party. Most Japanese, however, would probably agree that religious freedom has brought far more benefit than distress to both state and religion. Nonetheless, conservatives continue to pine for moral education in the schools and the sense of national spiritual unity of prewar days, though not necessarily for state control of religion.

A word should be said about the complex and often misunderstood role of the emperor in the relation of religion to the state. The roots of the imperial position are in the archaic sacred king, descended from the gods, whose rituals brought not only order to the society but also magical security from enemies and fertility for nature. This role is evident in the *Kojiki* and *Nihonshoki* accounts of ancient sovereigns and is crystallized, as we shall see in a moment, in the state rituals of Heian times—a ritual pattern that has never died out, thanks to the conserving character of Japanese religion and culture.

It would not be correct to say, however, that belief in archaic sacred kingship has persisted equally over all those centuries. Instead, during most of the long years of feudalism, the emperor was such a remote and powerless figure that ordinary people probably gave him very little thought; their religious lives were far more preoccupied with Buddhism or local Shinto. When imperial claims came into play it was inevitably because a group in power or seeking power, such as the Heian Fujiwara or the various shogunal houses, sought out the unique authority of the emperor to legitimate their authority. For this purpose the mythological heavenly descent of the emperor, the sacred symbols, and the ritual pattern needed to be kept reasonably intact.

Between 1868 and 1945, the imperial institution enjoyed a more central role. Great play was made of the "imperial will" as justifying national regimentation and expansionism. But it seems clear that Emperor Hirohito (r. 1926–) harbored considerable skepticism about such business, and that when he made his famous renunciation of divinity in 1946 he was renouncing not only what he had himself never believed but also what was largely a fabrication of recent propaganda. For although ancient Shinto spoke of the emperor as "manifest kami," that was in the context of a time when many manifest kami were in the world and when the distinction between priest and god was blurred. But the view that the emperor is ultimate legitimator of the state has persisted in postwar times; the new democratic constitution makes him a symbol of the state and its unity.

Last of all we must consider ethics and Japanese religion. As we have seen, the steel frame of Japanese ethical patterns is Confucianism; or more exactly, the values of the ancient clan and village expressed philosophically in Confucian terminology. To these patterns and values Shinto and Buddhism have respectively contributed the ideals of purity and compassion. In Buddhism, except for the most devout, the more non-Confucian values (for example, celibacy) have received little attention.

The role of religion in ethics has been to create a cleansed state of mind (makoto, sincerity in intellectualized Shinto, or enlightenment in Buddhism) in which one freely and spontaneously sees and does the right thing without thought of self. This means, as has often been remarked, that Japanese ethics are a "situation ethic," which hold no absolutes and no inflexible rules, but rather the right response in each situation depends on the requirements of sincerity and compassion and of course on the nature of the relationship between the people involved. In practice this means that religious realization liberates one to adopt ungrudgingly the behavior expected by Confucian and pre-Confucian values in a given situation: to express loyalty, acknowledge dependency, sacrifice self for the common good, and to sacrifice oneself for one's children or parents. For rare individuals, religious experience may free one for a highly unconventional life—like that of Zen master Ikkyu (1394–1481). But in most cases Japanese religion, like religion in any culture, has been the chief source and basis of the society's normative values.

It is now time to look at specific examples of Japanese religion at work in society.

## EXEMPLARY PATTERNS IN RELIGIOUS COMMUNITY

### Shinto Court Rituals as Socio-Religious Patterns

For our first example we will go back to those Shinto practices associated with the imperial court that preserved in crystallized form the world of archaic, sacred kingship. These rites were standardized after the Taika Reform of 745 C.E., and the priestly Nakatomi clan was instrumental in their development. These rites were set forth in the Taiho Codes of 701 and its commentaries, the foundational documents of what is called the Ritsuryo State, that is, the "state based on the rules and regulations [of the Code]." The Code provided for a court and administration based on Chinese models but adapted to Japanese interest in matters pertaining to Shinto and the traditions of ancient houses, including the imperial house. In it, religion, ritual, and government were rolled up together in a single center of sacred and political power.

This pattern flourished in the Nara and Heian periods, and the most extensive documentation of its rituals in their classic form is the *Engishiki* of 930 C.E. Though ritual practice declined in the chaotic middle ages,[3] in theory the ritsuryo (rules) of the Taiho Code was the fundamental law of the Japanese state until the modern constitutions. Through such rituals we can glimpse socio-religious patterns at the highest levels of ancient Japanese society, and we can begin to appreciate the power of ritual to maintain those patterns.

The major Shinto court rites in that time centered around two poles: the imperial palace and the Grand Shrine of Ise some sixty miles distant. The principal rituals were the toshigoi or spring prayers for the crops at the palace, the *niiname-sai* or harvest festival performed by the emperor at the palace (especially the daijo-sai or the harvest festival performed by the emperor the first year of his reign), the "ordination" of the imperial princess who went to Ise to serve as priestess and so became a link between the palace and the Grand Shrine, and the rites of Ise Shrine itself.

It is clear from the preeminence of seedtime and harvest in this ritual pattern that however exalted their courtly setting, the ceremonies had their roots in the agricultural cycle. They were rites to promote fertility and to commune with the gods in thanksgiving for bountiful harvests. This significance is closely allied with their role as functions of an archaic sacred king, for a major obligation of such a king was to bestow fertility magically both in the fields and in the kingly house by generating an heir.

The Japanese emperor, however, did not perform these rituals alone, nor was their significance limited to the significance of imperial sacred power. As court rituals they involved and celebrated the socio-religious roles of those connected with the court; as national rites they had meaning for society as a whole. (Even today, though diminished in importance, vestiges of these rituals and their significance remain.) Court rituals were not the sole prerogative of the emperor so much as of a coterie of ruling houses, just as local shrine rituals were not simply those of the priest but of the community, with members of various families often holding traditional functions.

All such matters reflect the collective yet class-defined nature of leadership that has prevailed in Japan down to the present century. In practice, leadership has been exercised not so much by individuals apart from their family or clan connections, or by an abstract social class, as by clans that have made themselves ruling oligarchies: the Soga, the Fujiwara, the Minamoto, or the Choshu and Satsuma samurai of the Meiji Restoration. Sometimes the clan has produced great individual leaders, but they have in turn been supported by the broad base of clan loyalty. Whoever has been in the ruling position, however, has legiti-

---

3. Felicia G. Bock, *Engi-Shiki: Procedures of the Engi Era*, 2 vols. (Tokyo: Sophia University Press, 1970 and 1972).

mated that power by professed loyalty to the imperial house, often reinforced by intermarriage into it. All this was reflected in court rituals, so let us, therefore, look at the central court rituals: the toshigoi, the practices of the Grand Shrine of Ise, the rites of the saigu, and the daijo-sai accession/harvest rituals.

The toshigoi was a spring ritual offering prayers for the crops in the coming year. The emperor himself participated, and the major ritualists were the Mi-kannagi priestesses (successors of ancient court shamanesses), the Nakatomi priests who headed the government's Office of Shrines, and the Fujiwara Prime Minister. Thus three key houses were brought together in this ceremony. The court also sent toshigoi offerings to hundreds of other shrines, and rites were performed in them by the local court-appointed officials, symbolically uniting the court with its outlying territories.[4]

Prior to the Meiji Restoration the Ise Grand Shrine rituals were performed by the Nakatomi clan, who honored Amaterasu at Ise's Inner Shrine (Naiku) and by a local priestly house, the Watarai, who presented offerings to the kami Toyouke at the Outer Shrine (Geku). The entire system of shrines was under the supervision of the court's shrine administration branch (jingi-kan). The latter sent offerings to Ise at major festival times and reported major imperial events. The greatest Ise ritual was, and is, the shikinen sengu, the building of a new shrine on the alternate site every twenty years and ceremonially transferring the sacred objects from old to new housing at the *kanname-sai* (Ise's harvest ritual) of that year.[5]

We have already looked at the rituals of the saigu of the imperial princess assigned to serve as priestess at Ise, in Chapter 3. The sociological significance of this process should be clear. The various rituals associated with the selection of the princess, the procession to Ise, and her functions at Ise all involved the Nakatomi and Imbe clans of the jingi-kan, the Nakatomi and Watarai clans at Ise, and the general populace itself. Here again the rituals both reflect and help keep alive the socio-religious patterns and roles among the major clans and between the state and the shrine system.

The daijo-sai, or harvest festival performed by the emperor at the time of accession to the throne, is an extremely ancient and complex ritual. We have already noted that during it the sovereign bathed, entered successively two lodges filled with sacred objects, and in each lay out offerings and sipped rice wine in communion with the deities. Here we can only call attention to the sociological overtones. First, three of the five clans involved in the mythological imperial descent from the ancestral kami were (and are) represented by descendants in the rite, and probably the other two houses were represented under variant names. The ministers of state, largely Fujiwara in the Heian era, also had prom-

4. Robert S. Ellwood, "The Spring Prayer (*Toshigoi*) Ceremony of the Heian Court," *Asian Folklore Studies,* 30, no. 1 (1971), 1–30.

5. Robert S. Ellwood, "Harvest and Renewal at the Grand Shrine of Ise," *Numen,* 15, no. 3 (November 1968), 165–190.

inent roles. The unity of such offices under the throne, both in mythological past and political present, was ritually affirmed.

The country was brought into the rite. Rice to be used as offerings at the daijo-sai, and from which the rice wine of the rite was also prepared, was grown in two plots in provinces on either side of the capital selected by an elaborate divination procedure. When the harvest was ready a local female child was chosen by divination to cut the first sheaf, and a local man served as "priest of the rice," which was itself regarded as a kami. The grain was brought to the Heian capital in a colorful procession binding together countryside and city in the cultus of the sacred emperor.

## The Zen Monastery as a Community of Buddhist Practice

We will now look once again at the Zen life, this time with an emphasis on its sociological aspects.

The great Zen monasteries such as Daitokuji or Myoshinji in Kyoto, where priests are trained for service in local temples, are not single institutions but complexes of Zen institutions and subtemples. Linked together, they form an enclave against the outside world. The demarcation is symbolized by the huge gate, the "mountain gate," that allows access into the walled enclosure from the bustling outside world.

Within, life is just as busy but differently paced. By 4:30 in the morning the monastic households will be up. In the subtemples a resident abbot, who may have spent four or five decades in monk's robes, together with two or three disciples and a caretaker, go about their early morning chores. The junior disciple lights the cooking fires while others begin to recite sutras in the meditation hall, followed by zazen. A kitchen worker than enters with breakfast trays. The simple meal of rice and soup is presented, in tiny but carefully prepared portions, to the image of the founder of the temple and to the spirits of its departed inmates and benefactors. Then the living members of the religious family are fed.[6]

Breakfast is finished and the dishes washed by 6:30, and it is now time for the day's work. Meditation, study, and manual labor are interspersed throughout the day. The abbot may spend the morning hours among his books or accounts while the junior monks sweep and rake the buildings and garden. They may be of high school or college age, in which case they will be off to school at the appropriate time. But after hours the abbot may join them and the caretaker in heavier chores around the establishment. The day ends with zazen and chanting, followed by the hot bath that is such an important part of the routine in the daily life of any Japanese.

---

6. Based on Jon Covell and Yamada Sobin, *Zen at Daitokuji* (Tokyo, New York, and San Francisco: Kodansha International, 1974), chap. 6.

However simple the life of the subtemple may be, that of the *sodo,* or training hall for Zen priests, is far more rigorous. Those who aspire to the priesthood, either of a subtemple within the larger local complex or of a community temple, undergo several years of training here.

Entry into Zen training is a calculated ordeal. The postulant kneels outside the door of the temple he wishes to enter, dressed in traditional garb including straw hat and sandals, for two or three days. Except for being given meals and a place to sleep at night, he is ignored. Then, when he is finally permitted to state what he wants, he will be told the monastery is full or the discipline is too hard. Only after several entreaties will he be deemed to have shown his seriousness of purpose and be allowed to stay in a special room for a few days to try meditating.

Beginning Zen students with high aspirations toward either Zen enlightenment or a Zen career, or both, will then be sent to the sodo. Today, perhaps half the students in the sodo of a major temple complex will be sons of local Zen priests following in their fathers' footsteps in accordance with the already discussed successor principle in Japanese religious institutioins; the other half will be a collection of persons of quite diverse background and age who wish to undertake Zen training out of a personal spiritual drive. For whatever reason, they have elected a demanding but—many would say—incomparably rewarding way of life.

During the day in the sodo, zazen alternates with hard physical labor performed in silence. The students eat their frugal meals in the zendo where they meditate and, in some instances, sleep in zazen posture. A *tatami* (woven straw mat) of some six by nine feet is the monk's "home" where he lives much of his life and keeps, on a shelf, his few belongings. The way in which everything is done, from morning toilet through taking meals to the five-hour evening meditation broken only by walking and chanting, is carefully regulated.

Sometimes the novice will have interviews with the roshi or spiritual mentor. This can be traumatic, for if any spiritual weakness is detected, the treatment might be the "shock therapy" of blows and abuse. Conversely, the student may demonstrate such deep understanding of Zen, and in particular of the koan or other technique he is working on, that the master greets him with twinkling smiles and pronounces that he has entered the "gateless gate" of enlightenment.

In all this we see the fundamental task of the sodo experience to discipline the student into a highly formal, regulated life, emptied of self-centered experiences and intentions. That, however, is only the foundation for the true achievement of Zen training, spontaneity and joy in the immediate present. It is represented in the bubbling happiness, the playful childlikeness, and penetrating wisdom of the great Zen heroes of past and present. Not all Zen students reach that summit, of course. Some drop out; some never become more than perfunctory adherents to the Zen way.

In its socio-religious pattern and structure, however, the Zen monastery reflects religious community. First, we note that it is a way of life lived in what the sociologist Irving Goffman has called a "total institution"—one that, whether prison, hospital, army, or monastery, controls one's behavior and expression of identity in nearly all areas of life.[7] In contrast to the relative freedom of choice in ordinary life, the total institution will prescribe for its members such things as dress, diet, daily schedule, and nature of work so that one's identity is closely tied to that single institution; one has no visible identity apart from it. (Of course, one may express the institution's "personality" in a somewhat special way. Senior Zen monks, like senior army officers, are often famous for vigorous and unique personality traits. This is not, however, expected of the training monk in the sodo or the soldier in boot camp.)

Second, we observe the symbols of separation between the monastery as total institution and the outside world. One notices not only the obvious walls and gates, but also monastic garb, traditional Zen foods, and the tea for which Zen is famous. On another level, there is the matter of style. Zen ways of doing things will be quickly noted by the observant visitor at a monastery. They largely center on neatness and cleanliness, suggesting that behind them lies an ancient Shinto ideal of purity as a supreme spiritual state. Zen houses and grounds are kept spotlessly neat, even to a special way of tying one's sandals together at the entryway to a building. The celebrated Zen gardens, often containing little more than moss, rocks, and raked sand, suggest first of all the purity of primordial nature unsullied by human hands, then the idea of transcending nature itself to communicate the ultimate purity of the "unborn mind" (emptiness awareness) realized in Zen meditation. But to sustain its image of purity, the monastery must be full of symbols of reversal showing it to be the opposite of the polluted outside world. Thus, like monks and nuns of all religious traditions, Zen monks arise while the world generally has more time to sleep, eat simpler (usually vegetarian) meals, uphold a tradition of celibacy (not always observed today), and meditate in calm joy.

Yet if the monastery is in some ways a reversal of the world, it parallels the world in other ways. The organization of the monastery, especially of the subtemples, clearly resembles a family. The abbot is *oyabun,* "parent substitute," playing the role of father to his disciple-children. This is a common pattern in Japanese life: in Japanese universities, businesses, even the underworld, juniors attach themselves to a senior oyabun in a pattern that goes back to the feudal practice of adopting heirs.

The subtemples, in turn, form a sort of village that, like the Japanese rural village made up of several "houses," also has its common center, the *hondo.* Early in the morning, three times a month, the great bell summons the abbots of the various subtemples to a service in the hondo, the great central hall of the monastery complex. They come through the gray dawn with the rapid, gliding step characteristic of Zen, and chant sutras for perhaps an hour and a half. Al-

---

7. Irving Goffman, *Asylums* (Garden City, N.Y.: Doubleday Anchor Books, 1961).

though each of the subtemples has its own traditions, indeed sometimes a highly distinctive style growing out of distinctive traditions and personalities, their unity in the reversal of the world is here also expressed. Zen expresses very deep aspects of the Japanese soul, yet it also presents a contrast to, and so implicitly a critique of, Japanese life as it is ordinarily lived.

## Soka Gakkai and the Importance of Community

Some years ago I [Ellwood] was a guest in the home of a Japanese woman and her young son. They were of modest means, and the house was neat but very tiny. This environment only highlighted the presence in the living room of a sheet inscribed with characters—the gohonzon ascribed to Nichiren that carries the phrase namu myoho renge kyo, "hail to the marvelous teaching of the *Lotus Sutra,*" and the names of prominent buddhas and bodhisattvas from that sutra.

The woman was very active in Nichiren Buddhism, having been converted to it by Soka Gakkai. Before I left she pressed into my hands a selection of Soka Gakkai literature. Her story made vividly clear the sort of experiences that lie behind the phenomenal postwar growth of that school.

She has lost all her family to the atomic bomb at Hiroshima. She came to Tokyo, married the man who fathered her son, but was soon abandoned by him. She then made a meager living selling newspapers on a street corner. A local Soka Gakkai group took an interest in her and her problems and acted as a family in which she was a loved and valued member. Her conversion, and her gratitude and enthusiasm toward Soka Gakkai, is easy to understand.

Not all Soka Gakkai converts were as desperate as this person, but undoubtedly most were in some way afflicted by the trauma of Japan's defeat in World War II—an event that called into question old established religions and left a spiritual vacuum. Of the many faiths that rushed in to fill that void, Soka Gakkai was overwhelmingly the most successful. With some sixteen million members by the early 1980s, it is by far the largest single religious organization in Japan. Its simple teaching and practice, its emphasis on benefits in this life, and its tight organization and vigorous recruitment policies all help account for that growth.

Nichiren himself taught that there are two ways of effecting conversions: *shakubuku,* the forceful method, and *shoju,* the mild and conciliatory path. In more recent years Soka Gakkai, with its growing interest in peace and cultural activities, has leaned toward the latter way. But in its postwar years of greatest growth the tactic was shakubuku. The word means literally "to break and subdue" and is interpreted to mean breaking the roots of error in the other person in order to allow true faith to take root itself. The technique called for vigorous argument and persistence in pursuing a prospect until success was attained. Shakubuku was criticized, but in an epoch now past it was also successful.

Whatever the method, however, a new convert is taken to a Nichiren Shoshu temple, where with appropriate rites a priest consecrates and presents a

Soka Gakkai Convention, Tokyo. (Soka Gakkai.)

gohonzon to be placed in his or her home. All objects pertaining to other religions must be removed and the gohonzon carefully enshrined and guarded, for damage to it is a very serious matter. From then on the convert's duties are to chant the daimoku (the namu myoho renge kyo) and the gongyo (passages from the *Lotus Sutra*) daily before the gohonzon, to practice shakubuku regularly toward others, and to participate in Soka Gakkai activities.[8]

The latter activities can be both pleasureful and time-consuming. One will first be introduced to the basic unit, the *kumi,* comprising perhaps a dozen families. The kumi meets often for discussion and group chanting; testimonials to the power of the daimoku are a conspicuous feature. Above the kumi are chapters and regional organizations leading up to the national headquarters. These control activities on a larger scale and provide occasion for the gala conventions that are such an important part of Soka Gakkai life and mystique.

Parallel to this structure is a horizontal organization of block units, for the kumi consists of people related by shakubuku who are not necessarily from the same geographical place. The block unit enables Soka Gakkai activity to be facilitated in a single community.[9] In addition, members will find themselves drawn into any number of special interest groups as well as special divisions devoted, for example, to drama, popular music, and other hobbies. All these have their

8. Kiyoaki Murata, *Japan's New Buddhism* (New York and Tokyo: Walker/Weatherhill, 1969), pp. 102–106, and Noah S. Brannen, *Soka Gakkai* (Richmond, Va.: John Knox Press, 1968), chap. 5.

9. Murata, *Japan's New Buddhism,* chap. 8.

ascending levels of organization. It is not uncommon for Soka Gakkai members to find almost all their free time taken up by the movement's organizations. Given the Japanese love of group life, and the sense of self-esteem that Soka Gakkai activity gives one's life, this for many may be more a joy than a burden.

More controversial is still another organization related to Soka Gakkai, the Komeito political party. Founded in 1964, the "Clean Government Party," as its name is officially translated, is ostensibly independent of Soka Gakkai. But its leaders and candidates are generally seasoned Soka Gakkai members, and the party makes no secret of being ultimately inspired by Nichiren's dictum that government and Buddhism should be harmoniously blended in an ideal society. But Soka Gakkai and the Komeito insist this is not interpreted in a way contrary to modern ideas of the separation of church and state. It simply means, they say, that good Buddhists should take an active part in civic affairs and, moved by Buddhist morality, should labor selflessly toward such political goals as elimination of corruption, equal justice to all, and world peace. In the late 1960s, when Japan was beset by bland, compromising leadership on the right and doctrinaire factions on the left, the new party proved attractive and quickly reached the status of Japan's third largest political group. It has, however, been accused of too generously exercising a minority's privilege of issuing only criticisms and platitudes and being too vague as to what concrete policies it would enact if given power.[10]

On a deeper level, however, the Komeito serves one purpose that is extremely important to Soka Gakkai, and that is the same purpose served by its multifarious organizations, its popular music groups, and its festive assemblies with squads of vivacious young people. Above all, Soka Gakkai wishes to give the ancient Buddhist faith a modern face and dispel the image of musty temples and ethereal monks in meditation. Buddhism, it feels, should speak to modern people living busy but happy lives in the modern world of politics, television, and jumbo jets. At its central temple, Taisekiji at the foot of Mt. Fuji, an ancient building is almost buried in splendid new auditoriums and other structures with futuristic architecture. Instead of meditation these Buddhists are more likely to chant at a rapid clip and then dance or sing to a modern beat. To them, the important thing is realizing eternity in the present moment amid a joyous and creative life here and now.

Because Soka Gakkai has been especially successful in bridging the gap between ancient faith and modern world, in both ideology and practice, it has had a powerful appeal in modern Japan. Similarly, it has been able to bridge social gaps from low to high and create a strong sense of solidarity among its members. All these factors are important to its success. Indeed, Soka Gakkai has taught the world that a religion that can fully accept the modern world has nothing to fear from it.

---

10. Brannen, *Soka Gakkai*, chap. 6, and James W. White, *The Sokagakkai and Mass Society* (Stanford, Calif.: Stanford University Press, 1970), chaps. 7 and 8.

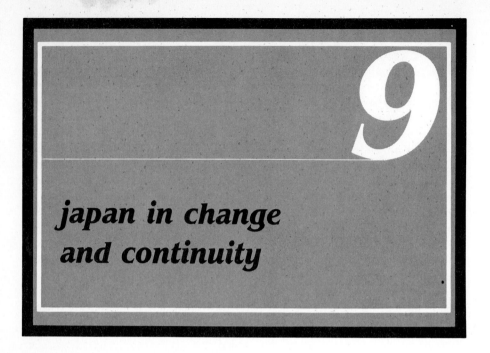

# japan in change and continuity

## RELIGION IN AN EVER-CHANGING WORLD

A book written by one of the authors of this present work, entitled *The Eagle and the Rising Sun,* discusses the nature and presence of certain of the New Religions of Japan in America.[1] This book, and others like it, indicate that the diverse cultures of our increasingly global community interact in multiple ways. We live in a world of mutual influence and mutual dependence.

The sociologist of religion, Peter Berger, tells us that we live in a qualitatively different world, where to choose among a variety of options is a modern necessity. Religiously, this choice is a matter of coming to terms with the meaning of one's own tradition as well as the views of other religions around the world. The major intellectual religious question is no longer "What does Jerusalem (i.e. Biblical revelation) have to do with Athens (i.e. reason)?" but "What does Jerusalem (i.e. Western religiosity) have to do with Benares (i.e. Eastern religiosity)?" In short, we live in a new situation of "contestation" between the "religions of interiority" (key Eastern religions) and "religions of confrontation" (Western religions). This contestation is not contest but rather mutual recognition and appreciation among the world's religions—a situation in which thoughtful and reflective people take seriously other religions in order to deepen their own.[2]

---

1. Robert Ellwood, *The Eagle and the Rising Sun* (Philadelphia: Westminster Press, 1974).

2. Peter Berger, *The Heretical Imperative* (Garden City, N.Y.: Anchor Press, 1979). See especially chaps. 1 and 6.

Such a state of affairs is true for Japan just as it is for America, Europe, or any other culture (or individual) that is part of the modern world. Religions, cultures, and human beings are constantly under internal and external pressure for change and are constantly facing new situations. Japan has been influenced in the last two centuries by Western religion and thought and has incorporated much of it at one level or another. Although one option in this new and ever-changing world is certainly nonreligious secularism, religious life in every culture tends to persist as a necessary part of human existence. In Japan, we have seen this in the persistence of traditional religion and the New Religions.

Japan—no less than the West—participates in a new situation in which it must come to terms both with its own tradition and with the religio-cultural traditions of the larger world. How it does this will determine its religious future. How *all* modern cultures understand their own traditions—yet remain open to the best of other traditions—will determine the world's religious future.

## CENTRAL PARADIGMS
## AND PERSISTENT PATTERNS

Although Japan, like every other modern culture, must face change in an ever-changing world, certain persistent patterns and central paradigms will no doubt continue, precisely because they reflect the very essence of the Japanese "way." We conclude this book by suggesting some of these patterns and paradigms that have persisted throughout Japanese religious life, in spite of ever-changing situations through history and in spite of the variety of "ways" that make up that life.

1. Although there are certainly exceptions, Japanese religion tends to find the sacred or ultimate within the natural/human realm, or at least in ready access to it. On balance, the "horizontal paradigm" discussed in Chapter 6 seems to predominate, and even the "vertical paradigm" is quickly qualified by easy passage between different realms of the sacred and the natural/human. This tends to lead the Japanese toward the sacralization of this world and this life itself and—in certain forms of Buddhism—toward a realization that this body/mind, this time and place, this world and life, are themselves the ultimate.

2. Religion in Japan is no abstract belief system or set of revealed truths; it is primarily a way that both leads toward some salvific goal and is itself a path or life to be lived. Ways imply not only that religion is always a matter of how life is lived but also that the practice of religion, actually living the religious life, is most crucial. It is only through the actual practice of specific religious disciplines and forms that the religious life is to be lived. This leads to the prominence of ritual order and ritual action within the religious life of Japan, or to what was called in Chapter 7 the "performance of religion."

3. Although much of Japanese religion is a practice of venerating or seeking benefits from externalized sacred powers, there remains a strong tendency

to affirm that the practice of religion is a process of disciplining the heart/mind (kokoro or *shin*) so as to be in harmony or unity with the sacred and to help one lead one's life authentically. This leads to a focus on the quality of certain kinds of intuitive sensitivity or modes of consciousness and to the centrality of aesthetic sensitivity.

4. Although much of Japanese religion focuses on the individual life, a tendency remains to see religious life in terms of collective religious communities that often intersect or overlap. Thus is religion lived out and understood in terms of the family, the clan, the village or area, the local shrine or temple group, sectarian communities, the "communities" of class and occupation, and ultimately the nation itself.

5. Finally, Japanese religion gives evidence of an easy interaction between mutually intersecting structures and forms, or, to put it another way, an aversion to definite and hard lines of demarcation, separation, or boundary between distinct groups. This can be seen in at least the following mutually interacting elements:

a. The various religions or ways are distinct but not mutually exclusive; they interact with and mutually influence each other (e.g. Shinto and Buddhism). Moreover, most Japanese are religious in more than one way simultaneously: they may honor both the kami and the buddhas while also fulfilling Confucian values.

b. The lines between religion and culture tend to break down, as do the lines between religion and daily life. Although religion can be discussed as a distinct aspect of Japanese life, the tendency is for religion to be lived out in a variety of cultural forms, from art and literature to national structures, and in the daily life of individuals and groups.

c. The old and the new, the traditional and the contemporary, seem to interact and intermix easily. The Japanese are often quite open to the new, but at the same time they like to maintain traditional patterns and structures. The new is accepted but changed in various ways to adapt it to older patterns (even as those older patterns are altered somewhat in the process).

d. The line of demarcation between the sacred and the profane breaks down easily and quickly. The tendency is to find the sacred permeating this life, and the nonsacred realm may easily become itself the realm of the sacred, or at least closely related to it.

e. The distinction between being and nonbeing can certainly be found in Japan, but being and nonbeing mutually and positively interact in the process of life. Although the Japanese affirm the beingness of things specifically and the world generally, they also appreciate a pregnant, meaningful nonbeing—the emptiness and/or intervals between things through which (or even by which) the sacred moves and is experienced. They affirm and find life permeated by those spaces, times, and experiences where being is cleared away and the sacred is allowed to appear right in the midst of being.

These five elements form what we might call central paradigms and/or deep and persistent structures that permeate Japanese religion; they are fundamental ways by which the Japanese have understood and lived their religious lives. They help provide continuity within a changing world and a changing Japan.

# appendix:
# brief summaries
# of major japanese
# religious traditions

## SHINTO

Shinto, ''The Way of the Gods,'' was the name given the ancient indigenous religion of Japan after the coming of Buddhism to distinguish it from the latter faith. Shinto focuses on the worship of the kami or gods associated with particular places and natural objects, as well as particular communities, clans, or occasionally occupations. The kami are generally worshiped in shrines where their spiritual presence is indicated by such symbols as the torii, or characteristic Shinto gate, and gohei, or zigzag strips of paper. Worshipers often approach shrines for individual worship, initiated by clapping the hands twice. Shinto public worship is conducted by priests who perform acts of purification, present offerings, and read norito or prayers. Shinto matsuri or festivals will also display lively and colorful features involving public participation such as dance, processions, and lighting fires; their nature varies according to the traditions of each shrine.

## CONFUCIANISM

Confucianism is a religious and philosophical tradition of immense importance in East Asia stemming from the teachings of the Chinese sage Confucius (551–479 B.C.E.). For Confucianism the supreme good is a good society, which in turn depends on right human motives and right relationships between humans. Right motives center on the virtue of rational humaneness, which expresses itself above all in "reciprocity" or "mutuality," realizing that everyone must live for the good of others rather than for oneself. If one lives in this way in accordance with the requirements of one's station in life, whether as parent or child, sovereign or subject, then one exemplifies the way of the true humanitarian; if everyone were to live this way, regardless of hardship, then society would work well for the good of all. Important to Confucianism are rules of decorum, which express the corporate nature of society and demonstrate its ideal harmony while elevating the minds of the people to social virtue. The family is the fundamental social unit, with the father-son relationship the paradigmatic one within it, involving varying obligations on both sides. The reverence for ancestors so much associated with Confucianism is simply an extension beyond the grave of the "filial piety" incumbent upon children toward their progenitors.

The personal veneration of Confucius that developed in China, along with other religious features, found relatively little expression in Japan. Shinto rituals and, in the Tokugawa period, even state-sponsored productions of noh plays, were seen as meeting the Confucian need for official rites. But Confucian moral philosophy has had a profound effect in articulating and refining fundamental Japanese values of social cooperation, family loyalty, work, and sense of interpersonal obligation.

## TAOISM

Taoism, or teaching about the tao (Jp., do) or "universal way," is a venerable Chinese tradition. Its philosophical wing finds its classic expression in the book called the *Tao te ching,* "The Book of the Way and its Power," ascribed to the semi-legendary Lao-tzu (fl. sixth century B.C.E.). This book inculcates a way of life that rejects the competitiveness and artificiality of conventional society in favor of a deep, intuitive, spontaneous rapport with the tao in nature and in the depths of oneself. On the other hand, so-called religious Taoism embraces a vast assortment of popular beliefs about gods, taboos, magic, and spirit-exorcism as well as colorful temple rites and esoteric techniques for attaining immortality. Both sides of Taoism are held together by the affirmation that rationalism has its limits, and that feeling, intuition, and imagination can transcend it. Taoism met needs in China unmet by the Confucian tradition for color, fancy, and spiritual techniques in dealing with personal as well as social issues. In Japan Taoism found expression chiefly in popular or folk religion, such as belief in taboo days and directions and in certain popular deities. Indirectly, it wielded an immense influence through its impact on Chinese Buddhism, especially Ch'an or Zen.

## BUDDHISM

Buddhism stems ultimately from the life and teachings of the historical Buddha Sakyamuni, the "holy man" (muni) of the Sakya clan in ancient India who was active around 550 B.C.E. His personal name was Siddhartha Gautama, and it was his followers who called him a "buddha" or "awakened one."

The Buddha is said to have attained enlightenment (bodhi) or nirvana (liberation) after meditating under a tree, and he subsequently taught others his dharma (truth, law, teaching) so that they might cross over the raging river of constant rebirth (samsara) and realize their own liberation from attachments and bondage to this world.

The teachings and practices of Buddhism, whether of the earlier sects in India (called the "Lesser Vehicle," or Hinayana, by Mahayana); the extension of those in Southeast Asia (Theravada); the many sects of Mahayana in India, China, Korea, and Japan; or the esoteric schools of Vajrayana out of Tibet, have one thing in common. They all see such teachings and practices as vehicles or ways (*yana*) for ultimate liberation from the suffering or negative character of existence. For some this liberation takes place within life itself, and one realizes (becomes awake to the fact) that this very world of samsara—seen from the wisdom of enlightenment—is itself the realm of nirvana. Others, especially more popular forms of Buddhism, see liberation as a distant goal, while in the meantime one must work for benefits in this life and for better rebirths in the future.

It is the Mahayana branch of Buddhism that has had the greatest impact on East Asia. This major reform movement began in India around the beginning of the Common Era and taught the "one vehicle" of the bodhisattvayana; that is, that all beings are potentially buddhas and that the proper, best, or great (*maha*) vehicle by which to realize buddhahood is the path of the bodhisattva, which leads to the realization of emptiness (sunyata), enlightenment (bodhi), the perfection of wisdom (*prajnaparamita*), and compassion (*karuna*) for others.

Mahayana not only sought reform and renewal at the very pinnacles of normative, orthodox Buddhism but subsequently developed tremendous appeal and flexibility, especially as it came to the Far East and flowered there. The now multiple buddhas and bodhisattvas, understood symbolically by the theological tradition, were taken literally by many others as a pantheon of cosmic powers standing by to help when called upon.

Sectarian developments of Mahayana Buddhism in the Far East reflect this vitality and diversity. In both China and Japan highly sophisticated sects such as Tendai or Zen had limited appeal for the masses, but kept alive the most profound Buddhist teachings. More popular sects (for example, Pure Land) carried their form of Buddha's message out to the farthermost villages and the lowliest peasants.

As the story of Japanese religion makes clear, the major sectarian developments in Japan included the early philosophical/monastic schools of the six Nara sects; the dominant Heian sects of Shingon and Tendai; the Kamakura schools of Zen, Pure Land, and Nichiren; and more modern versions of these in some of the New Religions. All have played long-lasting and important roles in Japanese religion.

Beyond these sectarian divisions and institutional forms, however, Buddhism has permeated Japanese society and culture to the point that it cannot be defined merely by such sects and their practices. Buddhism has taken on many forms in Japan, from local, popular cults devoted to this bodhisattva or that one to notions that the most refined artistic processes and products carry Buddhist meaning. Since Buddhism in general is more a practical way or path to be followed then a revealed set of truths to be believed, it opens itself to being shaped into any number of patterns and participating in any number of other "ways." The Buddhism of Japan is a perfect example of that.

## THE NEW RELIGIONS

The New Religions arose in Japan in the nineteenth and twentieth centuries. Although different in doctrine and practice, these religions have many common features. All have had founders who were strong charismatic figures, often in the shamanistic tradition and often female. Most have emphasized the coming of a new age. At the same time, they have stressed this-worldly benefits, healing, prosperity, and happiness. They have appealed chiefly to people of the lower classes, offering them sympathy, involvement in significant work, and institutions that have helped them adjust to modernity. Most of these religions have built imposing headquarters and even whole cities of great beauty, a focus for pride and pilgrimage, and a foretaste of the coming paradisal new world that they generally teach is on the way. At the same time, basic values and patterns of these religions have usually been consistent with Shinto, Buddhism, and Confucian morality and practice as popularly understood: karma, reincarnation, loyalty, family, and work. The following groups are some of the most important New Religions.

### Tenrikyo

Founded by Nakayama Miki (1798–1887), a farmwoman through whom a monotheistic God was believed to speak, Tenrikyo gives a distinctive account of the creation of the world. That narrative is enacted in its most important rites as means for calling humankind back to the Creator. Its central temple in Tenri City is constructed around the kanrodai, a pillar marking the place where the creation of humanity commenced. The religion also offers rites of healing.

### Konkokyo

The founder of this religion was a farmer, Kawate Bunjiro (1814–1883), who in 1859 believed himself to be commissioned by the monotheistic God to mediate between that God and humankind. Although devoted to this God, Konkokyo churches have altars and offerings similar to those of Shinto. There is, however, a unique rite called *toritsugi* in which a minister personally hears a parishioner tell of his or her spiritual state and seeks to reconcile that person to God, an activity often compared to Roman Catholic confession.

## Omoto

This religion is based on divined messages communicated through a farm-woman, Deguchi Nao (1836–1918), and subsequently interpreted by her son-in-law Deguchi Onisaburo (1871–1948), who also delivered voluminous revelations himself. Omoto teaches that the spiritual world is prior to the material world, that the human spirit is descended from the spirit world and will return to glory in it, that a new age is coming to be heralded by a new messiah, and that beauty reveals the spiritual realm. It also emphasizes healing. Onisaburo, who voiced social criticism, fell afoul of the government (together with his movement) in the 1920s and 1930s, and the group today is relatively small. Omoto's oceanic teachings have been an unfailing source of inspiration for other religious movements.

## World Messianity or Sekai Kyusei-kyo

Founded by a former member of Omoto, Okada Mokichi (1882–1955), this movement emphasizes the messianic and healing aspects of Omoto. It teaches that divine light is now increasingly coming into the world to cleanse it and create a paradisal new age; this light is also "channeled" through the hands of practitioners in a healing rite called *jorei*.

## PL Kyodan

The letters in the name of this religion stand for the English words Perfect Liberty. Also influenced by Omoto, this group was founded in 1946 by Miki Tokuchika (1900– ) on the basis of two prewar movements. Following the slogan "life is art," PL advocates living a balanced and harmonious life on the basis of divine law. Its graceful rituals of prayer, offering, and music are aesthetically pleasing. It also has rites for healing and offers personal divine guidance by senior priests of the religion.

## Seicho-no-Ie

This movement, whose name means "House of Growth," was founded by Taniguchi Masaharu (1893– ). Taniguchi, also a former member of Omoto, was influenced by the American "New Thought" tradition, which emphasizes the power of the mind and "positive thinking"; he taught that suffering is unreal and that all beings are absolutely perfect as children of God. It is only misguided attitudes that lead us into sickness and other suffering; through right understanding and change of attitude one can be healed. To aid in this process Seicho-no-Ie teaches certain chant-like affirmations and a method of mediation. In

Japan, Siecho-no-Ie has also long been associated with conservative and patriotic causes.

## Soka Gakkai

This movement, whose name means "Value-Creation Society," stems from an organization concerned with educational philosophy but closely linked to Nichiren Buddhism and founded in 1937 by Makiguchi Tsunesaburo (1871–1944). Influenced by pragmatism, it stressed the importance of immediate benefit as well as abstract truth in education, a view having some parallel to Nichiren's emphasis that true religion brings value in this present life. Soka Gakkai was reestablished by Toda Josei after World War II as a more actively religious organization aiming at conversion and teaching as a lay organization within the Nichiren Shoshu denomination. It is technically not a New Religion but has many features in common with them.

## Rissho Koseikai

This Nichiren denomination was founded in 1938 by Niwano Nikkyo (1906– ). It generally teaches Nichiren Buddhism but in an eclectic way that has allowed for shamanistic and spiritualistic practices as well as group counseling. Niwano has, since 1945, achieved worldwide recognition for his involvement in peace movements and interreligious dialogue.

## Reiyukai

This movement within the Nichiren group was established in 1925 by Kubo Kakutaro (1890–1944). It has much in common with Rissho Koseikai, and indeed is the latter's parent organization, for Niwano and other founders of it seceded from Reiyukai in 1938 because of personality conflicts. Reiyukai was long torn by internal troubles, but it can claim credit for pioneering modern, popular Nichiren Buddhism, including group counseling work.

# *Glossary*

This glossary includes terms that are of general importance to Japanese religion but are unfamiliar or not fully explained in the text. Terms not found here, including names of persons or places, may be pursued through the Index. (Please keep in mind that the Appendix consists of brief summaries of the major religions in Japan.)

The terms below appear in alphabetical order as they are spelled or transliterated in the text. Cross-listings are provided, where relevant, in the parentheses at the end of the listing.

*Amida* (Skt., Amitābha). Amida Buddha (*Amida-butsu*) is the great buddha of "infinite light/life" who is the focus especially of the various Pure Land sutras out of Indian Mahayana Buddhism and of the Pure Land sects of China and Japan. He "rules" in his "Pure Land" (Skt., Sukhāvatī; Jp., Jōdo) and, in popular faith, saves and receives the souls of the faithful into that land upon their death. Less literally understood, Amida is a metaphor or image of enlightenment itself. (See Namu Amida Butsu, Pure Land, Bodhi.)

*Aware* (See Mono-no-Aware).

*Bodhi* (Jp., *bo* or *bodai*). This is the Sanskrit word for "enlightenment." It encompasses a variety of specific ideas, all of which are understood to be aspects of or equivalent to enlightenment. These include the realization of emptiness (Skt., *śūnyatā;* Jp., *ku*), the realization of suchness (Skt., *tathatā;* Jp., *nyo* or *shinnyo*), the attainment of wisdom (Skt., *prajñā;* Jp., *hannya* or *chi-e*), the realization of truth (Skt., *dharma;* Jp., *hō*), the attainment of *nirvana* (Jp., *nehan*), and the attainment of buddha or bodhisattva status. (See Satori, Nirvana, Shinnyo, Ku, Hongaku, Dharma.)

*Bushido* (*bushido*). The "way of the warrior" has been a code of self-discipline, behavior, and cultural identity influenced by several religious and nonreligious factors in Japan. Among the former are Confucian values of loyalty, Zen values of ascetic self-denial and discipline, and Shinto ideals of purity and national loyalty.

*Dharma* (Jp., *ho*). Although this term is used in various ways in Mahayana Buddhism, its primary meaning refers to the teachings of Buddha. Beyond that it refers to the truth of Buddha and the very realization of that truth for oneself, namely, enlightenment itself. (See Bodhi.)

*Emptiness* (See Ku.)

**Enlightenment** (See Bodhi.)

**Harae** (*harai*). Ritual purity and/or the act of purification central to Shinto. Purification removes defilement in both internal and external "worlds" and allows kami to be harmoniously and beneficially present.

**Hijiri**. In Japanese folk religion, the "holy man" who works individually outside the institutional boundaries of any given religion and serves important religious functions among the common people of village and farm, especially in ancient Japan.

**Hitogami**. The "human-kami" system in Japanese folk religion indicates one major, distinctive religious pattern, namely, special kami associated with especially sacred persons (e.g. shamans, charismatic figures, saints, or sages). This system is strongly individualistic, as opposed to the ujigami system (See Ujigami.)

**Hongaku**. Heian Buddhism particularly emphasized a teaching already found in Indian Mahayana Buddhism, namely, that all beings are "essentially" or "fundamentally enlightened." To put it another way, enlightenment or nirvana is right here simply waiting to be recognized and awakened. (See Bodhi.)

**Honji Suijaku**. The theory of "true nature, manifest traces" was an important way for articulating the de facto mixing of Buddhism and Shinto, especially in the early medieval period. Shinto kami were understood, thereby, as manifested traces of essential Buddhist realities; or, in a Shinto reversal of that, buddhas and bodhisattvas were seen as manifest traces of the great Shinto deities.

**Jiriki**. The notion of "self-power" came to refer to traditional, monastic Buddhism and its dependence on the person's own mind/body to effect its own salvation. This arose in distinction to tariki, or the dependence on "other power" as taught primarily in the Pure Land sects. (See Tariki.)

**Kagura**. This refers to sacred music and dance in the Shinto tradition and is central to the ritual of classical Shinto. It is usually performed by young maidens called miko, and it has ancient roots in the shamanistic and mythological tradition in which calling forth and entertaining the kami were important.

**Kami** (*shin*). Literally, anything that is superior, above, or extra-ordinary. For Shinto it refers to the multiple sacred forces that inhabit the world (both human and natural) and are manifested in and through particularly sacred places, persons, or objects. (See Tama.)

**Kami-no-michi** (*shintō*). Literally the "way of the kami," this term is an alternate reading of the same Japanese characters otherwise read as "Shinto."

**Kokoro** (*shin*). This is the "mind" or "heart" as the locus of feelings and/or consciousness within the human being. Shinto has tended to use the reading "kokoro" in its emphasis on the refined sensitivities and emotions; Buddhism has tended to use the reading "shin" as reference to the nature of mind or consciousness.

***Ku*** (Skt., *śūnyatā;* Jp., *ku*). This is perhaps the most central category in Mahayana Buddhism. It means "emptiness" or void and refers to the particular mode of consciousness that appears when one empties the mind of its normal subject/object discrimination. (See Bodhi, Shinnyo.)

***Makoto.*** In a Shinto context this refers to truth as sincerity, honesty, and purity of intention. Some have claimed it is the essential category of Shinto and refers to the ideal human state, which is synonymous with the essence of kami as well.

***Mandala*** (Jp., *mandara*). Shingon, and/or esoteric Buddhism in general, have made important ritual and meditative use of the mandala as a symbolic, pictorial, or diagrammatic representation of reality as Buddhism sees it.

***Matsuri.*** Most specifically, this refers to all special Shinto festivals that call on the local kami, celebrate that kami and seek its benefits, and send it off until the next time. More broadly it could be understood to mean all Shinto ritual, even to the point of the ritualization of life itself.

***Mono-no-Aware.*** This is a central term for a particularly Heian-period religio-aesthetic sensitivity in which refined, delicate sensitivity to the wonder, beauty, and pathos of things was valued religiously.

***Mushin.*** Literally this means "no-mind," but it might better be understood (in Zen and Buddhism) as the "mu-mind," that is, the mind emptied of subject/object discriminations—the "no-thingness" (mu) mind beyond the ordinary discriminating mind. (See Ku.)

***Namu Amida Butsu.*** In Pure Land Buddhism, to pay "homage (or praise) to Amida Buddha" is to call on him in faith so as to be saved by his mercy and compassion. This is the central ritual/meditative act in Pure Land Buddhism and is more briefly referred to as the nembutsu. (See Amida, Pure Land, Tariki.)

***Nembutsu*** (See Namu Amida Butsu).

***Nirvana*** (Jp., *nehan*). Generally speaking, this term refers to enlightened existence as a state of being "blown out" or "extinguished," that is, as having put out the "fires" born of subject/object discriminations and attachments. In the Mahayana tradition, nirvana may be understood to await one beyond the grave, but its most central meaning is to live *this* life in an awakened, liberated manner as an "awakened one" (buddha). (See Bodhi.)

***Pure Land*** (Skt., *sukhāvatī;* Jp., *jōdo*). Understood as a literal place, this is Amida's paradisal world in the western sector of the cosmos and the place into which one is reborn if one has been faithful. Metaphorically, it is synonymous with this life lived as nirvana. (See Amida, Bodhi, Nirvana.)

**Satori**. The moment of "awakening," "realization," or "enlightenment," especially as understood by Zen. (See Bodhi, Nirvana.)

**Shinnyo** (Skt., *tathatā*). Often translated as "suchness" or "thusness," this term points to the other side of the coin of emptiness. It refers to the character of emptiness-realization as it engages a world of objects in their isness, thusness, suchness—as they immediately are without mental distancing. (See Bodhi, Nirvana, Ku.)

**Shintai**. This is the term for the object found in Shinto shrines that "houses" or "embodies" (tai) the kami (shin). It is not itself an object of worship, though it takes on sacrality in part because of its association with kami. Prevalent examples include mirrors, swords, jewels, and many natural objects.

**Shukyo** (*shūkyō*). Usually translated as "religion," this term more precisely means "sectarian teachings." It therefore indicates religion or religions in the narrow sense (as opposed to seishin as "spiritual", or do/michi as a "way" of spiritual significance), that is, institutionalized, sectarian groups and traditions with rather clearly defined parameters (e.g. *shin-shūkyō* as the "new religions" of Japan).

**Suchness** (See Shinnyo.)

**Tama**. This is a rather ill-defined term in the Shinto and folk traditions that generally refers to the soul or spirit of things, particularly people living or dead. As distinct from kami, it seems perhaps to be more ancient, more pervasive in the traditional folk Shinto, yet related in various ways to kami. Unlike kami, which are often rather well-defined and located, tama seem vague and in constant movement.

**Tariki**. This came to refer to an "other power" form of Buddhism, especially Pure Land Buddhism, which taught that one cannot rely on the self for salvation but only on the other power of Amida Buddha. (See Amida, Jiriki.)

**Ujigami**. Japanese folk religion has sometimes been discussed as revealing two distinct types of kami: hitogami and ujigami. The ujigami is the kami of the family or clan (uji) and is tied closely with ancestral spirits of a clan that have become kami of that clan (and/or of a related local area). (See Hitogami.)

**Wisdom** (Skt., *prajñā;* Jp., *hannya* or *chi-e* (See Bodhi.)

**Yugen** (*yūgen*). This is a central religio-aesthetic category in the Japanese tradition that has functioned particularly in Heian poetry and in the noh (*nō*) drama of Japan. It has referred to anything from refined elegance in style to the dark, mysterious beauty of the sublimely profound. In terms of a Buddhist-influenced aesthetic, it is the profoundly moving effect of an art that arises from mushin. (See Mushin.)

# Bibliography

## GENERAL

ANESAKI, MASAHARU, *History of Japanese Religion*. London: Kegan Paul, Trench, Trubner, 1930. Reprint, Rutland, Vt.: Charles E. Tuttle, 1963.

EARHART, H. BYRON, *Japanese Religion: Unity and Diversity*, 3rd ed. Belmont, Calif.: Wadsworth, 1982.

HORI, ICHIRO, ET AL., *Japanese Religion*. Tokyo: Kodansha International Ltd., 1972.

KITAGAWA, JOSEPH M., *Religion in Japanese History*. New York: Columbia University Press, 1966.

TSUNODA, RYUSAKU, WILLIAM THEODORE DE BARY, and DONALD KEENE, EDS., *Sources of Japanese Tradition*. New York: Columbia University Press, 1958.

VARLEY, H. PAUL, *Japanese Culture: A Short History*. New York: Praeger Publishers, 1977.

## FOLK AND POPULAR RELIGION

BERNIER, BERNARD, *Breaking the Cosmic Circle: Religion in a Japanese Village*. Cornell East Asie Papers, 5. Ithaca, N.Y.: Cornell China-Japan Program, 1975.

BLACKER, CARMEN, *The Catalpa Bow: A Study of Shamanistic Practices in Japan*. London: George Allen & Unwin, 1975.

BOWNAS, GEOFFREY, *Japanese Rainmaking and Other Folk Practices*. London: George Allen & Unwin, 1963.

DORSON, RICHARD M., *Studies in Japanese Folklore*. Bloomington: Indiana University Press, 1963.

HORI, ICHIRO, *Folk Religion in Japan: Continuity and Change*. Chicago: University of Chicago Press, 1968.

OUWEHAND, C., *Namazu-e and Their Themes*. Leiden: E. J. Brill, 1964.

SMITH, ROBERT J., *Ancestor Worship in Contemporary Japan*. Stanford, Calif.: Stanford University Press, 1974.

## SHINTO

HOLTOM, D.C., *The National Faith of Japan*. New York: Paragon Book Reprint Corp., 1965.

KATO, GENCHI., *A Historical Study of the Religious Development of Shinto*. Tokyo: Japan Society for the Promotion of Science, 1973.

KEGEYAMA, HARUKI, *The Arts of Shinto*. New York and Tokyo: John Weatherhill, 1973.

MATSUMOTO, SHIGERU, *Motoori Norinaga*. Cambridge: Harvard University Press, 1970.

ONO, SOKYO, *Shinto: The Kami Way*. Tokyo: Bridgeway Press, 1962.

PHILIPPI, DONALD, TRANS., *Kojiki.* Tokyo: University of Tokyo Press, 1968.

PICKEN, STUART, *Shinto: Japan's Spiritual Roots.* New York: Kodansha International, 1980.

ROSS, FLOYD H., *Shinto: The Way of Japan.* Boston: Beacon Press, 1965.

TANGE, KENZO, AND KAWAZOE, NOBORU, *Ise: Prototype of Japanese Architecture.* Cambridge: M.I.T. Press, 1965.

## CONFUCIANISM

ARMSTRONG, ROBERT C., *Light from the East: Studies in Japanese Confucianism.* Toronto: University of Toronto Press, 1914.

SMITH, WARREN W., JR., *Confucianism in Modern Japan,* 2nd ed. Tokyo: Hokuseido, 1973.

## BUDDHISM

ANESAKI, MASAHARU, *Nichiren the Buddhist Prophet.* Cambridge: Harvard University Press, 1916.

BLOOM, ALFRED, *Shinran's Gospel of Pure Grace.* Tucson: University of Arizona Press, 1965.

COLLCUTT, MARTIN, *Five Mountains: The Rinzai Manastic Institution in Medieval Japan.* Cambridge: Harvard University Press, 1981.

DUMOULIN, HEINRICH, *A History of Zen Buddhism.* New York: Pantheon Books, 1963.

EARHART, H. BYRON, *A Religious Study of the Mount Haguro Sect of Shugendo.* Tokyo: Sophia University, 1970.

ELIOT, SIR CHARLES, *Japanese Buddhism.* London: Edward Arnold, 1935.

HAKEDA, YOSHITO S., TRANS., *Kukai: Major Works.* New York: Columbia University Press, 1972.

KIM, HEE-JIN, *Dogen Kigen: Mystical Realist.* Tucson: University of Arizona Press, 1975.

KIYOTA, MINORU, *Shingon Buddhism: Theory and Practice.* Los Angeles: Buddhist Books International, 1978.

LAFLEUR, WILLIAM, *Buddhism: A Cultural Perspective.* Englewood Cliffs, N.J.: Prentice-Hall, 1985.

MATSUNAGA, ALICIA, *The Buddhist Philosophy of Assimilation.* Tokyo: Sophia University, 1969.

MATSUNAGA, DIAGAN, AND MATSUNAGA, ALICIA, *Foundation of Japanese Buddhism.* 2 vols. Los Angeles: Buddhist Books International, 1974.

PICKEN, STUART, *Buddhism: Japan's Cultural Identity.* Tokyo and New York: Kodansha International Ltd., 1982.

SANFORD, JAMES, *Zen-Man Ikkyu.* Chico, Calif.: Scholars Press, 1981.

SAUNDERS, DALE, *Buddhism in Japan.* Philadelphia: University of Pennsylvania Press, 1964.

————, *An Introduction to Zen Buddhism.* New York: Grove Press, 1964.

SUZUKI, DAISETZ, *Collected Writings on Shin Buddhism.* Kyoto: Shinshu Ontaniha, 1973.

————, *The Training of the Zen Buddhist Monk.* Berkeley: Wingbow Press, 1974 (orig. 1934).

## NEW RELIGIONS

McFarland, H. Neill, *The Rush Hour of the Gods.* New York: Macmillan. 1967.

Offner, Clark, B., and van Straelen, Henry, *Modern Japanese Religions.* Tokyo: Rupert Enderle, 1963.

Thomsen, Harry, *The New Religions of Japan.* Tokyo, and Rutland, Vt.: Charles E. Tuttle, 1963.

For a further reference for works on particular religions, see:

Earhart, H. Byron, *The New Religions of Japan: A Bibliography of Western-Language Materials.* Tokyo: Sophia University Press, 1970. (2nd ed., Ann Arbor, MI: University of Michigan, Center for Japanese Studies, 1983.)


## RELIGION AND JAPANESE CULTURE

Bancroft, Anne, *Zen: Direct Pointing to Reality.* London: Thames and Hudson, 1979.

Izutsu, Toshihiko, and Izutsu, Toyo, *The Theory of Beauty in the Classical Aesthetics of Japan.* The Hague: Martinus Nijhoff Publishers, 1981.

Keene, Donald, *Nō: The Classical Theatre of Japan.* Tokyo: Kodansha International Ltd., 1966.

LaFleur, William, *The Karma of Words: Buddhism and the Literary Arts in Medieval Japan.* Berkeley: University of California Press, 1983.

Leggett, Trevor, *Zen and the Ways.* Boulder, Colo.: Shambhala, 1978.

Nitobe, Inazo, *Bushido: The Soul of Japan.* Rutland, Vt.: Charles E. Tuttle, 1969.

Okakura, Kakuzo, *The Book of Tea.* New York: Dover Publications, Inc., 1964.

Pilgrim, Richard, *Buddhism and the Arts of Japan.* Chambersburg, Penn.: Anima Publications, 1981.

Suzuki, Daisetz, *Zen and Japanese Culture.* New York: Pantheon Books, Inc., 1959.

Ueda, Makoto, *Literary and Art Theories in Japan.* Cleveland, Ohio: Western Reserve University Press, 1967.

Warner, Langdon, *The Enduring Art of Japan.* New York: Grove Press, 1952.


## RELIGION IN MODERN JAPAN

Bellah, Robert, *Tokugawa Religion.* Boston: Beacon Press, 1957.

Kishimoto, Hideo, ed., *Japanese Religion in the Meiji Era.* Tokyo: Obunsha, 1956.

Morioka, Kiyomi, *Religion in Changing Japanese Society.* Tokyo: University of Tokyo Press, 1975.

————, and Newell, William, *The Sociology of Japanese Religion.* Leiden: E. J. Brill, 1968.

Murakami, Shigeyoshi, *Japanese Religion in the Modern Century.* Tokyo: University of Tokyo Press, 1980.

Norbeck, Edward, *Religion and Society in Modern Japan: Continuity and Change.* Houston: Tourmaline Press, 1970.

Piovesana, Gino K., *Recent Japanese Philosophical Thought, 1862–1962: A Survey.* Tokyo: Enderle Bookstore, 1963.

# Index